ACCOUNTS FOR SOLICITORS

ACCOUNTS FOR SOLICITORS

Jacqueline Kempton BA (Hons), Solicitor

Lesley King LLB, Dip Crim (Cantab), Solicitor

CLP

Published by

The University of Law,
2 Bunhill Row, London EC1Y 8HQ

British Library Cataloguing-in-Publication Data

A catalogue record for this book is available from the British Library.

ISBN: 978 1 80502 165 0

Typeset by Style Photosetting Ltd, Mayfield, East Sussex

Tables and index by Moira Greenhalgh, Arnside, Cumbria

Preface

This book is written primarily for the Legal Practice Course but it is hoped that it will be useful for others.

It is divided into two parts. The first part provides an introduction to business accounting. The second part deals with the accounts of solicitors and, in particular, the need to account for client's money.

The authors would like to thank their colleagues at The University of Law at Store Street for their help in the preparation of this book, and College of Law Publishing for their support during the production process.

The law is stated as at 1 April 2025.

JACQUELINE KEMPTON
LESLEY KING

Contents

PREFACE			v
TABLE OF STATUTES, RULES AND ACCOUNTING STANDARDS			xi
TABLE OF ABBREVIATIONS			xiii
INTRODUCTION			xv
Part I	**BUSINESS ACCOUNTS**		**1**
Chapter 1	INTRODUCTION TO BUSINESS ACCOUNTS		3
	1.1	Introduction	3
	1.2	Keeping records	3
	1.3	The nature of accounts	4
	1.4	Users of business accounts	4
	1.5	The role of accountants	4
	1.6	Accounts and tax	5
	1.7	Regulation of accounts	6
	1.8	Information provided by accounts	6
	1.9	Types of businesses	7
		Summary	7
Chapter 2	DOUBLE ENTRY BOOKKEEPING		9
	2.1	Introduction	9
	2.2	The purpose of double entry bookkeeping	9
	2.3	Principles of double entry	10
	2.4	The form of accounts	12
	2.5	Making entries	13
	2.6	Cash and ledger accounts	16
	2.7	Drawings	17
	2.8	Trial Balance	17
		Summary	18
		Solutions	18
Chapter 3	FINAL ACCOUNTS		21
	3.1	Introduction	21
	3.2	The purpose of final accounts	21
	3.3	The Profit and Loss Account	22
	3.4	Balance Sheet	25
	3.5	The importance of Final Accounts	29
		Summary	29
		Solutions	30
Chapter 4	ADJUSTMENTS		31
	4.1	Introduction	31
	4.2	The concept of accruals	31
	4.3	Outstanding expenses	32
	4.4	Payments in advance	33
	4.5	Work in progress	34
	4.6	Closing stock	35
	4.7	Bad and doubtful debts	36
	4.8	Depreciation	38
	4.9	Revaluation	40
	4.10	Disposal of a fixed asset	41

		Consolidation exercise	42
		Summary	42
		Solutions	43
Chapter 5	PARTNERSHIP ACCOUNTS		47
	5.1	Introduction	47
	5.2	The nature of partnerships	47
	5.3	Capital accounts	48
	5.4	Profit sharing	48
	5.5	The appropriation account	49
	5.6	Current account	49
	5.7	The Balance Sheet	50
	5.8	Details of movements on partners' current accounts	50
	5.9	Partnership changes	51
	5.10	Taxation of partnerships	51
		Summary	51
		Solutions	52
Chapter 6	INTRODUCTION TO COMPANY ACCOUNTS		53
	6.1	Introduction	53
	6.2	The nature of companies	53
	6.3	Shareholders	54
	6.4	Issuing shares	54
	6.5	Maintenance of capital and a company buying its own shares	56
	6.6	Debentures	56
	6.7	A Company Profit and Loss Account	57
	6.8	A Company Balance Sheet	59
	6.9	Consolidated accounts	63
	6.10	Deferred taxation	63
		Summary	66
		Solutions	66
Chapter 7	COMPANY ACCOUNTS: REGULATION AND FORMAT		67
	7.1	Introduction	67
	7.2	The role of regulation	67
	7.3	Statutory regulation	67
	7.4	Accounting principles	68
	7.5	Accounts formats	69
	7.6	Annual reports and accounts	73
		Summary	74
Chapter 8	ANALYSIS OF ACCOUNTS		75
	8.1	Introduction	75
	8.2	The purposes of analysing accounts	75
	8.3	Who will want to analyse accounts and why?	75
	8.4	The limitations of accounts	76
	8.5	What information do you need?	76
	8.6	Preliminary steps	77
	8.7	Some general considerations	79
	8.8	Trends and ratio analysis	80
		Summary	85
		Solutions	86
Part II	**SOLICITORS' ACCOUNTS**		**87**
Chapter 9	THE SRA ACCOUNTS RULES 2019		89
	9.1	Introduction	89
	9.2	Principles governing the Rules	90
	9.3	Who is bound by the Rules?	91

	9.4	Client money	92
	9.5	Client bank account	93
	9.6	Client bank account must not be used to provide banking facilities	93
	9.7	Paying client money into the client bank account	99
	9.8	Keeping client money separate from the firm's own money	100
	9.9	Withdrawals of client money from the client bank account	105
	9.10	Client accounting systems and controls	108
	9.11	Paying interest to clients	110
	9.12	Third party managed accounts	110
	9.13	Dealings with other money belonging to clients or third parties	110
	9.14	Obtaining and delivery of accountants' reports	111
		Summary	112
		Solutions	112
Chapter 10	ENTRIES FOR RECORDING SIMPLE CLIENT TRANSACTIONS		113
	10.1	Introduction	113
	10.2	The two sets of accounting records	113
	10.3	The format of the accounts	114
	10.4	Dealing with receipts of money	115
	10.5	Dealing with payments of money	116
	10.6	Recording the firm's professional charges	118
		Summary	120
		Solutions	120
Chapter 11	TRANSFERS		123
	11.1	Introduction	123
	11.2	Cash transfers	123
	11.3	Inter-client transfers	126
		Summary	128
		Solutions	128
Chapter 12	VALUE ADDED TAX		131
	12.1	Introduction	131
	12.2	General principles	131
	12.3	VAT and firms providing legal services	135
		Summary	145
		Solutions	147
Chapter 13	SPLITTING CHEQUES, MIXED RECEIPTS AND DEALING WITH BILLS		153
	13.1	Introduction	153
	13.2	Receipts partly of business and partly of client money	153
	13.3	Dealing with bills	155
	13.4	Revision of material in Chapters 9–13	155
		Summary	157
		Solutions	157
Chapter 14	MISCELLANEOUS MATTERS		161
	14.1	Introduction	161
	14.2	Receipt of a cheque made out to the client or a third party	161
	14.3	Dishonoured cheques	162
	14.4	Abatements	164
	14.5	Bad debts	165
	14.6	Petty cash	166
	14.7	Insurance commission	167
		Summary	168
		Solution	168
Chapter 15	ACCOUNTING TO THE CLIENT FOR INTEREST		171
	15.1	Introduction	171

	15.2	The obligation to account	171
	15.3	Use of separate designated deposit bank account	173
	15.4	Use of general client bank account	176
	15.5	SRA Consultation Paper	180
		Summary	181
		Solution	181
Chapter 16	FINANCIAL STATEMENTS		185
	16.1	Introduction	185
	16.2	Layout	185
		Summary	187
		Solution	187
Chapter 17	ACCOUNTING PROBLEMS FOR SOLICITORS		189
	17.1	Introduction	189
	17.2	Number of ledger accounts required	189
	17.3	Agency transactions	206
		Summary	209
		Solutions	209
Chapter 18	THIRD PARTY MANAGED ACCOUNTS		211
	18.1	Introduction	211
	18.2	Checks you should make before engaging a TPMA provider	212
	18.3	Engaging with the client	212
	18.4	What firms must tell clients	212
	18.5	Systems and procedures	213
	18.6	SRA Guidance	213
	18.7	Proposals for change	213
		Summary	214
Chapter 19	COMPLIANCE		215
	19.1	Introduction	215
	19.2	Accountants' reports	215
	19.3	Storage and retention of accounting records	217
		Summary	217
Part II Summary – Solicitors' Accounts			**219**
APPENDIX 1 TO PART II – MULTIPLE CHOICE QUESTIONS			221
APPENDIX 2 TO PART II – SRA ACCOUNTS RULES (EXTRACTS)			223
INDEX			227

Table of Statutes, Rules and Accounting Standards

Statutes
Companies Act 2006 61, 68, 73
Pt 15 (ss 380–474) 67
s 382 68
s 386(1) 68
ss 393–394 68
s 395 69–70
s 396 70
s 399 63
s 414A 74
s 415 74
s 423 68
s 426 68
ss 445–447 68
s 465 68
ss 475–476 68
s 580 55
s 610 61
s 658 56
s 690 56
s 733 62
Economic Crime and Corporate Transparency Act 2023 68
Financial Services and Markets Act 2000 96
Fraud Act 2006 109
Insolvency Act 1986
s 127 97
Legal Services Act 2007
Sch 2 91
Mental Capacity Act 2005 98
Code of Practice 98
Partnership Act 1870 47
s 10 98
Solicitors Act 1974 172, 181
s 85(2) 93
Value Added Tax Act 1994 156
s 4(1) 131
s 6(2)–(3) 133
s 6(4)–(6) 134
s 19(2) 133
s 25(2) 133
Sch 8 132
Sch 9 132

Statutory instruments
Companies (Receipt of Accounts and Reports) Regulations 2013 (SI 2013/1973) 68
Large and Medium-sized Companies and Groups (Accounts and Reports) Regulations 2008 (SI 2008/410) 70
Money Laundering, Terrorist Financing and Transfer of Funds (ingormation on the Payer) Regulations 2017 (SI 2017/692) 94
Payment Services Regulations 2017 (SI 2017/752) 225
Small Companies and Groups (Accounts and Directors' Report) Regulations 2008 (SI 2008/409) 70

Rules and codes
Solicitors' Accounts Rules 2011 90
Solicitors' Accounts Rules 2011 – *continued*
r 14.2(c) 105
r 14.5 93, 97, 98
r 20.3 102
SRA Accounts Rules 2019 89–112, 103, 105, 113, 114, 145, 214
text extracts 223–5
r 1.1 91
r 1.2 91
r 1.3 91
r 2 92, 110, 111
r 2.1 92, 110, 162, 223, 225
r 2.1(a) 92
r 2.1(b) 92
r 2.1(c) 92, 99
r 2.1(d) 92, 99, 100, 103, 158
r 2.2 92, 99, 100, 159, 219, 223
r 2.3 99, 128, 147, 162, 219, 223
r 2.4 100, 223
r 2.5 96, 100, 105, 126, 224
r 3 92, 110, 111
r 3.1 93, 224
r 3.2 93, 224
r 3.3 93–6, 97, 98, 99, 216, 224
r 4 92, 103, 104, 110, 111, 112
r 4.1 92, 100, 150, 219, 224
r 4.2 100, 101, 149, 153, 154, 158, 159, 162, 163, 197, 202, 224
r 4.3 92, 101–4, 128, 148, 150, 159, 224
r 4.4 104
r 5 103, 104, 110, 111, 123, 159, 219
r 5.1 104, 105, 147, 149, 224
r 5.1(c) 106–7
r 5.2 105, 224
r 5.3 105, 112, 116, 123, 128, 148, 150, 162, 163, 219, 224
r 6 105, 110, 111
r 6.1 162
r 7 110, 111, 112, 220
r 7.1 110, 171, 176
r 7.2 110, 171
r 8 110, 111, 112, 113, 114, 219
r 8.1 115, 158, 173, 190, 191, 194, 216
r 8.1(a) 108, 123, 161
r 8.1(b) 108
r 8.1(c) 108, 114
r 8.2 108, 110, 111, 216
r 8.3 108, 111, 216
r 8.4 108, 110, 111
r 9 110
r 10 111
r 10.1 111
r 10.2 111
r 11 110, 211
r 11.1 211, 212
r 11.1(b)(i)–(ii) 212
r 11.2 110, 211, 212
r 12 111

SRA Accounts Rules 2019 – *continued*
r 12.1 215
r 12.1(b) 215
r 12.2 216
r 12.4 112, 216
r 12.6 217
r 12.8 216–17
r 13.1 217
SRA Code of Conduct for Firms 2019 90, 99, 101, 110, 213, 214
para 1.2 171
para 2.1 213
para 5.1 167, 171
para 5.2 211
SRA Code of Conduct for Solicitors 2019 90, 101, 213, 214
para 4.2 211
para 8.6 212
para 8.11 213
SRA Financial Services (Scope) Rules 225
SRA Principles 90–1, 94, 101
SRA Principles – *continued*
Principle 1 90, 94
Principles 2–3 91, 94
Principle 4 91
Principle 5 91, 94, 99, 171
Principle 6 91
Principle 7 91, 99, 171, 211

Accounting standards
Financial Reporting Standards 6, 69
FRS 102 69, 73, 74
International Accounting Standards (UK Adopted IAS) 69, 71, 73, 74
International Financial Reporting Standards 69, 74

Generally accepted accounting practice
German GAAP 69
New UK GAAP *see* Financial Reporting Standards, FRS 102
UK GAAP 69, 74
US GAAP 69

Table of Abbreviations

COFA	Compliance Officer for Finance and Administration
COLP	Compliance Officer for Legal Practice
FRS	Financial Reporting Standards
GAAP	generally accepted accounting principles
HMRC	HM Revenue and Customs
IAS	International Accounting Standards
IASB	International Accounting Standards Board
IFRS	International Financial Reporting Standards
pa	per annum
PAYE	pay as you earn
TPMA	third party managed account
VAT	value added tax
VATA 1994	Value Added Tax Act 1994

Introduction

WHY DO I NEED TO KNOW ABOUT ACCOUNTS?

The short answer is because a knowledge of accounting principles is a required element of all Legal Practice Courses. However, that does give rise to a further question – 'Why?' The answer to this question is that knowledge and understanding of accounting principles will help you enormously in your professional and personal life, in the following ways.

To deal with the affairs of clients

A great deal of the work done by solicitors requires an understanding of accounts:

- In commercial work, you may be involved in shares or asset takeovers and will need to be able to 'read' the accounts of the company involved to understand the problems of the transaction.
- In private client work, you may be involved in the valuation of shares for taxation purposes.
- In family work, you may have to look critically at the accounts of a business run by a spouse when you are trying to agree the amount of a financial settlement.

To liaise with accountants

Particularly in commercial work, you may have to work closely with accountants on certain aspects of transactions. You will find it helpful to understand some of the concepts and jargon accountants use. Accountants have studied law and have some understanding of the solicitor's job. Therefore, as a profession, we will be at a disadvantage if we have no understanding of their job.

To deal with your own financial affairs

It is likely that you will have money to invest, if not now then in the not too distant future. An understanding of the principles of investment is vital to your financial well-being.

To run your own business

If you become a partner you will have to manage the financial affairs of your firm. To do so adequately you must understand profitability and solvency, and the crucial importance of cash flow.

To comply with the SRA Accounts Rules

The SRA Accounts Rules require anyone regulated by the SRA who handles money belonging to clients to keep particular accounts and to record dealings with such money in a particular way. While you are unlikely to have to make the entries yourself, you will be responsible if errors are made by others. You may have to decide whether a payment which is to be made by your firm for a particular client can be made from the client bank account or must be made from the firm's own bank account. Similarly, when money is received from a client, you may have to decide whether it should be paid into the client bank account or the firm's own bank account.

HOW TO USE THIS BOOK

This book is not designed for passive reading. It is a work book. You will find that there are exercises for you to do throughout the text. These exercises are an integral part of the course. They are designed to develop your understanding and confidence, not merely to test you on the material you have just read. Solutions to the exercises appear at the end of the relevant chapter. It is essential that you study these solutions as you go through the text.

PART I

BUSINESS ACCOUNTS

CHAPTER 1

INTRODUCTION TO BUSINESS ACCOUNTS

1.1	Introduction	3
1.2	Keeping records	3
1.3	The nature of accounts	4
1.4	Users of business accounts	4
1.5	The role of accountants	4
1.6	Accounts and tax	5
1.7	Regulation of accounts	6
1.8	Information provided by accounts	6
1.9	Types of businesses	7

LEARNING OUTCOMES

After reading this chapter you will be able to:

- explain the importance for a business of keeping financial records
- describe the role of accountants
- explain the basic information to be found in business accounts
- distinguish between different business types.

1.1 INTRODUCTION

In this chapter you will be introduced to the topic of business accounts. You will begin by looking at the purpose and importance of record keeping, before going on to examine some key accounting concepts.

1.2 KEEPING RECORDS

Most people keep some sort of record of what happens to their money. You probably keep paper or digital pay slips, bank and building society statements, loan agreements and credit card bills. These documents provide a useful personal record. These records enable you to calculate your financial position and are essential when dealing with His Majesty's Revenue and Customs (HMRC) as they provide the information necessary to calculate your tax liability.

Anyone who runs a business needs similar information to keep track of the financial position of the business. However, because so many different events occur in the life of a business, it is impractical to rely on individual documents to provide the full picture. It is preferable to take the relevant information from the individual documents and enter it on separate records. These records summarise the individual documents and are usually referred to as accounts.

While a business is small, the proprietor will probably do everything personally, including keeping the accounts. However, once a business expands, it is common to employ a bookkeeper to undertake the vital but time-consuming task of keeping the accounts on a day-to-day basis. This leaves the proprietor free to concentrate on securing the success of the business by planning strategy, and improving the quality of the product and the level of customer satisfaction.

1.3 THE NATURE OF ACCOUNTS

Accounts then are nothing more, and nothing less, than summaries of financial information. The term 'accounts' is frequently used in two senses. It is used to describe the day-to-day records which a business keeps of its financial transactions – you will also hear these records referred to as 'the books'. The term is also used to describe the summary statements which a business produces at the end of its accounting year.

The focus in the first part of this book will be on understanding and interpreting accounts in the sense of the year-end summary accounts. However, in order to be able to read a set of year-end accounts you must first understand the day-to-day record keeping which underlies them.

1.4 USERS OF BUSINESS ACCOUNTS

The financial affairs of a business will be of interest to a variety of individuals, both inside and outside the business itself. A number of people will therefore need to use the accounts for a variety of different purposes.

1.4.1 Internal users

The person most directly interested in the accounts of a business will be its owner or proprietor. The proprietor needs the accounts to provide accurate, up-to-date information which the proprietor can interpret correctly to draw conclusions about the past performance of the business. This enables the proprietor to make decisions as to future development and plan a business strategy. The proprietor therefore uses the accounts retrospectively, to see what has already occurred, and prospectively, to see where the business might be headed.

In anything but the smallest of businesses, there will also be employees and executives, managers and directors, who will similarly need to use the accounts to manage and direct the affairs of the business. Employees may also demand information about the financial health of the business, usually as a prelude to pay negotiations

1.4.2 External users

Those who deal with the business, such as its bankers, those who lend money or advance credit to it, will often need to look at the accounts. The main purpose is to monitor the performance of the business in order to safeguard their position against financial loss.

Those who work alongside the business and are involved in its financial affairs – for example analysts, lawyers and accountants – will look at the accounts to assess the state of the business in order to advise on past events and assist in the planning of future decisions.

Those who invest in the business will want to review the accounts to see what is happening to their investment and what returns or gains they can expect.

1.4.3 Government

The government body that will need to see the accounts regularly will be HMRC. The accounts are the starting point for establishing liability for tax. Other government agencies, such as the Competition and Markets Authority or the Registrar of Companies, will need to see the accounts from time to time.

1.5 THE ROLE OF ACCOUNTANTS

A business may have its own in-house accountant or, more commonly, it will buy in accountancy services in much the same way as it buys in legal services.

A business will involve accountants in one or more of a number of different aspects of managing the finances of a business.

1.5.1 Recording information

We have already seen that it is very important to have records so that the proprietor of a business can make informed decisions. The accountant will follow rules that govern the way in which information is recorded. It is important that there are rules, since it means that anyone who has learnt the rules can understand accounts kept by another person on the basis of those rules.

1.5.2 Reporting

The accountant will analyse the information contained in the day-to-day accounts, summarise it and present it to management. Management can then use that information as the basis for decisions on strategy. However, it is not just management who need financial reports. As we have seen, there is also a demand for information from outside the business – HMRC demands tax returns and, in the case of companies, the Government, potential investors and shareholders require published accounts.

1.5.3 Auditing

Not all accountants are qualified to audit accounts. Only those who are registered auditors are authorised to sign a statutory audit report.

Most companies are required to have their accounts examined by a qualified auditor, who must provide an opinion as to whether the accounts give a 'true and fair' view of the affairs of the company and its profit (or loss) for the relevant period. The auditors will have access to all the books, records and documents of the company. They are under an obligation to the members of the company and are also subject to disciplinary action by their professional body for misconduct.

In addition to the statutory audit required by the Companies Acts, auditors may be invited by management to carry out an audit as a means of obtaining an independent appraisal of the efficiency of the organisation.

1.5.4 Dealing with HMRC

Accountants frequently prepare tax returns for submission to HMRC on behalf of individuals and businesses. They can advise on the availability of deductions, exemptions and reliefs, and on the correct treatment of income and capital gains.

1.6 ACCOUNTS AND TAX

Accounts are very important as a record for taxation purposes. The Government imposes a variety of different taxes, all of which require detailed records. The accounts of the business are the starting point for assessing tax liability in a number of situations.

If the business is unincorporated, the proprietor (or proprietors, if it is a partnership) will include the profit or profit share of the business (ie the financial benefit which they derive from the business) in their income tax return. If the business is a company, the company itself will be liable for corporation tax based on the information given in the accounts.

If the business employs staff, it will have to operate the Pay As You Earn (PAYE) scheme. This requires the employer to deduct income tax from the employees and to account for it to HMRC. Records will have to be kept of salaries so that HMRC can check that the correct amount of tax has been deducted and so that certificates of deduction of income tax can be issued to employees. The business will also have to deduct National Insurance contributions from the employees. Again, detailed records will have to be kept for HMRC.

Lastly, if the business is registered for value added tax (VAT), it will need to keep records of VAT charged to customers and of VAT charged to the business by suppliers. It will have to account to the Government for the correct amount of VAT every quarter.

1.7 REGULATION OF ACCOUNTS

There is a great deal of regulation of accounts. Some of it is self-imposed by the accountancy profession and some of it is imposed externally, for example the Government insists that companies produce final accounts at the end of the accounting year in a particular form.

A person could prepare a set of accounts for their own use on any idiosyncratic basis they wished, but such accounts would be useless to an outsider trying to understand the affairs of the business. Clearly, if accounts are prepared on a uniform basis (ie if the same conventions have been followed and the same practices adopted), they will be usable by anyone.

Frequently, people want to compare the accounts of one business with the accounts of another (eg when investing or considering the purchase of a business). It is impossible to make a valid comparison unless the accounts have been prepared on a uniform basis. The accounting profession has therefore tried to achieve a measure of uniformity.

The UK Financial Reporting Council (FRC) (the main standard setter in the UK) lays down definitive standards of financial accounting and reporting (known as Financial Reporting Standards (FRSs)). These standards describe methods of accounting for application to all financial accounts (although we will consider them in the context of company accounts in **Chapter** 7). They stipulate how financial dealings should be recorded with the aim that the accounts give a true and fair view of the financial position of an enterprise and its profit or loss. Although these standards have no statutory force, non-compliance by an accountant could lead to disciplinary action by the appropriate governing body in a similar way to disciplinary proceedings against a solicitor. (In the King's Speech in July 2024, the newly elected Labour government made a commitment to create a new body, the Audit, Reporting and Governance Authority to replace the FRC.)

In recent years, accounts regulation has begun to reflect the increasing globalisation of commerce and finance. The International Accounting Standards Board sets standard applicable at an international level.

1.8 INFORMATION PROVIDED BY ACCOUNTS

Accounts provide information about the financial affairs of the business. A business needs to know:

(a) the income it has generated in a particular period; and
(b) the expenses it has incurred in the same period.

Deducting expenses from income enables the business to calculate the profit it has made.

A business also needs to know:

(a) the assets it has at a given moment; and
(b) the liabilities it has at a given moment.

Deducting the total liabilities from the total assets will establish the net worth or value of the business.

On a daily basis, therefore, a business must keep records of income, expenses, assets and liabilities. The classification of items into these four categories is a fundamental aspect of bookkeeping and accounts.

Income is what the business is trying to produce. It is the result either of the labour of the business's employees, or of the investment of its capital. Examples of income are professional charges for services supplied, the price charged for stock sold, interest received and insurance commission received.

Expenses are items paid, the benefit of which is obtained and exhausted in a relatively short time (often within a single accounting period) and where the expenditure is necessary to maintain the earning capacity of the business. Examples of expenses are the price paid for stock bought for resale, gas, electricity, wages, interest paid, hire charges, petrol and repairs.

Assets must be carefully distinguished from expenses. Like expenses, assets are the result of expenditure. The difference is that an asset gives rise to a benefit which can be spread over a longer period and which will increase the earning capacity of the business. Examples of assets are premises, machinery, fixtures and fittings, vehicles, cash and debtors.

Liabilities are amounts owing from the business. Examples of liabilities are bank loans and creditors.

Accounts show and distinguish between the income, expenses, assets and liabilities of the business. The classification is crucial to gaining an understanding of accounts. You will therefore need to keep this classification in mind as you work through the book.

1.9 TYPES OF BUSINESSES

Businesses may take a variety of forms. In this first part of the book we shall be looking at the accounts of two different types of business: a trading business, which generates income through the buying and selling of stock; and a professional business, such as a firm of solicitors, which sells services to its clients.

We shall also consider three different business mediums:

(a) businesses which are run by a single individual as a sole trader or practitioner;

(b) partnerships where two or more people join forces to run the business together; and

(c) companies which are owned by shareholders and run by directors.

SUMMARY

(1) Accounts are summaries of financial information.

(2) Accounts are read by a number of different users for a variety of purposes.

(3) Financial items can classified as income, expenses, assets and liabilities.

CHAPTER 2

DOUBLE ENTRY BOOKKEEPING

2.1	Introduction	9
2.2	The purpose of double entry bookkeeping	9
2.3	Principles of double entry	10
2.4	The form of accounts	12
2.5	Making entries	13
2.6	Cash and ledger accounts	16
2.7	Drawings	17
2.8	Trial Balance	17

LEARNING OUTCOMES

After reading this chapter you will be able to:

- explain the purpose of bookkeeping
- explain the rules which underlie double entry bookkeeping
- make basic entries using the double entry system
- draw up a trial balance.

2.1 INTRODUCTION

In order to be able to interpret a set of business accounts you must first understand the records on which those accounts are based. In this chapter you will be introduced to the system businesses use to collate financial information – double entry bookkeeping.

2.2 THE PURPOSE OF DOUBLE ENTRY BOOKKEEPING

In order for the accounts to provide accurate information, the business must have a system in place to record its financial dealings. The process of recording financial transactions in the accounting records of a business is called bookkeeping. This terminology harks back to the days when these records were hand-written, or 'entered', into large bound books; and indeed these day-to-day records are often referred to as 'the books' of the business. Today, of course, businesses usually keep their financial records using computerised systems.

All businesses use the same bookkeeping system to record their day-to-day transactions. This system is called the double entry bookkeeping system. The double entry system was developed in the 15th century by Venetian traders. The fact that it continues to be used today is a tribute to their ingenuity and its efficiency.

There is nothing to stop anyone inventing their own personal accounting system. However, there is a great deal to be said for uniformity. We have seen that the accounts need to be understood by outsiders. This is achieved by using the double entry system, which has been developed over hundreds of years and is understood by people all over the world.

Double entry bookkeeping is a system of recording financial dealings built upon a series of rules. As we look at the double entry system some of the rules may appear arbitrary to you, perhaps even counter-intuitive. The fact is that the Venetian traders could have decided to set up the whole system differently, but they chose not to. However, once you have accepted that initial decision, everything which follows builds methodically, and you will soon appreciate that the system has its own internal logic.

2.3 PRINCIPLES OF DOUBLE ENTRY

Double entry bookkeeping is based on one very simple idea: every business transaction has two aspects to it, so, to give an accurate picture of the state of the business, both aspects need to be recorded. Consider the following examples which illustrate the two aspects of a number of transactions:

(a) The business pays cash to buy premises:
Aspect 1 – The business has less cash
Aspect 2 – The business has acquired premises

(b) The business sells goods to a customer for cash:
Aspect 1 – The business has earned income
Aspect 2 – The business has more cash

(c) The business provides services to a client on credit:
Aspect 1 – The business has earned income
Aspect 2 – The business has a debt owing to it

(d) The client pays the business the money owed:
Aspect 1 – The business has lost the debt that was owing to it
Aspect 2 – The business has more cash

(e) The business pays wages:
Aspect 1 – The business has less cash
Aspect 2 – The business has incurred an expense

No matter what type of transaction you consider, there will always be two aspects to it.

Both aspects of a transaction are recorded in the books of the business. Each aspect must be recorded in a different account. The double entry bookkeeping system requires the business to have a number of separate accounts, so, for example, there is one account for cash, one account for each type of asset, one for each type of expense, one for each person to whom the business owes money, one for each debtor that owes money to the business.

In order to record the two aspects, accounts are divided into two sides. The two aspects of any transaction are recorded on different sides of the two accounts.

2.3.1 Rules for recording transactions

The rules for recording transactions may conveniently be summarised as in the following table:

Left column	**Right column**
Expense incurred	Income earned
Asset acquired/increased	Asset disposed of/reduced
Liability reduced/extinguished	Liability incurred/increased
Cash gained	Cash paid

We have seen that every transaction has two aspects. When an individual transaction is recorded, one aspect appears in the left-hand column of the grid and will therefore be recorded on the left-hand side of one account. The other aspect appears in the right-hand column of the grid and will therefore be recorded on the right-hand side of another account. For every transaction these two aspects must first be identified and then each of them recorded in two separate accounts.

There is no magic about whether entries are made on the left or the right. The system would have worked just as well if the different aspects were recorded on the opposite sides. The rules summarised in the grid simply need to be learned and followed.

Example

A business carries out the following transactions:

(a) *The business buys a machine for £20,000 cash.*

Expense incurred	Income earned
Asset acquired/increased	Asset disposed of/reduced
Liability reduced/extinguished	Liability incurred/increased
Cash gained	Cash paid

The business gains an asset in the form of a machine (recorded on the left of the machine account) and pays cash (recorded on the right of the cash account).

(b) *The business buys stock for £1,000 cash.*

Expense incurred	Income earned
Asset acquired/increased	Asset disposed of/reduced
Liability reduced/extinguished	Liability incurred/increased
Cash gained	Cash paid

The purchase of stock is an expense of the business. The business incurs an expense (recorded on the left of the purchases account); there is a payment of cash (recorded on the right of the cash account).

(c) *The business sells stock for £3,000.*

Expense incurred	Income earned
Asset acquired/increased	Asset disposed of/reduced
Liability reduced/extinguished	Liability incurred/increased
Cash gained	Cash paid

By selling stock the business earns income (recorded on the right of the sales account); there is a gain of cash (recorded on the left of the cash account).

You may have noticed already an important point about the double entry system. At this stage of recording the transactions, there is no need to worry about how well the business is doing. Transactions are simply recorded as they occur. The system is a mechanical method of recording transactions as they happen and involves no value judgements about the state of the business. In the above example, when recording the initial purchase or sale of stock, there is no need to worry about whether the goods bought were 'worth' £1,000, or whether the sale price of £3,000 was a high or low price. A record is simply made of what happens.

2.3.2 The business is separate from the proprietor

Another important principle of double entry bookkeeping is that the business is regarded as completely separate from its proprietor. So, when a proprietor sets up a business and puts in some cash, the transaction must be recorded from the point of view of the business. The two aspects of the transaction are that the business is gaining cash and is incurring a liability, in that it now owes money to the proprietor. This liability to repay its proprietor is normally referred to as the 'capital' of the business.

Exercise 2A

Yasmin starts a business buying and selling goods.

Identify the two aspects involved in the following transactions and say whether they would be recorded on the right or the left of the accounts:

(1) To start the business, Yasmin puts in £20,000 cash.

(2) Business buys premises for £90,000 cash.

(3) Business buys trading stock for £2,000 on credit from Fred, a supplier.

(4) Business sells some of the trading stock for £4,000 cash.

(5) Business pays Fred, the supplier, £2,000.

2.3.3 Debit and credit

So far, when talking about the two sides of the accounts, we have referred to the left-hand side and the right-hand side. However, the double entry system uses the labels 'Debit' and 'Credit'.

'Debit' is used as a label for the left-hand side and 'Credit' as a label for the right-hand side. They are shortened to 'DR' and 'CR' respectively.

Example

(a) Joe sets up a business and pays in £120,000 to start it.

The business gains cash (recorded on the left of the cash account with a DR entry) and incurs a liability to its proprietor (recorded on the right of the capital account with a CR entry).

(b) The business buys premises for £100,000.

The business pays cash (recorded on the right of the cash account with a CR entry) and gains an asset in the form of the premises (recorded on the left of the premises account with a DR entry).

2.4 THE FORM OF ACCOUNTS

Accounts may be presented in a variety of different forms. The most common is the tabular form, as shown below:

Name of Account				
Date	Details	DR	CR	Balance

When the transaction is recorded, the date of the transaction is entered in the 'Date' column. The 'Details' column contains a cross-reference to the name of the account where the other part of the double entry is made, often with a brief description of the nature of the transaction as well. The amount involved is entered in the left-hand debit column (DR) or the right-hand credit column (CR), as appropriate. The 'Balance' column shows the running balance on the account. If the DR entries exceed the CR entries, the balance is described as a DR balance, and vice versa.

Example

A business pays three electricity bills: £1,000, £2,000 and £3,000. Each payment will be recorded on the electricity account and the cash account. The electricity account will show debit entries as the business is incurring an expense, and will look as follows:

Electricity				
Date	Details	DR	CR	Balance
1	Cash	1,000		1,000DR
2	Cash	2,000		3,000DR
3	Cash	3,000		6,000DR

The corresponding entries appear in the cash account as credit entries because the business is paying cash, and will look as follows:

Cash				
Date	Details	DR	CR	Balance
1	Electricity		1,000	1,000CR
2	Electricity		2,000	3,000CR
3	Electricity		3,000	6,000CR

2.5 MAKING ENTRIES

Every financial transaction must be recorded in the accounts of the business as it happens. To help you to understand how the double entry system works in practice, we shall now look at a series of simple transactions which may typically occur in the early stages of the life of a business.

Example

Miriam sets up a business selling handmade designer knitwear. She buys the knitwear from a small group of producers in Scotland, and she then sells it to the public from a rented shop in Camden.

The following financial transactions occur:

June

1 Miriam starts a business and puts in £10,000 cash
2 Business buys a computer for £2,000
4 Business pays rent of £1,000
7 Business buys knitwear for £2,000
8 Business sells knitwear for £750

To record these events the business will need the following accounts:

- a capital account
- a cash account
- an asset account for the computer
- two expense accounts: one for rent, and one for the purchase of the knitwear stock
- an income account for the sale of the knitwear stock

The following entries are required in the accounts of the business:

1 June Miriam puts in £10,000 cash

The two aspects of this transaction are that the business:

- gains cash
- incurs a liability to Miriam

There will be a DR entry on the cash account and a CR entry on the capital account:

Cash				
Date	Details	DR	CR	Balance
1 June	**Capital**	**10,000**		**10,000DR**

Capital				
Date	Details	DR	CR	Balance
1 June	**Cash**		**10,000**	**10,000CR**

2 June Business buys a computer for £2,000

The two aspects to this transaction are that the business:

- loses cash
- gains an asset

There will be a CR entry on the cash account and a DR entry on the computer account:

Cash				
Date	Details	DR	CR	Balance
1 June	Capital	10,000		10,000DR
2 June	**Computer**		**2,000**	**8,000DR**

Computer				
Date	Details	DR	CR	Balance
2 June	**Cash**	**2,000**		**2,000DR**

4 June Business pays rent of £1,000

The two aspects of this transaction are that the business:

- pays cash
- incurs an expense

There will be a CR entry on the cash account and a DR entry on the expense account for rent:

Cash				
Date	Details	DR	CR	Balance
1 June	Capital	10,000		10,000DR
2 June	Computer		2,000	8,000DR
4 June	**Rent**		**1,000**	**7,000DR**

Rent				
Date	Details	DR	CR	Balance
4 June	**Cash**	**1,000**		**1,000DR**

7 June Business buys knitwear for £2,000

The two aspects of this transaction are that the business:

- pays cash
- incurs the expense of purchasing stock

There will be a CR entry on the cash account and a DR entry on the expense account for purchases:

Cash				
Date	Details	DR	CR	Balance
1 June	Capital	10,000		10,000DR
2 June	Computer		2,000	8,000DR
4 June	Rent		1,000	7,000DR
7 June	**Purchases**		**2,000**	**5,000DR**

Purchases				
Date	Details	DR	CR	Balance
7 June	**Cash**	**2,000**		**2,000DR**

8 June Business sells knitwear for £750

The two aspects of this transaction are that the business:

- gains cash
- earns income by selling stock

There will be a DR entry on the cash account and a CR entry on the income account for sales:

Cash				
Date	Details	DR	CR	Balance
1 June	Capital	10,000		10,000DR
2 June	Computer		2,000	8,000DR
4 June	Rent		1,000	7,000DR
7 June	Purchases		2,000	5,000DR
8 June	**Sales**	**750**		**5,750DR**

Sales				
Date	Details	DR	CR	Balance
8 June	**Cash**		**750**	**750CR**

The above example is of a trading business. Trading businesses make their profit by buying and selling goods (stock). They may do so for cash or on credit. The purchase of stock is considered an expense of the business and is recorded in the purchases account. The business earns income by selling stock and this is recorded in the sales account.

Solicitors and other professionals do not sell trading stock to produce income; they sell their services. When a bill is issued, a solicitor wants to record the two aspects of the transaction. The first aspect is the sale of the solicitor's services and the second aspect is the gain of the debt now owed by the client to the firm. Charges for professional services are recorded as a CR entry on an income account, often called 'profit costs'. The client's debt is recorded as a DR entry on an account in the name of the client. When the client eventually pays, the solicitor will record a receipt of cash and the loss of the debt owed by the client to the business. It is important to notice that no entry is made on the profit costs account when the client pays the cash due. The profit costs account merely records the bill issued. It does not show whether or not clients have paid their bills.

Exercise 2B

Using the blank accounts below, make the double entries to record the following transactions:

1 July Sally starts to practise as a solicitor. She puts in £5,000 cash.

2 July Business pays £1,000 rent for office premises.

8 July Business sends out a bill for £300 profit costs to Sidney, a client.

10 July Business pays £1,000 cash in staff wages.

Cash				
Date	Details	DR	CR	Balance

Date	Details	DR	CR	Balance

Date	Details	DR	CR	Balance

Date	Details	DR	CR	Balance

Date	Details	DR	CR	Balance

Date	Details	DR	CR	Balance

2.6 CASH AND LEDGER ACCOUNTS

You will have noticed that a large number of transactions have one aspect which will be recorded in the cash account. Most businesses operate by banking all receipts and making virtually all payments by electronic transfer or cheque. The so-called 'cash' account is in reality a record of receipts into and payments out of the bank account. However, a business will usually need a small amount of cash in the office to cover small, day-to-day expenses. This is referred to as 'petty cash'. A petty cash account is required to record the periodic receipts of cash from the bank and the various payments made from petty cash.

We mentioned earlier that, traditionally, accounts were kept together in a bound book referred to as the 'ledger'. The cash account was the busiest account and was kept in a separate book. This distinction is of no practical importance, as accounts are now usually computerised.

However, it makes a difference in terminology, since all the accounts are referred to as 'ledger accounts' apart from the cash account and, where there is one, the petty cash account.

2.7 DRAWINGS

Anyone running a business will almost certainly need to withdraw some cash from time to time to live on. A withdrawal by the proprietor reduces the cash in the business and also reduces the amount the business owes to the proprietor. Rather than record these withdrawals on the capital account each time, it is usual for a business to keep a separate account entitled 'Drawings' on which to record withdrawals made by the proprietor during the accounting period.

The drawings account is a temporary account. At the end of the accounting period, the balance on the drawings account is transferred to the capital account so that the picture on the capital account is brought up to date, showing the total amount now owed to the proprietor.

2.8 TRIAL BALANCE

Periodically, a bookkeeper checks the accuracy of the bookkeeping. Depending on the nature of the business and the frequency with which financial transactions occur within it, this may be done at the end of every day or every month. However, every business will always carry out a check of its bookkeeping at the end of its accounting period (usually one year).

We have seen that every transaction has two aspects, and the double entry system requires that, for every DR entry made on an account, a CR entry for an identical amount must be made on another account. If every transaction has been properly recorded, the total of DR entries will equal the total of CR entries. If an entry has been made on only one side of the accounts, or if an entry has been written incorrectly on one side of the accounts, there will be a discrepancy between the two totals.

It should therefore be possible to check the accuracy of bookkeeping by comparing the two totals. However, over an entire accounting period, a bookkeeper will make an enormous number of entries. Adding them all up would be a tedious task. As a short-cut, it is possible to add together all the DR balances from the various accounts and then all the CR balances; if no errors have been made, the two totals will agree. You will see why this works if you think about what the balance on an individual account represents. It is the difference between the DR and CR entries on each account. If the correct DR and CR entries have been made on each account, the differences between the DR and CR sides of each and every account should agree. The process of adding together all DR and CR balances and comparing the total is referred to as preparing a 'Trial Balance'.

Example

Look at the solution to Exercise 2B below. We are going to use the figures to prepare a Trial Balance.

Trial Balance

	DR	CR
	£	£
Capital		5,000
Cash	3,000	
Wages	1,000	
Rent	1,000	
Profit Costs		300
Debtors (Sidney)	300	
	5,300	5,300

The Trial Balance is used as a check on the accuracy of the bookkeeping. If one half of an entry has been omitted or written as a wrong amount, the error is revealed because the total debits will not equal the total credits. However, the Trial Balance will not reveal all bookkeeping errors. If, for example, the bookkeeper has failed to make any entries relating to a particular transaction, the Trial Balance will not reveal the error because the debit and credit totals will add up to the same amount, but it will be the wrong amount.

Exercise 2C

Prepare a Trial Balance from the following list of balances:

Profit Costs	£10,000CR
Rent	£5,750DR
Electricity	£150DR
Wages	£2,500DR
Cash	£2,000DR
Creditors	£300CR
Debtors	£750DR
Fixtures and Fittings	£1,400DR
Capital	£1,750CR
Bank Loan	£500CR

Preparing a Trial Balance enables the bookkeeper to check the accuracy of the records. However, a Trial Balance will always be prepared at the end of the accounting period as a first step in preparing the year-end summary accounts, or 'Final Accounts', of the business. We examine Final Accounts in **Chapter 3** below.

SUMMARY

(1) Businesses use the double entry bookkeeping system when recording day-to-day transactions.

(2) The double entry bookkeeping system recognises that every business transaction has two aspects.

(3) Each aspect is recorded on an account.

(4) There will be one DR entry and one CR entry for each transaction.

(5) There are conventions which govern whether a DR entry or a CR entry is made.

(6) A Trial Balance is a list of the debit and credit balances on the accounts of the business.

(7) A Trial Balance is used:
- (a) to check the accuracy of the bookkeeping;
- (b) as a preliminary to drawing up Final Accounts.

SOLUTIONS

Exercise 2A

(1) Business gains cash	(1) Business incurs liability to proprietor
(2) Business gains asset (premises)	(2) Business pays cash
(3) Business incurs expense (cost of stock)	(3) Business incurs liability to Fred
(4) Business gains cash	(4) Business earns income
(5) Business extinguishes liability to Fred	(5) Business pays cash

Exercise 2B

Cash				
Date	**Details**	**DR**	**CR**	**Balance**
1 July	Capital	5,000		5,000DR
2 July	Rent		1,000	4,000DR
10 July	Wages		1,000	3,000DR

Capital				
Date	**Details**	**DR**	**CR**	**Balance**
1 July	Cash		5,000	5,000CR

Rent				
Date	**Details**	**DR**	**CR**	**Balance**
2 July	Cash	1,000		1,000DR

Profit Costs				
Date	**Details**	**DR**	**CR**	**Balance**
8 July	Sidney		300	300CR

Sidney				
Date	**Details**	**DR**	**CR**	**Balance**
8 July	Profit Costs	300		300DR

Wages				
Date	**Details**	**DR**	**CR**	**Balance**
10 July	Cash	1,000		1,000DR

Exercise 2C

Trial Balance

	DR	CR
	£	£
Profit Costs		10,000
Rent	5,750	
Electricity	150	
Wages	2,500	
Cash	2,000	
Creditors		300
Debtors	750	
Fixtures and Fittings	1,400	
Capital		1,750
Bank Loan		500
	12,550	12,550

CHAPTER 3

Final Accounts

3.1	Introduction	21
3.2	The purpose of final accounts	21
3.3	The Profit and Loss Account	22
3.4	Balance Sheet	25
3.5	The importance of Final Accounts	29

LEARNING OUTCOMES

After reading this chapter you will be able to:

- explain the purpose of Final Accounts
- draw up a basic profit and loss account
- draw up a basic balance sheet
- interpret the information provided by a simple set of Final Accounts.

3.1 INTRODUCTION

So far we have looked at the bookkeeping entries made by a business to record its financial transactions as they occur day to day. We have also seen that periodically the bookkeeper will prepare a Trial Balance. In this chapter we shall see how the basic financial information recorded using the double entry system may be presented as Final Accounts. Understanding this method of presentation will enable you to begin to use the accounts to make assessments as to the performance of the business.

3.2 THE PURPOSE OF FINAL ACCOUNTS

The records kept using the double entry system give the business information on every single transaction carried out, for example payment of a gas bill, purchase of a fixed asset, delivery of a bill to a client, receipt of cash from a client in payment of costs. However, neither the records produced using the double entry system nor the Trial Balance are particularly helpful in enabling us to assess the financial state of the business.

Consider the following Trial Balance:

Trial Balance as at . . .

	DR	CR
Sales		15,000
Purchases	12,000	
Cash	5,000	
Rent	3,000	
Capital		10,000
Bank Loan		5,000
Wages	5,000	
Machinery	5,000	
	30,000	30,000

At first sight it is difficult to work out how well the business is doing. All the information that we need is there, but it is not presented in a way that makes interpretation easy.

For any proprietor, of course, it is vital to know how well the business is doing. The proprietor will want to know:

(a) Has the business made a profit?

(b) How much is the business worth?

The profitability of the business may be calculated by preparing a Profit and Loss Account. The worth or value of the business may be seen by preparing a Balance Sheet. The purpose behind preparing a Profit and Loss Account and a Balance Sheet is essentially to bring together the detail of the day-to-day records as summarised in the Trial Balance and present it in such a way that this key information about the performance of the business may readily be seen.

Typically a business prepares a Profit and Loss Account (also known as an Income Statement) and a Balance Sheet (also known as a Statement of Financial Position) once a year at the end of the accounting period. Collectively these end-of-year accounts are referred to as 'Final Accounts'. (Other year-end statements are produced, such as cash flow statements, which are extremely important to investors and lenders, but we shall consider these in the context of company accounts in **Chapter** 7.)

We shall now consider the Profit and Loss Account and the Balance Sheet in turn. Remember that the starting point for both is the Trial Balance. The figures from the Trial Balance are transferred across to the Final Accounts.

3.3 THE PROFIT AND LOSS ACCOUNT

The first element of the year-end Final Accounts is the Profit and Loss Account. The purpose of the Profit and Loss Account is to present information from the Trial Balance, so that it can readily be seen whether the business has made a profit during the accounting period.

3.3.1 The period covered

The accounting period will normally (but not necessarily) be one year. The Profit and Loss Account is headed with the period to which it relates.

Examples

Profit and Loss Account for ABC & Co for year ended 30 September [202–]
Profit and Loss Account for ABC & Co for 1 October [202–] to 30 September [202–]

3.3.2 Income and expenses

In essence the Profit and Loss Account shows us a very simple calculation:

Income – Expenses = Profit

Using this calculation, you will see that if the income of the business exceeds its expenses, the business has made a profit. Conversely, if the expenses exceed the income then the resulting figure will be a negative one, showing that the business has made a loss.

An important point to note here is that only those items appearing on the Trial Balance which can be classified as income and expenses will appear on the Profit and Loss Account. It is therefore vital to identify these items accurately, and to distinguish them from the assets and liabilities of the business. Those items which can be classified as assets and liabilities will appear on the Balance Sheet. We considered this classification at **1.8**.

Having prepared the Trial Balance, looking at the items to distinguish between income and expenses on the one hand and assets and liabilities on the other is the next step in preparing the Final Accounts.

Exercise 3A

Study the following Trial Balance. Identify those accounts which will appear on the Profit and Loss Account as income, and those which will appear as expenses.

Trial Balance as at . . .

	DR	CR
Capital		61,000
Bank Loan		50,000
Premises	200,000	
Machinery	6,000	
Rent Paid	1,500	
Wages	3,500	
Electricity	700	
Interest Paid	450	
Interest Received		300
Professional Charges		114,000
Cash	4,850	
Debtors	12,000	
Creditors		3,700
	229,000	229,000

3.3.3 Preparation

Once the items appearing in the Trial Balance as income and expenses have been identified, the balances on those accounts are transferred to the Profit and Loss Account. Essentially all the income figures are grouped together, followed by the expenses. Then the total expenses are deducted from the total income to calculate the profit.

The Profit and Loss Account is usually set out vertically. So the calculation of profit appears as:

Income

–

Expenses

=

Profit

Example

Here is an extract from the Trial Balance prepared for Ann, a solicitor in sole practice. It shows the income and expense accounts for the year 1 March 2024 to 28 February 2025.

Ann, a firm
Extract from Trial Balance 28 February 2025

	DR	CR
Profit Costs		120,000
Interest Received		20,000
General Expenses	10,000	
Wages	30,000	

Ann's Profit and Loss Account will show income less expenses and will look like this:

Profit and Loss Account for Ann for year ended 28 February 2025

	£	£
Income		
Profit Costs	120,000	
Interest Received	20,000	
		140,000
Expenses		
Wages	10,000	
General Expenses	30,000	
		(£40,000)
NET PROFIT		100,000

Although you will see that the figures on the Profit and Loss Account are shown in columns, these no longer represent debits and credits. The columns are simply used to make the Profit and Loss Accounts appear as clear as possible. The convention is to show workings in column(s) to the left and carry the main figures across to the right-hand column. You should also note the convention of indicating that a figure is to be deducted, or shown as a minus, by placing that figure in brackets.

The net profit shown on the Profit and Loss Account (£100,000 in the above example) is owed to the proprietor (Ann). However, this does not mean that the proprietor will simply take the profit out of the business at the end of the year. A business needs to retain at least some of its profits to fund investment and growth.

Exercise 3B

Prepare a Profit and Loss Account for Smith for the year ended 31 December 2024 based on the Trial Balance set out below:

Trial Balance as at 31 December 2024

	DR	CR
Profit Costs		20,000
Wages	14,000	
Rent	3,000	
Electricity	500	
Fixtures and Fittings	6,500	
Computers	7,000	
Debtors	2,000	
Creditors		2,000
Cash	2,000	
Drawings	2,000	
Capital		15,000
	37,000	37,000

Understanding the Profit and Loss Account enables the proprietor, or anyone else reading the accounts, to begin to assess the performance of the business. A key measure of the success of a business is whether it is making a profit; consequently if the business has low profits, the proprietor will usually want to take steps to improve them. From the simple calculation which we now know to be shown in the Profit and Loss Account (Income – Expenses = Profit) it is clear that there are only two ways of improving profits: increasing income and/or decreasing expenses. A business can increase its income by selling more stock (perhaps by better marketing or introducing new products), or by increasing prices (this will require careful consideration of the market and business competitors to see if it is viable). Decreasing expenses could be achieved by finding a cheaper supplier, but might involve taking commercial decisions such as cutting the number of staff. Sometimes it may be possible for a business to change the nature of its products sold to those with a higher 'mark up'; this will have the effect of increasing profits.

3.3.4 Trading Accounts

A business which buys and sells goods has a Profit and Loss Account, but it also has a preliminary account called a Trading Account. A business which provides professional services, for example a firm of solicitors, does not need a Trading Account.

The Trading Account shows income from sales less the cost of those sales (ie, the cost of buying the trading stock). The difference between the two is the gross profit. The gross profit is then carried forward to start the Profit and Loss Account; any other income is added and the expenses of running the business are deducted to produce the net profit.

To prepare the Trading Account the balance on the sales account for the year will be transferred from the Trial Balance to the Trading Account as income. The balance on the purchases account for the year will be transferred to the Trading Account as an expense. The difference between the sales income and the cost of buying trading stock will represent the gross profit.

Example

A business has the following balances on its sales and purchases accounts for the year 1 January to 31 December 2024. The balances are transferred to the Trading Account.

Extract from Trial Balance as at 31 December 2024

	DR	CR
Sales		**400,000**
Purchases	**280,000**	

Its Trading Account will show sales less the cost of the goods sold:

Trading Account for year ended 31 December 2024

	£
Sales	400,000
Less Cost of goods sold	
Purchases	(280,000)
Gross profit	120,000

The Profit and Loss Account then follows with the addition of any other income and the deduction of the remaining expenses to produce the net profit.

The reason for having a separate Trading Account is to highlight the difference between what the business pays for its trading stock and what it sells it for. This is achieved by separating these items from other income and expenses. This is then usually presented in the Final Accounts with the Trading Account at the top of the page and the Profit and Loss Account following below. Highlighting the gross profit in this way is helpful to the proprietor. If a business has a low net profit figure overall, the proprietor will try to identify the cause and take steps to try to improve the profitability of the business. A low net profit figure could be caused by high running expenses, or by stock being bought at too high a price. Separating the two types of expenses by moving the expense of purchasing stock into the Trading Account makes it easier to spot where the problems have occurred.

3.4 BALANCE SHEET

The second element of the year-end Final Accounts is the Balance Sheet. The purpose of the Balance Sheet is to present the figures from the Trial Balance in order to show the net worth or value of the business.

3.4.1 The date of preparation

The Balance Sheet is a list of the assets and liabilities of the business. It lists the assets and liabilities on the last day of the accounting period, and is accurate only for that one day. It must be headed with that date.

> **Example**
>
> Balance Sheet for ABC & Co as at 31 December [202–].

3.4.2 Assets and liabilities

We saw at **3.3.2** that only those items from the Trial Balance which can be classified as income and expenses for the year appear on the Profit and Loss Account to calculate net profit. The remaining items represent assets and liabilities, and these are the items which will appear on the Balance Sheet.

Just like the Profit and Loss Account, in essence the Balance Sheet shows a simple calculation, although, as we shall see later, the way in which the calculation is presented is a little more complicated. The calculation shown on the Balance Sheet is:

Assets – Liabilities = Net worth of the business

The presentation of the Balance Sheet shows that if all the assets of the business are added together and all the liabilities then deducted, the figure that remains is the net worth, or value, of the business. However, the Balance Sheet does not simply show assets in one section and liabilities in the other. It shows what the business is worth *to the proprietor*. Therefore, one section of the Balance Sheet shows the value of assets less liabilities owed to third parties; the other shows the amount owed to the proprietor as capital. The two amounts should be the same.

The Balance Sheet calculation (Assets – Liabilities = Net Worth) is shown vertically. In the example set out below, we show the first part of the calculation (Assets – Liabilities) followed by the value to the proprietor, labelling the sections 'Employment of Capital' and 'Capital Employed' respectively. Different titles are often used for the two sections of the vertical Balance Sheet. The assets section is often entitled simply 'Assets' and the liabilities section is often labelled 'Financed By' or 'Represented By'.

Example

Balance Sheet as at 30 September 202–

	£	£	£
EMPLOYMENT OF CAPITAL			
Fixed Assets			
Premises		50,000	
Machinery		50,000	
			100,000
Current Assets			
Debtors	10,000		
Cash	102,000		
	112,000		
Less Current Liabilities			
Creditors	(2,000)		
Net Current Assets			110,000
			210,000
Less Long-term Liabilities			
Five-year Bank Loan			(100,000)
Net Assets			**110,000**
CAPITAL EMPLOYED			
Capital			
Opening balance		80,000	
Net profit		60,000	
Drawings		(30,000)	
			110,000

You will see that a layer of complexity has been added here because, having identified the assets and liabilities from the Trial Balance, they must be sub-divided:

(a) Assets are divided into fixed assets and current assets:

Fixed assets are those which are bought not for resale but to improve the efficiency of the business, for example premises, machinery.

Current assets are short-term assets, for example cash and debtors. These are sometimes referred to as 'circulating assets' because they change their character as one asset turns into another: for example, when a debtor pays, the business no longer has the debtor as an asset; it has the cash paid instead.

(b) Liabilities are divided into current liabilities and long-term liabilities:

Current liabilities are those which are repayable in 12 months or less from the date of the Balance Sheet.

Long-term liabilities are those repayable more than 12 months from the date of the Balance Sheet.

By convention, assets are listed in decreasing order of permanence (or, to put it another way, in increasing order of liquidity). So, fixed assets are shown before current assets. Listing in decreasing order of permanence means that premises will always be shown first in the list of fixed assets. Within the current assets, debtors will always be shown above cash because cash is more liquid.

The Balance Sheet shows current liabilities being deducted from current assets to give a figure called 'net current assets'. This is an important figure for a business. It shows the extent of the assets which the business can most readily turn into cash in order to meet its most pressing liabilities. In other words, it represents the liquid funds available to the business. A business may have substantial assets and be very profitable, but if it has insufficient liquid assets, it will be unable to meet its debts as they fall due and will be unable to continue trading. The Balance Sheet therefore highlights this. A low (or negative) figure for net current assets is usually an indication that the business is in financial difficulty.

Long-term liabilities are deducted from the total of fixed and net current assets to give a figure for the net assets of the business. Net assets will always equal the amount owing to the proprietor as capital at the end of the year.

The 'Capital Employed' section reflects the value of the business to the proprietor. This starts with the balance on the capital account. The net profit from the Profit and Loss Account is 'owed' to the proprietor and must be added. Any withdrawals made by the proprietor during the accounting year will be shown on the drawings account, and therefore the balance on the drawings account is deducted.

As we have seen already, when the proprietor starts a business, they will normally contribute some money to the business. From the perspective of the business, the capital contributed is a liability owed to the proprietor. The proprietor of a business hopes that at the end of the accounting period the business will have made a net profit. Any profit the business makes will be 'owed' to the proprietor. Therefore, once the net profit has been calculated on the Profit and Loss Account, it will be credited to the capital account to increase the amount shown as owing to the proprietor.

Exercise 3C

Prepare a Balance Sheet for Smith as at 31 December 2024 based on the Trial Balance set out in Exercise 3B. Remember that in Exercise 3B you calculated the net profit. You will add this to the balance on the capital account.

Understanding the Balance Sheet enables the proprietor or anyone else reading the accounts to begin to assess the current state of the business. A business whose liabilities exceed its assets is in financial difficulty. If the business cannot meet its liabilities, there is a risk that unpaid creditors may take some kind of insolvency proceedings. The nature of the assets and liabilities is also important. A business may have high-value fixed assets but little cash. Whilst the net value of such a business may be high, the business lacks the cash with which to pay immediate liabilities. If a business has to start to sell fixed assets in order to pay current liabilities, it is usually an indication that the business is in financial difficulties.

3.4.3 Client bank account

A firm of solicitors will have an additional asset – a bank account containing money held for clients. This asset will always be equalled by the amount the firm 'owes' its clients. The two items are normally shown as self-cancelling items on the Balance Sheet after the net figure for current assets.

Example

	£	£
Net Current Assets		110,000
Client bank account	100,000	
Due to clients	(100,000)	

3.5 THE IMPORTANCE OF FINAL ACCOUNTS

The proprietor of a business will need to know how much profit the business made in the most recent accounting period, how much cash is in the bank, and what liabilities and other assets the business has at the end of the accounting period. All this information can readily be seen from the way in which the information is presented in the Final Accounts.

The Final Accounts also enable the proprietor, and others, to assess the past performance of the business and make informed decisions for the future. If the business is fundamentally profitable, but currently short of cash because of over-enthusiastic expansion, the proprietor may decide to borrow money in order to increase the cash in the business. If the machinery is outdated, it may be sensible to scrap the existing machinery and to buy something more modern. If the business is thriving, the proprietor may consider taking on more staff and expanding the business.

Whatever the type of business medium you are considering, however large or small the business may be, at the heart of its Final Accounts will be a Profit and Loss Account and a Balance Sheet. You will often see some added complexity, and you will certainly see different terminology. However, whenever you are looking at any set of Final Accounts, remember that they will in essence be showing you this basic information – the Profit and Loss Account, revealing the profit that the business has made, and the Balance Sheet, showing the net worth of the business.

SUMMARY

(1) The Final Accounts of a business comprise a Profit and Loss Account and a Balance Sheet.

(2) A Profit and Loss Account shows income less expenses to give net profit.

(3) Businesses which buy and sell goods have a Trading Account as well as a Profit and Loss Account. The Trading Account shows income from sales, less the cost of goods sold to give gross profit. The Profit and Loss Account shows gross profit less expenses to give net profit.

(4) The Balance Sheet shows assets and liabilities. It is set out as follows:

  (a) first fixed assets are added together;

  (b) then the net current assets figure is calculated – this is total current assets less total liabilities;

  (c) the total fixed assets and net current assets are added together;

  (d) any long-term liabilities are deducted;

  (e) the result is labelled 'Net Assets';

  (f) it should equal the new capital figure found by adding net profit to the figure for capital on the Trial Balance and deducting drawings.

SOLUTIONS

Exercise 3A

Expenses	Income
Rent Paid	Professional Charges
Wages	Interest Received
Electricity	
Interest Paid	

The remaining items represent assets or liabilities which will appear on the Balance Sheet.

Exercise 3B

Profit and Loss Account for Smith for year ended 31 December 2024

	£	£
Income		
Profit Costs		20,000
Expenses		
Wages	14,000	
Rent	3,000	
Electricity	500	
		(17,500)
NET PROFIT		2,500

Exercise 3C

Balance Sheet for Smith as at 31 December 2024

EMPLOYMENT OF CAPITAL		
Fixed Assets		
Fixtures and Fittings	6,500	
Computers	7,000	
		13,500
Current Assets		
Debtors	2,000	
Cash	2,000	
	4,000	
Less Current Liabilities		
Creditors	(2,000)	
Net Current Assets		2,000
Net Assets		15,500
CAPITAL EMPLOYED		
Capital		
Opening Balance	15,000	
Net profit	2,500	
Drawings	2,000	
		15,500

CHAPTER 4

ADJUSTMENTS

4.1	Introduction	31
4.2	The concept of accruals	31
4.3	Outstanding expenses	32
4.4	Payments in advance	33
4.5	Work in progress	34
4.6	Closing stock	35
4.7	Bad and doubtful debts	36
4.8	Depreciation	38
4.9	Revaluation	40
4.10	Disposal of a fixed asset	41

LEARNING OUTCOMES

After reading this chapter you will be able to:

- explain the concept of accruals
- describe the purpose of year-end adjustments
- make the key adjustments required to produce accurate Final Accounts.

4.1 INTRODUCTION

Up to now we have recorded financial transactions as they occur. So, the recording of the payment of, say, an electricity bill is made when the bill is actually paid, and the appropriate entries are made on the electricity and cash accounts respectively. If an electricity bill has been received but not yet paid, there will be no entries in the accounts. This can mean that the books present a somewhat distorted picture with, for example, expenses being recorded in the accounting period when they happen to be paid, rather than being recorded in the accounting period to which they relate. In this chapter we shall look at how the figures recorded using the double entry system may be adjusted so that the Final Accounts present a more accurate picture of the performance of the business.

4.2 THE CONCEPT OF ACCRUALS

The Final Accounts of most businesses are prepared and adjusted on what is called the 'accruals basis'. The accruals basis requires that income and expenditure are recorded in the period to which they relate rather than that in which payment or receipt happens to occur. Relying simply on when cash is paid would result in the Final Accounts being distorted by the almost accidental timing of payments in relation to the beginning and end of the accounting year. Using the accruals basis instead means that the Final Accounts provide a more accurate picture of how the business has performed during the accounting year.

Final Accounts, then, must include all expenses which relate to the accounting period, irrespective of whether the expense has yet been paid or whether bills have yet been received. So far as income is concerned, the accruals basis requires the Final Accounts to include all income 'earned' during the period, irrespective of whether cash has yet been received or whether bills have yet been delivered.

Conversely, if an expense has been paid in the current accounting period which actually relates to an earlier or later period, it will not be included in the current Final Accounts. Similarly, income received in the current accounting period which actually relates to an earlier or later period will not be included in the current Final Accounts. Instead, such items will be included in the Final Accounts for the earlier or later period.

You can think of the process of determining which items relate to which period as 'matching'. The task is to 'match' the expense to the period in which the benefit of the expense was obtained, and to 'match' the income to the period in which the work producing the income was done.

Exercise 4A

You are preparing Final Accounts for Smith & Co for the accounting year ending 31 December 2024. Decide which of the following items relate to the accounting year ending 31 December 2024:

(a) electricity bill paid 10 January 2024 for period July–December 2023;

(b) electricity bill paid 10 July 2024 for period January–June 2024;

(c) electricity bill unpaid for period July–December 2024;

(d) stationery bill paid 30 November 2024. Three-quarters of the stationery purchased remains in the stationery cupboard on 1 January 2025;

(e) rent for new premises paid in advance on 28 December 2024 for period January–March 2025;

(f) work done for clients during 2024 but not yet billed by 31 December 2024, estimated at £15,000.

We have seen that the Final Accounts are prepared using the figures from the Trial Balance. These Trial Balance figures are themselves derived from the records made using the double entry system, and so it is sometimes necessary to make adjustments to the Trial Balance figures before inserting them into the Final Accounts in order to ensure that the Final Accounts follow the accruals concept.

We are now going to look at a number of different types of adjustments. However, there are a couple of general points to bear in mind. First, adjustments are always made *after* the preparation of the Trial Balance at the end of the accounting period. Secondly, each adjustment will always be reflected on both the Profit and Loss Account and the Balance Sheet.

4.3 OUTSTANDING EXPENSES

As and when expenses are paid during an accounting period, entries are usually made on the cash account and on the relevant expense account. Assume that a Trial Balance for a business includes a balance on the electricity account of £1,000. This figure reflects those electricity bills paid during the accounting period. We shall assume that the business receives a further bill for £200 for electricity used during the current year, but the bill has not been paid by the time the Trial Balance is prepared at the end of the accounting period.

As the electricity bill has not been paid, no double entries have been made and the bill is therefore not included in the Trial Balance figure. The electricity has been used in this accounting year and it therefore properly relates to this year. The Trial Balance figure for electricity is consequently too low. In order for there to be an accurate reflection of the expense incurred in relation to electricity for this year, we need to adjust the Trial Balance figure. The adjustment is made by increasing the Trial Balance figure of £1,000 by the amount of the outstanding bill of £200. The increased expense of £1,200 is then shown on Profit and Loss as the true expense for the current accounting period.

The adjustment will also be reflected on the Balance Sheet. The amount of the unpaid bill, £200, is shown on the Balance Sheet as a current liability. This shows that the business will start the next accounting year with the bill still owing. The unpaid expense can simply be shown as an additional item in the current liabilities section of the Balance Sheet. However, in practice a business is likely to have a number of unpaid expenses at the year end, it is usual to add these together and show one composite figure for unpaid expenses, labelled 'Accruals'.

Example

(Extract) Profit and Loss Account Year ended . . .

	£	£
Income		
Expenses		
Electricity	1,200	
Wages		
Stationery		

(Extract) Balance Sheet as at . . .

	£	£
Current Liabilities		
Creditors		
Accruals	200	

4.4 PAYMENTS IN ADVANCE

Payments in advance are essentially the opposite of outstanding expenses. It will sometimes be the case that a business pays an expense this year but will not get the benefit until next year, for example rent paid in advance. The payment will have been made and recorded in the current accounting year, but the expense properly relates to the following year.

Assume that the Trial Balance for a business includes a balance on the stationery account of £600, which includes £50 for stationery bought this year but which the business will use next year. The Trial Balance figure for the expense of stationery is too high. We need to adjust the Trial Balance figure of £600 by reducing it by the amount of the payment in advance, £50. The reduced expense of £550 is then shown on Profit and Loss as the true expense for stationery for the current accounting period.

The amount of the payment in advance is shown on the Balance Sheet as a current asset (usually after cash). The 'asset' for the business is the benefit of the payment already having been made. It shows that the business will begin the next accounting year being able to use something in the future without any further payment. As with outstanding expenses, it is usual to add all payments in advance for the year together and show one composite figure in the current assets section of the Balance Sheet labelled 'Prepayments'.

Example

(Extract) Profit and Loss Account Year ended . . .

	£	£
Income		
Expenses		
Electricity		
Wages		
Stationery	550	

(Extract) Balance Sheet as at . . .

	£	£
Current Assets		
Work in Progress		
Debtors		
Cash		
Prepayments	50	

4.5 WORK IN PROGRESS

A firm of solicitors, like any other business providing services, earns income by sending a bill to a client for the work done on the client's behalf. This is recorded when the bill is delivered to the client, and the relevant entries are then made in the client's account and the profit costs account. It will often be the case that a solicitor will reach the end of the accounting year having done work for a client which has not yet been billed. As a bill has not been delivered, no entries will have been made on the profit costs account to show the income earned, and yet the work has been done in the current year and it properly relates to the current year. A firm of solicitors will therefore want to adjust its profit costs account at the end of the year to reflect the value of this work in progress at that date.

The estimated value of work done but not yet billed increases the profit costs properly attributable to the current period and must be added to the balance on the profit costs account appearing on the Trial Balance. The increased figure for profit costs must be shown in the income section of the Profit and Loss Account. It is usual, however, to show the costs actually billed and the value of work in progress at the end of the year as two separate items, which are then added together on Profit and Loss Account.

The estimated figure for work in progress at the end of the year is also shown on the Balance Sheet. The figure will appear as an additional item in the current assets section. Work in progress is normally shown as the first of the current assets. This shows that the business will start the next accounting period with the benefit of that work in hand.

A firm of solicitors will begin each year with some work in progress from the previous year. It is normal to show the value of work in progress at the start of the year as a deduction on Profit and Loss Account from the value of bills issued during the year.

Example

(Extract) Profit and Loss Account Year ended . . .

	£	£
Income		
Professional Charges	478,000	
Less Opening Work in Progress	(30,000)	
Plus Closing Work in Progress	40,000	
		488,000
Expenses		

(Extract) Balance Sheet as at . . .

	£	£
Current Assets		
Work in Progress	40,000	
Debtors		
Cash		
Prepayments		

A point to note here is that the modern approach generally adopted by professional firms is to calculate work in progress by treating the right to payment as accruing gradually as the work is done. The result is that much work in progress is shown as part of the debtors figure on the Balance Sheet instead of as a separate item. However, in order to illustrate the principles clearly, we shall show work in progress separately in our examples and exercises.

4.6 CLOSING STOCK

When we calculated gross profit on the Trading Account (see **3.3.4**), we deducted the cost of goods sold from sales and we used the purchases figure to represent the cost of goods sold. However, the purchases figure does not, by itself, represent the correct value for cost of goods sold. It is highly unlikely that a business will buy, say, £10,000 worth of stock during the year and then reach the end of the year with each and every item of stock having been sold and its warehouse empty. In reality the business will have some stock which remains unsold. It is therefore necessary for a trading business to make an adjustment for the value of any stock purchased during the year and left unsold at the end of the year. The adjustment is made by showing the value of closing stock appearing in the Trading Account as a deduction from purchases in order to calculate the cost of goods sold.

The figure for closing stock will also appear as an additional item in the current assets section of the Balance Sheet. This shows that the business will be starting the next accounting year with the benefit of that stock having already been purchased. Closing stock is usually shown as the first item in the current assets section.

Unless it is the first year of trading, the business will have started the year with some stock in the warehouse left over from the previous year and still waiting to be sold. The value of this opening stock must also be taken into account when calculating the cost of goods sold.

Example

Trading Account for . . .

	£	£
Sales		12,000
Less Cost of Goods Sold		
Purchases	5,000	
plus Opening Stock	1,000	
less Closing Stock	(2,000)	
		(4,000)
GROSS PROFIT		8,000

You will see from the above example that the cost of goods sold is calculated as follows:

Cost of Goods Sold = Purchases + Opening Stock – Closing Stock

By convention, stock is valued in the Final Accounts at the *lower* of its acquisition cost or its realisable value. There is of course no guarantee that the stock left over at the end of the year can be sold even for the price that the business paid for it in the first place. The goods may be perishable or have become unfashionable, or they may have been damaged or lost. The business should inspect its stock at the end of the year to check its condition and place a realistic value on it. The value given for closing stock is therefore an estimate. This means that when you are analysing accounts, you should always look critically at the figure given for closing stock. The value given may not be a realistic assessment of its value. Overvaluing stock is an easy way to distort the accounts by making the profit figure look better. This is illustrated in the following example.

Example

In its first year of trading, a business has sales of £20,000 and purchases of £10,000. The closing stock is valued at £1,000. The Trading Account will be as follows:

Trading Account for . . .

	£	£
Sales		20,000
Less Cost of Goods Sold		
Purchases	10,000	
less Closing Stock	(1,000)	(9,000)
GROSS PROFIT		11,000

We shall now set out the Trading Account again, but this time on the basis that the closing stock is valued at £7,000. Look at the effect this has on the gross profit.

Trading Account for . . .
Year 1

	£	£
Sales		20,000
Less Cost of Goods Sold		
Purchases	10,000	
less Closing Stock	(7,000)	(3,000)
GROSS PROFIT		17,000

You will see that increasing the value for closing stock has the effect of increasing gross profit. Obviously, therefore, it is very important that the closing stock figure should be accurate. If it is not, the gross profit figure will also be inaccurate.

4.7 BAD AND DOUBTFUL DEBTS

4.7.1 Bad debts

Debtors are a current asset of a business, and they therefore increase the net value of the business appearing on the Balance Sheet. However, in reality not every debtor will pay the amount owed to the business. A debtor may become insolvent and be unable to pay; or a debtor may simply refuse to pay, and the business takes the commercial decision that it is not worth the time and expense of suing for the debt. If these so-called bad debts were to continue to be included in the Balance Sheet figure for debtors, that figure would be inaccurate and as a consequence the net value of the business would be inflated. Periodically, therefore, a business will review its debtors during the year to ascertain whether any should be declared bad and written off.

The effect of writing off a debt as bad is that the debtor is no longer shown as owing the firm money. The debtors figure from the Trial Balance is adjusted by deducting the amount of the bad debt. This adjusted figure for debtors appears on the Balance Sheet, and therefore the total of assets will be reduced.

Bad debts are regarded as an expense of the business. The value of a bad debt which has been written off will appear in the Profit and Loss Account as an additional item of expense labelled 'Bad debts'.

As well as writing off debts during the accounting period, it is common to review debtors at the end of an accounting period, to consider whether any further debts need to be written off as bad. It is the final figure for bad debts which will be shown on Profit and Loss as an expense reducing the net profit. Any further bad debts written off at that point will be deducted from the debtors figure and added to the bad debts figure before these are transferred across to the Final Accounts.

Exercise 4B

At the end of an accounting period you have already written off £1,500 debts as bad. Your remaining debtors amount to £20,000. You decide to write off a further £1,000 of debts as bad.

(a) What figure will you show on the bad debts account?
(b) What figure will you show on Profit and Loss for bad debts?
(c) What figure will you show on the Balance Sheet for debtors?

4.7.2 Doubtful debts

At the end of an accounting period after the known bad debts have been written off, the books will still show that the business is owed a certain amount by its debtors. The business may be owed this amount on paper, but the business will know from past experience that whilst it may not be able to identify any more specific debts as bad, in practice it never manages to collect all its debts.

The business knows that the debtors figure in the Trial Balance is likely to be too high and that it would therefore be inaccurate to calculate net profit on the basis that all debtors will pay, and inaccurate to include the full debtors figure on the Balance Sheet. An adjustment must be made to take account of the uncertainty regarding the debtors by making provision for doubtful debts.

To make this adjustment a business will calculate the value of debtors it thinks may never pay. Doubtful debts are considered an expense of the business. There will therefore be an additional item of expense in the Profit and Loss Account labelled as 'Provision for Doubtful Debts' (although sometimes this is added to the bad debts to give a composite figure for 'Bad and Doubtful Debts').

The adjustment must also be reflected on the Balance Sheet to demonstrate that some of the debtors figure is considered doubtful. It is usual to show the amount of the 'Provision for Doubtful Debts' on the Balance Sheet as a deduction from debtors.

Example

At the date of the Trial Balance a business has written off £15,000 of debts as bad and has £82,000 of debtors remaining. The business then decides to write off an additional debt of £2,000. Having reviewed its debtors, it concludes that £8,000 of them are doubtful; it therefore makes a provision for doubtful debts of £8,000.

The Final Accounts will appear as follows:

(Extract) Profit and Loss Account Year ended . . .

	£	£
Income		
Expenses		
Bad Debts		17,000
Provision for Doubtful Debts		8,000

(Extract) Balance Sheet as at . . .

	£	£
Current Assets		
Debtors	80,000	
Less Provision	(8,000)	
		72,000
Cash		
Prepayments		

Exercise 4C

Mabel is a solicitor in practice on her own. The bookkeeper prepares a Trial Balance and then has to make the following adjustments. There are outstanding electricity expenses of £200 to take into account, and stationery left over at the end of the year amounts to £300. A provision is to be made for doubtful debts of £175.

For questions (1)–(3) below, tick which *one* of the options you think is correct.

(1) **In relation to the £200 outstanding electricity bill:**

(a) The £200 will increase the amount shown on Profit and Loss for electricity. It will not appear on the Balance Sheet.

(b) The £200 will reduce the amount shown on Profit and Loss for electricity and will appear on the Balance Sheet as a current asset.

(c) The £200 will increase the amount shown on Profit and Loss for electricity and will appear on the Balance Sheet as a current asset.

(d) The £200 will increase the amount shown on Profit and Loss for electricity and will appear on the Balance Sheet as a current liability.

(2) **In relation to the pre-paid stationery stock of £300:**

(a) The £300 will increase the amount shown on Profit and Loss for stationery. It will not appear on the Balance Sheet.

(b) The £300 will reduce the amount shown on Profit and Loss for stationery and will appear on the Balance Sheet as a current asset.

(c) The £300 will increase the amount shown on Profit and Loss for stationery and will appear on the Balance Sheet as a current asset.

(d) The £300 will increase the amount shown on Profit and Loss for stationery and will appear on the Balance Sheet as a current liability.

(3) **Making provision for doubtful debts will:**

(a) Increase debtors.

(b) Reduce debtors.

(c) Reduce bad debts.

(d) Have no effect on debtors.

4.8 DEPRECIATION

We have seen that when a business acquires fixed assets, such as cars, computers or machinery, this will be recorded in the books of the business. The price paid for an asset will be included in the Final Accounts at the year end in the fixed assets section of the Balance Sheet. The business will have acquired the asset to benefit the business in the long term, and is therefore likely to own the asset for several years. In reality many fixed assets lose some of their value each year. You may have experienced this yourself. If, for example, you have ever owned a car, you will know that when you come to sell it, the sale price is likely to be much less than the price you paid for the car. This annual loss in value is called 'depreciation'.

Depreciation is a hidden expense of the business and must be shown on the Profit and Loss Account as an item reducing net profit.

> **Example**
>
> A business buys a machine in Year 1 for £15,000. By the end of Year 5 it is worn out and has to be scrapped. Over the five years, it has depreciated by £15,000. To look at it another way, it has cost the business £3,000 a year to keep the machine for the five years. The Profit and Loss Accounts for those years must show the annual expense of keeping the machine.

The Balance Sheet will not show just the original purchase price of the asset. Instead, it will show the original purchase price with a deduction for the amount of depreciation incurred to date. This depreciation is referred to as 'accumulated depreciation'.

> **Example**
>
> A business bought a van at the beginning of Year 1 for £20,000. Each year, the business depreciates the van by £3,000. At the end of Year 3, the business will have depreciated the van three times (once at the end of Years 1, 2 and 3). Accumulated depreciation will therefore amount to £9,000. The Balance Sheet as at the end of Year 3 would include the following item for vans:

	£	£
Fixed Assets		
Van	20,000	
less Depreciation	(9,000)	
		11,000

The £11,000 in the above example is referred to as the 'book value' of the van – its value in the business's books or accounts. Each year, the amount of accumulated depreciation shown on the Balance Sheet will increase by £3,000.

The Profit and Loss Account each year will record the loss in value over the one-year period. Thus, each year, the depreciation expense shown on Profit and Loss will be £3,000.

4.8.1 Calculation

Accountants have different methods of calculating the amount of depreciation, for example the 'straight line' method and the 'reducing balance' method. In this book, we look only at the 'straight line' method.

A business using the straight line method will decide on the likely length of the life of an asset. The loss in value is spread evenly over the projected life of the asset. Thus, if the projected life is 10 years, the business will use up 10% of the asset's original value each year. If the projected life is four years, the asset will be reduced by 25% of its original value each year.

The reason that this method is called 'straight line' is that the asset suffers the same amount of depreciation each year. If the asset is kept for the whole of its projected life, the value of the asset will eventually be reduced to zero.

The straight line method of calculating depreciation is to some extent artificial in that it presupposes an even loss of value year by year, whereas in reality an asset is likely to suffer a greater drop in the value of the asset in the first years of its life. Calculating depreciation by the straight line method also depends on an estimate being made of the useful life of an asset. The business will therefore keep the depreciation of its assets under review. If, for example, an asset looks likely to last for longer than expected, its rate of depreciation should be slowed down.

4.8.2 Date of purchase and sale

It is common practice:

(a) to depreciate all assets held at the end of an accounting period for an entire accounting period, irrespective of the point in the period at which the purchase was made;

(b) not to depreciate assets sold part way through an accounting period.

This helps to simplify the calculations.

Exercise 4D

Ruddle has been in practice as a solicitor for some years. The Trial Balance for the year ended 31 December 2024 includes the following:

	£
Interest Received	22,567
Furniture and Library at cost	15,000
Motor Cars at cost	40,000
Provision for Depreciation at start of 2024:	
Furniture and Library	4,500
Motor Cars	16,000

Depreciation is to be charged at the following rates (straight line basis):
Furniture and Library 15% pa
Motor Cars 20% pa

For questions (1)–(3) below, tick which *one* of the options you think is correct.

(1) **Depreciation on furniture and library will be:**

(a) £2,250 on Profit and Loss.

(b) £1,500 on Profit and Loss.

(c) £4,500 on Profit and Loss.

(d) £450 on Profit and Loss.

(2) **Depreciation on the furniture and library will be:**

(a) £4,500 on the Balance Sheet.

(b) £6,750 on the Balance Sheet.

(c) £2,250 on the Balance Sheet.

(d) £1,500 on the Balance Sheet.

(3) **Depreciation on motor cars will be:**

(a) £16,000 on Profit and Loss.

(b) £8,000 on Profit and Loss.

(c) £8,000 on the Balance Sheet.

(d) £16,000 on the Balance Sheet.

4.9 REVALUATION

Assets which are not depreciated, such as premises, will continue to be recorded at their acquisition value. Over time, the real value may increase. As it does so, the value recorded in the accounts will become increasingly inaccurate.

The proprietor of a business may decide to revalue the asset. The figure given for the asset in the Balance Sheet will be increased to its true value.

A business may revalue an asset at any time, but typically a proprietor will want to do so if they are considering bringing someone else into the business to run it jointly with them as a partner. The revaluation is made just before admitting the partner, so that the accounts show the increase in value as belonging to the original proprietor.

4.10 DISPOSAL OF A FIXED ASSET

4.10.1 Disposal at 'book' value

When a fixed asset is sold, this will be recorded in the books to show that the business has lost the fixed asset and gained cash.

Provided the asset is sold for exactly the value at which it is recorded in the accounts of the business, no gain or loss over book value arises as a result of the transaction. The only effect of the sale will be on the Balance Sheet, where there will be fewer fixed assets and more cash. The business has simply transformed one asset (premises) into a different sort of asset (cash). Therefore, total assets on the Balance Sheet remain the same.

4.10.2 Disposal not at 'book' value

It is fairly unusual for an asset to be sold for exactly the amount recorded in the accounts. If the asset is sold for more than its book value, the excess will be a profit on the sale. The profit will be recorded on the Profit and Loss Account and will increase net profit. If the asset is sold for less than its book value, there will be a loss on the sale. The loss will be recorded on the Profit and Loss Account and will reduce the net profit.

Only the excess or shortfall over book value is recorded on Profit and Loss. It is important to differentiate profits and losses of this type from trading profits and losses. Failure to do so will make the Final Accounts misleading. Accounts should show profit resulting from trading activities and other items such as gains and losses on sale of assets separately.

Exercise 4E

Premises recorded in the accounts at £170,000 are sold for £200,000.

(a) What is the gain over book value?

(b) What will be recorded on Profit and Loss?

(c) What effect will the sale have on the Balance Sheet, assuming the Balance Sheet is prepared immediately after the sale?

CONSOLIDATION EXERCISE

Exercise 4F

Consider the following Trial Balance.

TRIAL BALANCE AS AT 31 DECEMBER 2024

	DR	CR
Sales		250,000
Purchases	150,000	
Opening Stock	6,000	
General Expenses	60,000	
Debtors	15,000	
Capital		70,000
Drawings	10,000	
Creditors		4,000
Office Furniture	55,000	
New Cars	23,000	
Cash	1,000	
Rent Paid	3,000	
Bad Debts	1,000	
	324,000	324,000

Prepare a Profit and Loss Account and Balance Sheet, taking into account the following year-end adjustments:

(a) unpaid general expenses of £2,000;

(b) rent has been paid in advance but £1,000 of it relates to the following year;

(c) the firm wishes to create a provision for doubtful debts of £2,000;

(d) closing stock at the end of the year is estimated at £7,000;

(e) the firm decides to depreciate the new cars by 10% pa.

SUMMARY

(1) *Accruals and prepayments*

(a) Adjustments are made to income and expense accounts at the end of each accounting period to make sure that the figures on those accounts accurately reflect the expenditure and income of the accounting period.

(b) An outstanding expense will increase the expense figure on the Profit and Loss Account and it will produce an additional current liability on the Balance Sheet.

(c) A prepayment will reduce the expense figure on the Profit and Loss Account and it will produce an additional current asset on the Balance Sheet.

(2) *Closing Work in Progress and Closing Stock*

(a) Closing Work in Progress will be added to the Profit Costs figure and so will increase the income of the current year; it will be shown on the Balance Sheet as a current asset.

(b) Closing Stock will be deducted from the Cost of Goods Sold figure and so will increase the income of the current year; it will be shown on the Balance Sheet as a current asset.

(3) *Provision for doubtful debts*

(a) The business will estimate the debts which are doubtful.

(b) The estimate (called a provision) is included on Profit and Loss as an extra expense and deducted from Debtors on the Balance Sheet.

(4) *Depreciation*

(a) Many fixed assets lose value over time. One method of recording this loss of value is the 'straight line' method. The annual fall in value is recorded on the Profit and Loss Account.

(b) Each year the asset will lose a percentage of the original value – this will be the same figure each year.

(c) Each year the Balance Sheet will show the original value of the asset less all the depreciation incurred to date (the 'book value' of the asset). Each year the book value of the asset will fall.

(5) *Disposing of fixed assets*

(a) If the asset is sold for more than book value, the gain will be shown on Profit and Loss (it should be clearly differentiated from ordinary profits from trading activities).

(b) If the asset is sold for less than book value, the loss will be shown on the Profit and Loss Account (it should be clearly differentiated from ordinary business expenses).

SOLUTIONS

Exercise 4A

(a) This expense relates to an earlier accounting period and will not be included in the Profit and Loss Account for the current year even though it is paid in the current period. The amount of the expense will have been included in the previous year's Profit and Loss Account.

(b) This expense relates to the current accounting year and will be included in the Profit and Loss Account for the current year.

(c) This expense relates to the current accounting year and will be included in the current Profit and Loss Account even though not yet paid.

(d) The stationery bill should be apportioned. One-quarter of the stationery purchased has been used in the current accounting period; three-quarters will not be used until the following period. Therefore, one-quarter of the bill should be shown as an expense on the current Profit and Loss Account, and three-quarters should be carried forward as an expense to the Profit and Loss Account for the following period.

(e) The rent has been paid in the current accounting period, but the benefit will not be obtained until the following period. Therefore, the whole of the expense should be carried forward to the Profit and Loss Account for the following period.

(f) The work has been done in the current accounting period and therefore the benefit of it should be attributed to the current accounting period. It will be included on the current Profit and Loss Account as additional income.

Exercise 4B

(a) £2,500. Bad debts were £1,500; you have now written off a further £1,000.

(b) £2,500.

(c) £19,000. The debtors on the last day of the accounting period, having already written off bad debts of £1,500, were £20,000. You then wrote off a further £1,000, which will reduce debtors to £19,000.

Exercise 4C

(1) (d) Outstanding expenses increase expenses shown on Profit and Loss and are shown on the Balance Sheet as a current liability.
(2) (b) Prepaid amounts reduce expenses shown on Profit and Loss and are shown on the Balance Sheet as current assets.
(3) (b) Making provision for doubtful debts reduces debtors and appears as an expense on the Profit and Loss Account.

Exercise 4D

(1) (a) Depreciation on furniture charged to Profit and Loss is 15% of the acquisition value shown on the Trial Balance:
15% × £15,000 = £2,250
(2) (b) Accumulated depreciation shown on the Balance Sheet is the total of accumulated depreciation from previous years plus current depreciation:
£4,500 + £2,250 = £6,750
(3) (b) Depreciation on cars charged to Profit and Loss is 20% of the acquisition value shown on the Trial Balance:
20% x £40,000 = £8,000

Exercise 4E

(a) Book value was £170,000. The sale was for £200,000. Therefore, the gain over book value is £30,000.

(b) Only the gain over book value, £30,000, is recorded on Profit and Loss. Thus, the net profit of the business will be increased by £30,000.

(c) Premises will no longer be shown in the fixed assets section of the Balance Sheet. Fixed assets will therefore be reduced by £170,000.

Cash will be increased by £200,000. Overall, therefore, the assets of the business will have been increased by £30,000. The Capital Employed section will also be increased by £30,000, since the net profit of the business goes up by £30,000 and net profit is shown in the Capital Employed section of the Balance Sheet representing an amount owed to the proprietor by the business.

Exercise 4F

TRADING AND PROFIT AND LOSS ACCOUNT YEAR ENDED 31 DECEMBER 2024

Income			
Sales			250,000
Less: Cost of Goods Sold			
Purchases		150,000	
Opening Stock		6,000	
Closing Stock		(7,000)	
			(149,000)
GROSS PROFIT			101,000
Less: Expenses			
General (£60,000 + £2,000)		62,000	
Rent Paid (£3,000 – £1,000)		2,000	
Bad Debts		1,000	
Provision for Doubtful Debts		2,000	
Depreciation on cars		2,300	
			(69,300)
Net Profit			31,700

BALANCE SHEET AS AT 31 DECEMBER 2024

EMPLOYMENT OF CAPITAL

Fixed Assets			
Office Furniture		55,000	
Vehicles	23,000		
Depreciation	(2,300)		
		20,700	
			75,700
Current Assets			
Closing stock		7,000	
Debtors	15,000		
Less Provision For Doubtful Debts	(2,000)		
		13,000	
Cash at Bank		1,000	
Prepayments		1,000	
		22,000	
Current Liabilities			
Creditors	4,000		
Accruals	2,000		
		(6,000)	
NET CURRENT ASSETS			16,000
NET ASSETS			**91,700**
CAPITAL EMPLOYED			
Capital	70,000		
Drawings	(10,000)		
Profit	31,700		
			91,700

CHAPTER 5

Partnership Accounts

5.1	Introduction	47
5.2	The nature of partnerships	47
5.3	Capital accounts	48
5.4	Profit sharing	48
5.5	The appropriation account	49
5.6	Current account	49
5.7	The Balance Sheet	50
5.8	Details of movements on partners' current accounts	50
5.9	Partnership changes	51
5.10	Taxation of partnerships	51

LEARNING OUTCOMES

After reading this chapter you will be able to:

- explain how the nature of a partnership affects the form of its Final Accounts
- draw up an appropriation account
- distinguish between capital and current accounts
- describe how partnership changes are reflected in the accounts.

5.1 INTRODUCTION

So far we have concentrated on the accounts of a sole trader or sole practitioner. We are now going to turn to those businesses owned by two or more people in partnership.

5.2 THE NATURE OF PARTNERSHIPS

In a partnership, capital is contributed by a number of different proprietors (the partners) and the firm's profit is 'owed' to those partners. The business will have to keep separate records for each partner, showing:

(a) the amount of capital contributed;

(b) the amount of profit 'owed' at the end of each year by the business to the partner;

(c) the amount withdrawn from the business during the year by the partner.

The accounts of a partnership will have to show this information. This joint ownership means that there will therefore be some differences between the accounts of a business run by one person and the accounts of a partnership. The keeping of records and the presentation of the Final Accounts for the partnership will still follow the same format we have been considering so far, but there will be some additional elements in the accounts which reflect the joint nature of the business.

When a partnership is set up, the partners will usually reach an agreement on how they intend to run the business. Even if the partners themselves fail to turn their minds to this, the Partnership Act 1890 will imply terms into their business arrangement. The accounts will reflect the financial terms of the partnership agreement.

Both trading and professional businesses can be run through the medium of a partnership. In this chapter, for convenience, we shall use a solicitor's firm for our illustrations.

5.3 CAPITAL ACCOUNTS

By definition a partnership has more than one proprietor. At the outset each will contribute money to start the business. The partners may decide to contribute in equal or unequal amounts.

Each partner will have a capital account in their own name. This account will show the amount contributed by the partner.

Example

Mary and Syed set up a partnership and contribute £30,000 and £20,000 respectively as capital. The capital employed section of the Balance Sheet will show separately the balance on each capital account

Extract Balance Sheet as at ...

Capital Employed		
Mary	30,000	
Syed	20,000	
		50,000

The capital account will also show the partner's share of an increase (or decrease) in value of an asset recorded in the accounts by way of revaluation. The ratio in which partners are to share increases and decreases in the value of capital assets may be set out in the partnership agreement. If the partnership agreement is silent on this point, the partners will share capital increases and decreases in the ratio in which they agreed to share profits and losses.

5.4 PROFIT SHARING

You will now be familiar with the idea of the profit produced by a business being 'owed' to the proprietor. In a partnership, the profit will be owed to the proprietors or partners and shared between them.

A well-drafted partnership agreement should set out the profit-sharing ratio upon which the parties have decided. So, for example, if partners A and B have agreed to a profit-sharing ratio of 2:1, this means that the net profit will be divided so that A receives two-thirds and B receives one-third. If the partnership agreement is silent, the partners will share profits and losses equally.

The partnership agreement may provide for a simple profit-sharing ratio. Alternatively, the agreement may contain a more complex method of dividing the profits, whereby the partners receive 'interest on capital' and/or 'salaries'. The terminology here can be confusing because we are not using these terms in the same way as we have been using them so far, ie as an additional source of income (interest) and the wages paid to employees (salaries). In partnership accounts, 'salaries' and 'interest on capital' are simply labels given to different shares of net profit.

A salary is a set sum taken from the profit. So the partnership agreement may provide for Partner A to receive a salary of £10,000. This means that A will receive the first £10,000 of profit. This type of agreement is common where one partner is doing more of the day-to-day work in the business – the salary reflects the extra workload.

If the partnership agreement provides for the partners to receive interest on capital, this simply means that the partners will receive a share of profit calculated by reference to how much capital each partner contributed to the business. So if partners A and B contributed capital of £5,000 and £2,000 respectively, and the partnership agreement provides for them to receive 10% interest on capital, this means that A will receive £500 and B will receive £200 from the net profit. This type of agreement is common where the partners have contributed capital unequally; the interest on capital reflects the extra investment made by those partners who have contributed more.

When the net profit of the partnership has been calculated, the partners must then take that net profit figure and share it between the various partners in accordance with the terms of the partnership agreement. The amount due for 'interest' and 'salaries' is allocated first, and then any balance is divided amongst the partners in the agreed profit-sharing ratio.

Unless the partnership agreement provides otherwise, 'salaries' and 'interest' must be appropriated to partners by the partnership irrespective of whether the net profit is sufficient to cover the amount due. The result may be to produce a loss for the year, which must then be appropriated among all partners in the agreed profit-sharing ratio. A well-drafted partnership agreement should, therefore, provide that salaries and interest are due only if profits are sufficient to cover them.

5.5 THE APPROPRIATION ACCOUNT

The Profit and Loss Account of a partnership is prepared in exactly the same way as the Profit and Loss Account of a sole trader or practitioner. However, the Profit and Loss Account is extended to an appropriation account on which the allocation of net profit among the partners is shown.

Example

Wendy and Peter set up in partnership. Wendy contributes capital of £5,000 and Peter contributes £2,000. The net profit for the year has been calculated at £21,700. The partnership agreement provides for interest on capital of 10% pa, a salary for Peter of £1,000 pa and remaining profits to be divided 3:1.

Extract Profit and Loss Account for year ended ...

	£	£	£
Net Profit			21,700
Appropriations	**Wendy**	**Peter**	
Interest on Capital	500	200	700
Salary	–	1,000	1,000
Profits	15,000	5,000	20,000
	15,500	6,200	21,700

You will note that the column on the right keeps a running total of how the profits have been allocated.

5.6 CURRENT ACCOUNT

The net profit is owed to the proprietor(s) of the business. Where there is only one proprietor, we have seen that the profit is usually credited directly to the capital account. In the case of a partnership, it is usual to have a separate current account for each partner to which the appropriation of net profit (including salary and interest) is added and from which drawings are deducted. The reason for separating capital and current accounts is that, as we have seen, partners are often entitled to interest on capital contributed. It is therefore desirable to keep the original capital contribution of each partner readily identifiable and unaffected by subsequent appropriations of profits and drawings.

Exercise 5A

Pam and Theresa are in partnership as solicitors. The partnership agreement provides for interest on capital of 10% pa. Theresa is to receive a salary of £9,000 pa. Remaining profits are to be shared equally.

The Trial Balance of Pam and Theresa as at 31 December is as follows:

Trial Balance

		DR	CR
		£	£
Capital:	Pam		120,000
	Theresa		80,000
Current:	Pam		2,000
	Theresa		1,000
Drawings:	Pam	3,000	
	Theresa	2,000	
Bank Loan			34,000
Premises		200,000	
Profit Costs			260,000
General Expenses		150,000	
Travel Expenses		4,000	
Debtors		153,000	
Creditors			25,000
Cash		10,000	
Client Bank Account		400,000	
Due to Clients			400,000
		922,000	922,000

Prepare a Profit and Loss and Appropriation Account from the above figures.

5.7 THE BALANCE SHEET

The capital and current account balances of each partner are shown separately on the Balance Sheet in the capital employed section.

Example

(Extract) Balance Sheet at at ...

Capital Employed		
Capital		
Partner A	50,000	
Partner B	40,000	
Current		
Partner A	20,000	
Partner B	10,000	
		120,000

5.8 DETAILS OF MOVEMENTS ON PARTNERS' CURRENT ACCOUNTS

You will notice that, in the previous example, we showed only the final balances for the current accounts on the Balance Sheet. This is because the Balance Sheet would be very cluttered if full details of salaries, interest, profit shares and drawings were included, especially where there are several partners. It would be difficult to pick out the important figures. However, it is helpful to show information as to how the balances were arrived at. It is therefore usual to provide an appendix to the Balance Sheet which sets out the detailed picture of movements on partners' current accounts.

A common form of presentation is set out in the practical example below.

Example

Movements on partners' current accounts

	A	B
	£	£
Balance at start of accounting period	2,000	2,000
Appropriations	40,000	34,000
Drawings	(22,000)	(18,000)
Closing balance	20,000	18,000

Exercise 5B

Prepare a Balance Sheet and details of movements on partners' current accounts from the figures given in Exercise 5A and your calculation of the net profit from that exercise.

5.9 PARTNERSHIP CHANGES

The number of partners may change part of the way through an accounting period either because a new partner is admitted, or because an old partner leaves. Unless the partners agree otherwise, the net profit for the year of the change will be apportioned on a time basis to the period before and the period after the change.

Two appropriation accounts will be prepared, one allocating the pre-change profit in accordance with the pre-change partnership agreement and one allocating the post-change profit in accordance with the post-change partnership agreement.

5.10 TAXATION OF PARTNERSHIPS

Each individual partner makes a tax return claiming personal allowances. The senior partner of the firm makes a return of partnership income. HMRC then makes a joint assessment to tax in the partnership name. This assessment is based on each partner's share of profit less reliefs and charges, and supplies the senior partner with information on the method of calculation so that the tax burden may be apportioned among the partners. The tax liability of the individual partners is not shown in the partnership accounts.

SUMMARY

(1) The Profit and Loss Account of a partnership is continued to an Appropriation Account which shows the allocation of profit (interest on capital, salary and profit share) amongst the partners.

(2) Each partner has a separate capital and current account.

(3) The current account records the partner's share of net profit and drawings.

(4) The capital and current account balances for each partner are shown on the Balance Sheet.

SOLUTIONS

Exercise 5A

Profit and Loss Account for year ended 31 December ...

Income			
Profit Costs			260,000
Expenses			
General Expenses		150,000	
Travel Expenses		4,000	
			(154,000)
NET PROFIT			106,000
Appropriations			
	Pam	Theresa	
	£	£	£
Interest	12,000	8,000	20,000
Salary		9,000	9,000
Profits	38,500	38,500	77,000
	50,500	55,500	106,000

Exercise 5B

Movements in Partners' Current Accounts

	Pam	**Theresa**
	£	£
Opening Balance	2,000	1,000
Appropriations	50,500	55,500
Drawings	(3,000)	(2,000)
	49,500	54,500

Balance Sheet as at 31 December . . .

Employment of Capital		
Fixed Assets		
Premises		200,000
Current Assets		
Debtors	153,000	
Cash	10,000	
	163,000	
Current Liabilities		
Creditors	(25,000)	
Net Current Assets		138,000
Client Bank Account	400,000	
Due to Clients	(400,000)	
Less Long-term Liabilities		
Bank Loan		(34,000)
Net Assets		**304,000**
Capital Employed		
Capital: Pam	120,000	
Theresa	80,000	
Current: Pam	49,500	
Theresa	54,500	304,000

CHAPTER 6

INTRODUCTION TO COMPANY ACCOUNTS

6.1	Introduction	53
6.2	The nature of companies	53
6.3	Shareholders	54
6.4	Issuing shares	54
6.5	Maintenance of capital and a company buying its own shares	56
6.6	Debentures	56
6.7	A Company Profit and Loss Account	57
6.8	A Company Balance Sheet	59
6.9	Consolidated accounts	63
6.10	Deferred taxation	63

LEARNING OUTCOMES

After reading this chapter you will be able to:

- explain how the nature of a company affects the form of its Final Accounts
- describe how company profits are allocated
- explain the concept of reserves
- outline the purpose of deferred taxation.

6.1 INTRODUCTION

So far we have considered the Final Accounts of sole traders and partnerships. In this chapter we turn to the accounts of companies.

6.2 THE NATURE OF COMPANIES

The accounts of a company are prepared on exactly the same accounting basis as those of a sole trader or a partnership. Financial transactions will be recorded using the double entry system, and the information will be summarised and presented in the Final Accounts at the end of the year. There are, however, some differences in the presentation of the Final Accounts because of the different legal nature of a company. Understanding company accounts therefore requires an understanding of how a company operates.

A company is a distinct legal entity which is separate from its owners. A company can enter into contracts in its own name and has its own tax liabilities. A company is owned by its members (also called 'shareholders') who put money into the business by buying a 'share' in the company. A company is run on a day-to-day basis by its directors.

The directors manage the company, but they do not own the company unless they also happen to be shareholders. In small companies it is common for an individual director to be a shareholder too. In the case of large companies the directors and shareholders will usually be different.

People who want to run a business will often choose to do it through the medium of a limited company for a number of reasons. An important consideration is that there is less financial risk to the owners. Shareholders have no financial liability to the company beyond paying for their shares. If the company runs into financial difficulties, it may be wound up as insolvent but the shareholders will not be asked to cover the company's debts. The separation between those running the business and the owners also means that there is the opportunity to raise capital from 'outsiders' – the shareholders can provide the funding, leaving the directors to run the business.

Company accounts are closely regulated by a combination of legislation and accounting practices. We consider regulation in **Chapter 7**, but for now you just need to be aware that part of this regulation does influence the form and content of accounts.

The different nature of companies and the regulative requirements means that you will see some differences in layout and terminology between company accounts and the accounts of a sole trader/practitioner or partnership that we have been looking at in previous chapters. However, you should remember that the accounts are still showing the same basic information that we have seen in the Profit and Loss Account and the Balance Sheet.

6.3 SHAREHOLDERS

A person who wants to invest money will often buy shares in a company as a way of profiting from a successfully-managed business without having to fund the whole of the cost of the business. Each year the directors of the company will review the profits of the company and will decide how much of the profit, if any, can be returned to the shareholders. The payment to the shareholders is called a dividend.

For example, a company with 40,000 shares may make a £100,000 profit in a particular year. The directors may decide that they need to retain £80,000 within the company to cover expected liabilities and future expansion, but that they can pay £20,000 to the shareholders. Each shareholder will receive a dividend of 50p per share held.

Dividends are normally paid at the end of the company's trading period, although some companies will make smaller payments during the year. Dividends paid at the end of the year are referred to as 'final' dividends; those paid during the year are referred to as 'interim' dividends.

There is an element of uncertainty for the shareholders, since they depend on the decision of the directors as to the amount they will receive by way of dividend. Directors may decide, if profits are low or if substantial expansion is required, to pay no dividends in a particular year. The level of dividends paid by many companies is often quite low, and many people who invest in shares do so to obtain the increase in the value of the shares themselves as the business prospers.

Example

Mark sets up a company. He contributes £10,000 and his father contributes £40,000. In return Mark is issued with one-fifth of the shares in the company and his father is issued with four-fifths. The company's assets are currently £50,000, ie the cash contributed by Mark and his father. So if Mark's father tried to sell his shares he would probably get £40,000. Suppose that the company trades successfully for the next 10 years and the assets increase to £1 million. If a third party offers to buy the shares, Mark's father would receive four-fifths of £1 million (£800,000). The third party would then own the shares and would receive any future dividends and the benefit of any further increases in asset values.

6.4 ISSUING SHARES

A shareholder puts money into a company and in return the company issues shares to the shareholder. When a company issues shares, this is recorded in the same way as when a sole trader/practitioner or partner introduces capital. However, rather than use a separate capital account for each shareholder, the company will record the transaction in a composite share capital account.

Using one share capital account makes recording the entries much easier. There could be a large number of different shareholders, for example, so that having a separate capital account for each one would be unmanageable. Having one account also avoids the company having to keep updating the names of different capital accounts every time a shareholder sells their shares.

You will now be familiar with the capital account for a sole trader/practitioner or for individual partners appearing in the 'capital employed' section of the Balance Sheet. This is also the case for the capital introduced by the shareholders when being issued with their shares. However, in a company Balance Sheet this section is usually headed differently. There is no absolute consistency in the terminology used, but 'Financed By', 'Equity' and 'Capital and Reserves' are commonly seen as headings.

Example

Extract from Balance Sheet for X Ltd as at 31 December 202–

Net Assets	**200,000**
Capital and Reserves	
Share capital	200,000
	200,000

6.4.1 Issuing shares at par

A company may issue shares either at par or at premium. (It is not possible for shares to be issued at a discount: see Companies Act (CA) 2006, s 580.) Each share has a nominal or par (ie face) value, eg £1. The issue of shares at par means that the shares are 'sold' to the shareholder for their nominal value.

6.4.2 Issuing shares at a premium

The issue of shares at a premium means that the shares are 'sold' to the shareholders for more than their nominal value. So, a share with a nominal value of £1 may be issued to a shareholder for £1.50; the premium is 50p. When the issue of shares is recorded in the books, the premium element is recorded separately in a share premium account and is shown separately from the share capital on the Balance Sheet.

6.4.3 Types of shares

A company may issue shares of different types. For example, it may issue ordinary shares, which carry the usual rights of a shareholder to receive dividends and vote when company decisions are referred to the shareholders, and preference shares, which carry preferential rights such as entitling the preference shareholder to dividends in priority to ordinary shareholders. If there is only a small profit, the preference shareholders may receive a dividend and the ordinary shareholders nothing. A company may also issue shares of the same type carrying different rights, for example voting and non-voting ordinary shares.

The company law distinctions between these different shares are beyond the scope of this book. The important point to appreciate is that, whatever type of share is issued, the basic entries are precisely the same. However, the different kinds of shares will be shown separately in the Balance Sheet.

Example

(Extract) Balance Sheet for Y Ltd as at 31 December Year 1

Net Assets	**500,000**
Capital and Reserves	
Preference Shares	100,000
Ordinary Shares	300,000
Share Premium Account	100,000
	500,000

6.5 MAINTENANCE OF CAPITAL AND A COMPANY BUYING ITS OWN SHARES

6.5.1 Maintenance of capital

A general principle of company law is that capital, once raised, must be maintained. After members have paid for their shares, the money produced constitutes the company's capital. Creditors will expect this fund to remain in the company to be available to meet the company's debts and, because the liability of the members of the company is limited, this capital sum should not be diminished (although, of course, assets can be lost through unsuccessful trading).

To provide this protection for creditors of companies, it is not normally permissible for the company to return the shareholders' initial investment during the lifetime of the company. The impact of this on the members of the company is that, having bought their shares, they cannot normally hand back their share certificate to the company in exchange for the consideration they originally provided. However, if the business is successful the owners will often be able to sell their shares to third parties. They will receive a price based on the value of the company's assets at the date of the sale, plus something for the 'goodwill' of the business generated by their successful past trading.

6.5.2 Company buying its own shares

One of the consequences of the need for a company to maintain its share capital is that a company must not generally purchase its own shares (CA 2006, s 658).

However, there are often circumstances where it is helpful for a company to be able to buy its own shares. This is particularly the case for small and medium-sized private companies because there is not usually a ready market for the shares of such companies. A small company might want to buy out a dissident shareholder who may be harming the company's business, buy the shares of a deceased shareholder where the personal representatives or beneficiaries under the will do not wish to keep them, or buy the shares of a proprietor of a company who is retiring to make way for new management.

The CA 2006, s 690 permits a company, provided various conditions are complied with, to purchase its own shares. Once purchased, the shares are cancelled and the issued share capital reduced by the nominal amount of the shares.

6.6 DEBENTURES

If a company borrows money, it will commonly do so by issuing debentures. A debenture is a document evidencing a loan made to the company. Thus, if a company issues debentures of £50,000, this basically means that the company is borrowing £50,000.

A debenture differs from a share in that a debenture holder is not an owner of the company (ie they are not a shareholder) and the payment of interest on a debenture is not dependent on the making of profits by the company. From the point of view of the company, this has advantages and disadvantages.

Exercise 6A

You are a director of a company. You wish to raise additional capital of £50,000 and are trying to decide whether to issue more shares, or whether to borrow.
What are the advantages and disadvantages of each course of action from the company's perspective?

6.7 A COMPANY PROFIT AND LOSS ACCOUNT

Whether a company is in the business of dealing in goods or services, much of the Profit and Loss Account will look very similar to the accounts of a sole trader practitioner business. It will show the same type of trading income and other types of income, as well as similar expenses. The same accounting principles and concepts, such as accruals, depreciation, etc, will govern the way in which the figures are arrived at.

The Profit and Loss Account of a company shows the company's income and deducts expenses to show the company's profit. There are, however, some minor differences in the types of expense which may appear on a company's Profit and Loss Account. These differences flow from the fact that a company is a separate legal person, with its own legal identity separate from those of its shareholders and directors. A salary paid to a director is, from the company's point of view, an expense incurred in earning profit and will therefore appear on the Profit and Loss Account as an expense. This is so even if the director is a shareholder and therefore an 'owner' of the business. It is an expense in the same way as wages paid to ordinary employees. In contrast, a 'salary' paid to a partner under the terms of the partnership agreement is merely a method of allocating the profit and will appear on the appropriation section of the account.

6.7.1 The appropriation of profit

The Profit and Loss Account of a partnership shows the calculation of net profit and then continues into an appropriation account to show how that profit is to be allocated or appropriated. The net profit of a company is also allocated for particular purposes. For a company there are three main purposes: taxation; dividends; and retention of profits.

6.7.1.1 Taxation

Tax is not a feature of the accounts of sole traders/practitioners or partnerships simply because these types of business do not have a tax liability. Instead tax is paid by the sole trader/practitioner or the individual partners on the benefits they derive from the business. In contrast, a company has its own tax liability, and this will appear in the accounts.

The first item to be considered after the net profit has been ascertained is the company's liability to corporation tax on that profit. A company is no different from an individual in that it has a legal liability to pay tax and must be sure that provision is made to meet its tax bill. Until tax has been provided for, the directors cannot make a decision on the declaration of a dividend.

For most companies corporation tax is not normally payable until nine months after the end of the accounting period. So when the Final Accounts are prepared at the end of that accounting period, the company will not actually have paid any tax on its profits from that year. On its Profit and Loss Account the company will show that a certain amount of profit is needed to pay the company's tax bill by setting out the company's profits before and after tax.

Example

In its first year of trading, a company has income of £200,000 and expenses of £100,000. It estimates that corporation tax of £20,000 will be payable

(Extract) Profit and loss Account for the year ending ...

Net Profit before tax	**100,000**
Tax	(20,000)
Post Tax Profit	**80,000**

The company has a liability to pay the tax when it falls due. The amount of tax due to HMRC will therefore appear on the Balance Sheet as a current liability.

Example

(Extract) Balance Sheet as at ...

Current Assets		
Cash	30,000	
Current Liabilities		
Creditors	(xxx)	
Provision for Tax	(20,000)	
Net Current Assets		xxx

When the tax is eventually paid the provision will disappear from the current liabilities section and cash will be reduced in the current assets section.

Large companies are treated rather differently for tax purposes. A 'large' company for this purpose is one whose profits in the accounting period in question exceed a set amount (currently £1.5 million). Most large companies have to pay their corporation tax in four instalments.

In practice, the company will makes the first payment six months and 14 days after the start of the company's accounting period, and subsequent payments will be made quarterly. The first instalments will obviously have to be based on an estimate of the company's profits. At the date of the Balance Sheet at the end of the accounting period a large company will already have paid two instalments of tax and the rest will still be outstanding.

Very large companies (ie those whose profits exceed £20 million in the accounting period) also pay corporation tax in four instalments, but on different dates. The first instalment is due two months and 13 days after the first day of the accounting period, and quarterly thereafter.

6.7.1.2 Dividends

A dividend represents a distribution of part of the net profit to the owners of the company (ie the shareholders). A company is most unlikely to distribute the whole of its profit after tax. There are two reasons for this:

(a) it will need to retain funds to meet future costs of running or expanding the business;

(b) much of the profit is not actually available in the form of cash – profit may be represented by any assets (eg stock, debtors or fixed assets).

The directors will decide how much cash can, in their opinion, safely be distributed to the shareholders by way of a dividend. The balance of the profit after tax is retained within the company. Company law requirements mean that the company cannot actually pay the dividend until the shareholders approve its size in the annual general meeting, which will take place after the end of the accounting period.

Strictly speaking, dividends which have been recommended but not approved are not yet payable. A recommended dividend will not be shown in the accounts, but it will be mentioned in the accompanying Notes to the accounts.

Once a dividend has been paid, it could, as it is an allocation of profit, be shown in an appropriation account in the same way as a partnership's allocation of profit appears in an appropriation account. However, in practice, the payment of a dividend is usually included in the Notes to the accounts or in a separate statement (see **Chapter 7**).

6.7.1.3 Retained profit

Once provision has been made for taxation and dividends, the balance of the net profit is retained in the business.

The retained profit is profit which could be distributed to the shareholders should the directors decide to distribute it. The retained profit is therefore 'owed' to the shareholders and will be shown on the Balance Sheet. In just the same way as the net profit for a sole trader is transferred across to the 'capital employed' section of the Balance Sheet to show the total amount owed to the proprietor, so in a company the retained profit is carried across to the Balance Sheet. The retained profits are often referred to as a 'Profit and Loss Reserve', and are normally shown on the Balance Sheet immediately after the share capital to show the total amount 'owed' to the shareholders.

6.8 A COMPANY BALANCE SHEET

6.8.1 Capital and reserves

The main difference in a company Balance Sheet is contained in the 'Capital Employed' or, as it is often headed in company accounts, 'Capital and Reserves' section.

Example

(Extract) Balance Sheet as at . . .

NET ASSETS	**220,000**
CAPITAL AND RESERVES	
Share Capital	100,000
Debenture Redemption Reserve	20,000
Profit and Loss Reserve	100,000
SHAREHOLDERS FUNDS	**220,000**

We have already looked at the 'capital' element of this as the shareholders' original capital contribution to the company in return for the issue of shares. Now we shall turn to the reserves element.

6.8.2 Reserves

The term 'reserve' can be confusing, because at first sight it suggests an extra pot of cash at the company's disposal. However, this is not the case. The reserves appear in the equivalent to the 'Capital Employed' section of the Balance Sheet. This section of a Balance Sheet shows the amount which a business 'owes' to its owners. So, reserves are 'owed' to the shareholders but not distributed to them. Reserves essentially arise through profits being retained within the company.

A company Balance Sheet may show different types of reserves. The principal division is between revenue reserves and capital reserves. A revenue reserve is one which (in theory at least) could be distributed to the shareholders at any time, for example through the payment of a dividend. A capital reserve is one which is not available for distribution in this way.

6.8.2.1 Revenue reserves

Most reserves are revenue reserves. A revenue reserve may be created by retaining profits for a specific purpose, or merely by retaining profit generally. In either case, the assets represented by the reserve profit can be used for the payment of dividends in future years, always assuming that the necessary cash is available.

The Profit and Loss Reserve is the main example of a revenue reserve. We have seen that after tax has been provided for and a decision taken on the payment of a dividend, the remaining profits will be retained in the company. This figure will appear on the Balance Sheet as the Profit and Loss Reserve. As the company generates profits year on year, they will be added to this figure so that over time the retained profit figure increases.

Exercise 6B

Study the following extract from the Profit and Loss Account and Balance Sheet.

Profit and Loss Account for year ending . . .

	£
Profit before tax	**70,000**
Tax	(22,000)
Profit after tax	**48,000**

Balance Sheet as at . . .

Share Capital	100,000
Reserves	100,000

Tick which one you think is correct.

Assume no dividend has been paid. On last year's Balance Sheet, reserves would have been:

(a) £100,000;
(b) £148,000;
(c) £52,000;
(d) £48,000.

It is often difficult for people not directly involved in the management of the company (eg shareholders, employees) to understand why large amounts of profit are being retained in the company instead of being returned to the shareholders as dividends or being used to pay salaries for employees. It is quite common, therefore, for directors to indicate why profits are being retained by attaching labels to portions of retained profit, such as 'debenture redemption reserve', indicating that some of the profits have been retained in anticipation of the company having to repay a debenture in the future. A debenture redemption reserve is a revenue reserve. It is important to realise that the labels are for convenience only; the reserves remain undistributed profits *owed* to shareholders.

Example

Consider the following Balance Sheet. The company has a debenture and has created a Debenture Reserve to show that profits are being retained in the company so that the debenture can be paid back when required.

Balance Sheet as at ...

	£	£
ASSETS		
Fixed Assets		40,000
Current Assets		
Cash	25,000	
less Current Liabilities		
Creditors	(5,000)	
Net Current Assets		20,000
		60,000

Long-term Liabilities		
Debenture		(10,000)
		50,000
CAPITAL AND RESERVES		
Share Capital	20,000	
Debenture Reserve	10,000	
Profit and Loss	20,000	
		50,000

Now we shall look at the Balance Sheet as it will appear after the debenture has been paid back:

Balance Sheet as at ...

	£	£
Fixed Assets		40,000
Current Assets		
Cash	15,000	
less Current Liabilities		
Creditors	(5,000)	
Net Current Assets		10,000
		50,000
CAPITAL AND RESERVES		
Share Capital	20,000	
Debenture Reserve	10,000	
Profit and Loss	20,000	
		50,000

Cash has been reduced by £10,000. The debenture of £10,000 has disappeared. Notice that the debenture redemption reserve has remained on the Balance Sheet. This is because it is merely undistributed profit 'owed' to the shareholders. Nothing has been distributed to the shareholders, so this 'liability' remains. The company may decide to relabel the reserve.

Retaining profit for a particular purpose does not mean that the cash will be available for that purpose when it is required in the future. Although the value of the assets as a whole will have increased as a result of making a profit, the increase is likely to be in the form of extra fixed assets or trading stock, rather than extra cash. Therefore, in order to ensure that the required amount of cash is available, it will be necessary to set aside an equivalent amount of cash in a reserve fund (sometimes called a 'sinking fund') at the same time as profit is retained within the business.

6.8.2.2 Capital reserves

Capital reserves are reserves which, for legal or practical reasons, are not available for distribution by way of dividend. They are part of the long-term capital of the company and therefore not free to be returned to shareholders. The CA 2006 requires some capital reserves to be shown separately on the Balance Sheet.

We have already encountered one type of capital reserve, namely the share premium account (see **6.4.2**). We saw that when a company issues shares at a premium, it is required to record the surplus over the nominal value of the shares on the share premium account (CA 2006, s 610). The share premium account must be shown separately on the Balance Sheet.

A revaluation reserve is an example of a capital reserve. A revaluation reserve is created when a company decides to revalue its assets. As in the case of a partnership, when a company decides to increase the value of an asset to a more realistic amount, the value of assets shown in the Balance Sheet is increased. There must be a corresponding increase in the 'Capital Employed' section of the Balance Sheet. Unlike a partnership, however, it is not the capital accounts which will record this increase; instead, a reserve account will be opened which will be credited with the revaluation increase. A revaluation reserve simply records the fact that asset values have increased.

Example

A company decides to revalue its fixed assets. The revaluation produces a net increase of £100,000 over the assets' previous book value of £140,000. The Balance Sheet will therefore appear as follows:

(Extract) Balance Sheet as at ...

	Before	After
Fixed Assets	140,000	240,000
Net Current Assets	180,000	180,000
	320,000	420,000
CAPITAL AND RESERVES		
Share Capital	100,000	100,000
Revaluation Reserve	–	100,000
Profit and Loss Reserve	220,000	220,000
	320,000	420,000

A new reserve has been created, fixed assets have increased and net current assets remain unchanged.

A capital redemption reserve is required where a company buys back shares out of profits. The company can buy its own shares only if it has the funds available to do so. This usually means distributable profits. To avoid reducing its capital, the company is required to transfer to a capital redemption reserve an amount equivalent to the share capital bought back (CA 2006, s 733).

6.8.2.3 Capitalisation of reserves

The result of retaining part of the net profit in the business is that, after a number of years, a company will have built up substantial reserves of undistributed profit. Although these reserves are in theory 'owed' to the shareholders, in reality they will be represented by fixed assets and net current assets, and there will not be sufficient cash to pay the shareholders everything 'owed'. To recognise this state of affairs, the company may decide to capitalise some of these reserves by making a bonus issue of shares to its members.

The effect of a bonus issue is that each shareholder will own a greater number of shares, but the value of each individual share will be less since the shares as a whole will still be represented by the same total value of assets. In addition, future dividends are likely to be declared at a lower rate because a similar amount of net profit will have to be apportioned among a larger number of shares.

Exercise 6C

Study the following extract from a Balance Sheet.

Balance Sheet as at [date]

Assets	**600,000**
Capital and Reserves	
Share capital	**50,000**
Reserves	**550,000**
	600,000

Assume that the company decides to make a 'two for one' bonus issue against reserves. Which one of the following statements is correct?

(a) Assets will be reduced by £100,000.
(b) Reserves will increase by £100,000.
(c) Reserves will be reduced by £100,000.
(d) Share capital will be increased by £50,000.

6.9 CONSOLIDATED ACCOUNTS

It is very common for a company which is expanding its business activities either to acquire control of other companies, or to compartmentalise parts of its own organisation so that each part can be run as a separate company (this is sometimes described as 'ring fencing' hazardous parts of the company's business undertaking). The resulting business combinations are referred to as 'groups'. The controlling company is referred to as the 'parent' and the controlled company as the 'subsidiary'.

With some exceptions (mainly for small companies), s 399 of the CA 2006 requires group accounts to be prepared by a 'parent company'. A parent company is essentially a company which holds a majority of the voting rights in a subsidiary, or which has some other significant influence over decision making in the subsidiary, for example by having the power to appoint and remove a majority of the directors.

Shareholders in the parent company need additional financial statements to show the combined results of all the companies in the group if they are to be able to assess performance of their company.

A parent company is normally required to produce:

(a) a consolidated Profit and Loss Account showing the profit or loss of the group; and
(b) a consolidated Balance Sheet showing the assets and liabilities of the group as a whole.

Although each company retains its own legal identity and must prepare its own Final Accounts, the requirements as to group accounts reflect the commercial reality that the group as a whole is a single unit.

6.10 DEFERRED TAXATION

A company pays corporation tax on its profits. However, the profit figure on which tax is payable is not the same as the profit figure which is calculated on the Profit and Loss Account. This is because tax legislation is not in the same terms as accounting rules. Some of the expenses which appear on the Profit and Loss Account, such as depreciation, are not deductible from income for tax purposes. In addition, tax legislation allows some deductions which do not feature on the Profit and Loss Account, such as capital allowances. Also, some items of income, such as government grants, are not taxable. The result is that it is often difficult to relate the tax figure to the accounting profit without further information.

6.10.1 The concept

Accountants like to spread expenses evenly over the period to which they relate. Straight line depreciation (see **4.8.1**), where the reduction in value of the assets is spread evenly across the life of the assets, is an example of this.

HMRC is not concerned with matching income and expenses to the appropriate period in the same way. Depreciation is not regarded as a deductible expense for tax purposes, so the tax liability of a company must be calculated on its net profit before deducting depreciation.

Although depreciation is not a deductible expense for tax purposes, the Government wishes to encourage companies to expand and improve. Companies are allowed to deduct part of the cost of some types of assets against their profits for tax purposes under the capital allowance scheme. The rules on the amount which can be deducted in the form of capital allowances vary according to the policies of the current Government.

In some tax years, companies are allowed large 'first year' capital allowances on the cost of purchasing assets. When this is possible, the company obtains a great deal of tax relief in that year, resulting in a low tax bill and consequently large post-tax profits for that year. Once the allowance has been claimed, there will be little or no tax relief for later years, which means larger tax bills and, therefore, smaller post-tax profits for those years.

A distorting effect on a company's post-tax profit is produced by the fact that the benefit of the capital allowance on the purchase of an item of plant or machinery is usually greater initially than the figure treated as an annual accounting expense for depreciation. (Correspondingly, in later years it is generally smaller.) In simple terms, from an accounting point of view, 'too much' tax relief is being allowed initially and, as a result, too much tax will be charged in later years. Accountants would describe such a situation by saying that a timing difference exists.

6.10.2 Object of deferred tax accounting

The object of deferred tax accounting is to redistribute the tax liability shown on the Profit and Loss Account as though timing differences did not exist, and to iron out the distortions which they produce.

The figure for post-tax profits is used by many as a measure of a company's performance. Ordinarily, therefore, a reduction in the post-tax profits from one year to the next would be a cause for concern. However, it may be the case that in the first year the business received large capital allowances, which reduced its tax liability and thus increased its post-tax profit. In the following year, the business may have received lower capital allowances, which increased its tax liability, thus reducing its post-tax profit.

Accountants preparing accounts generally deal with timing differences by creating a provision for tax in a year in which they consider too little tax is being charged. This provision is used in later years to reduce the burden of the tax charged against current profits.

6.10.3 A basic illustration

First, consider how, in the absence of deferred tax accounting, the accounts of the following business (AB Ltd) would appear. For convenience, the example assumes an unchanging corporation tax rate of 30% for all of the years mentioned, and also that 100% capital allowances were available to the company. These assumptions highlight the problems caused by timing differences and make the illustration easier to follow.

Example

AB Ltd is a company which in recent years was making (after depreciation and other overheads) a profit of £15,000 per annum. Assume that in the first year covered by the example, it bought a machine for £15,000. The machine has an expected working life of three years, so that (calculated on the straight line basis) depreciation is for accounting purposes being treated as an annual expense of £5,000.

Since depreciation does not qualify as a deductible expense for tax purposes, the £5,000 will have to be added back to calculate the profit on which tax is payable.

The company took a 100% capital allowance in the year of acquisition in respect of the machine.

You will see from the example that the capital allowance has a distorting effect on the post-tax profit figures because the tax relief is taken in the first year and not spread over the machine's working life.

	Taxable profit	Tax @ 30%	Post-tax profit
Year	£	£	£
1	20,000		
less allowance	(15,000)		
	5,000	1,500	13,500
2	20,000	6,000	9,000
3	20,000	6,000	9,000

Over the three-year period, the company pays a total of £13,500 in tax. If this were spread evenly over the three-year period, the company would pay £4,500 pa. This means that in Year 1 the company paid £3,000 too little in tax. In each of the next two years, the company pays £1,500 too much.

To iron out this distortion, AB Ltd should create in Year 1 a provision for deferred tax equal to the amount of tax 'saved' as a result of the excess tax relief (the originating difference). This provision would be shown on the Profit and Loss Account in Year 1, and would have the effect of reducing the post-tax profit for that year. In subsequent years, the provision would be used, and therefore shown on the Profit and Loss Account as a deduction from the taxation figure. This would have the effect of increasing the post-tax profit for subsequent years.

Example

The Profit and Loss Account for Year 1 should show the actual tax paid as well as a provision for the amount of tax saved as a result of the excessive relief.

(a) Using the figures from the example above, it will be necessary to create a provision of £3,000 for Year 1:

Profit and Loss Account for Year 1

	£	£
Net Profit		15,000
Tax	1,500	
plus Provision	3,000	
		(4,500)
Post-tax Profit		10,500

In subsequent years, the accounts will have to show the actual tax paid of £6,000 pa. However, part of the provision created in Year 1 on the Profit and Loss Account will be used to reduce the amount finally shown as charged against profits.

(b) Each year, £1,500 of the provision will be used to reduce the amount of tax charged in the Profit and Loss Account.

Profit and Loss Account for Years 2 and 3

	£	£
Net Profit		15,000
Tax	6,000	
less Provision	(1,500)	
		(4,500)
Post-tax Profit		10,500

When looking at a set of accounts, you should certainly be concerned if no provision at all has been made, since this may mean that the business will face heavy tax bills in the future. This would mean a dramatic fall in post-tax profits.

SUMMARY

(1) A company has a separate legal identity from its owners (the shareholders) and the people who run it (the directors).

(2) A company has its own tax liability.

(3) A company's net profit is allocated to:

   (a) payment of tax;

   (b) dividends;

   (c) retention within the company.

(4) A company which has a subsidiary must produce consolidated accounts which show the position of the group as a whole.

(5) Because capital allowances may cause fluctuations in post-tax profit, it is usual to make a provision for deferred tax designed to iron out distortions.

SOLUTIONS

Exercise 6A

Shares

Advantages

Dividends need only be paid if profits are sufficient, and the directors will decide on any amount to be paid.

Shares are not normally bought back by the company, so once issued the company has no further capital liability to the shareholder during the lifetime of the company.

Disadvantages

Shareholders have voting power in relation to some company decisions.

Debentures

Advantages

Debenture holders have no voting power.

Disadvantages

The interest under the loan agreement must be paid even if profits are poor.

Cash will have to be available to pay back the debenture in the future.

Exercise 6B

(c) This year's reserved profits will be added to accumulated reserves. As the result is £100,000, last year's reserves must have been £100,000 less £48,000, ie £52,000.

Exercise 6C

(c) Each shareholder will receive two shares for every one share held. Therefore the company will issue 100,000 £1 shares. Share capital will increase by £100,000. Reserves will be reduced by £100,000. Assets will not be affected.

CHAPTER 7

Company Accounts: Regulation and Format

7.1	Introduction	67
7.2	The role of regulation	67
7.3	Statutory regulation	67
7.4	Accounting principles	68
7.5	Accounts formats	69
7.6	Annual reports and accounts	73

LEARNING OUTCOMES

After reading this chapter you will be able to:

- explain the importance of the regulation of company accounts
- describe the origin of accounts regulation
- describe the different formats of company accounts used in the UK.

7.1 INTRODUCTION

You have seen that the legal nature of a company is reflected in its Final Accounts. In this chapter you will examine how statutory and non-statutory regulations determine the format in which company accounts are presented.

7.2 THE ROLE OF REGULATION

Regulation is means of achieving uniformity. Earlier we highlighted the fact that there is a lot to be said for uniformity in the preparation and presentation of accounts. Uniformity means that accounts can be read and interpreted by anyone who understands the rules, and enables direct comparisons to be made between the accounts of different businesses.

The desirability of uniformity is heightened in relation to companies, where large numbers of individuals, some of whom may not be financially sophisticated, become directly involved by investing as shareholders.

Consistency in the preparation of accounts helps to create transparency. It is important that investors and others can trust and rely upon the information contained in the accounts.

Companies are an integral part of the economy. Regulation exists for the protection of the general public. Society generally has an interest in transparency, reliability, equivalence and comparability of published information about companies.

7.3 STATUTORY REGULATION

Companies are a creation of statute. It is not surprising, therefore, that their accounts are also subject to a substantial amount of statutory regulation.

The statutory regulation of company accounts is contained mainly in Part 15 of the CA 2006. Part 15 contains the procedural requirements for company accounts for all UK companies.

The Act imposes slightly different requirements on different kinds of company. The main distinction for this purpose is between companies which are subject to the small companies regime and companies not subject to that regime. A company is subject to the small companies regime if it is a private company which satisfies two or more of the following requirements contained in s 382: its turnover is not more than £10.2 million; its Balance Sheet total is not more than £5.1 million; and it does not employ more than 50 employees (the turnover and Balance Sheet limits are set to increase to £15 million and £7.5 million respectively with effect from 6 April 2025). Broadly speaking, for these companies the statutory requirements have historically been more relaxed.

At the most basic level, s 386(1) requires every company to keep 'adequate accounting records'. The directors and other officers of the company commit a criminal offence if they fail to keep such records.

The directors must prepare accounts for the company for each of its financial years (s 394). Section 393 provides that directors of a company must not approve accounts unless they are satisfied that they give a true and fair view of the assets, liabilities, financial position and profit or loss, and auditors must have regard to that obligation when carrying out their functions.

In addition, the CA 2006 requires certain accounts to be filed with the Registrar of Companies. Companies subject to the small companies regime must file a copy of a Balance Sheet drawn up on the last day of the financial year, and a copy of the auditor's report unless the company is exempt from audit. Medium-sized companies may file abbreviated accounts. A company is medium-sized if it satisfies two or more of the following requirements: its turnover is not more than £36 million; its Balance Sheet total is not more than £18 million; and it does not employ more than 250 employees (s 465) (the turnover and Balance Sheet limits are set to increase to £54 million and £27 million respectively with effect from 6 April 2025). All other companies must file full accounts (ss 445–447).

Every company must send a copy of its annual accounts and reports for each financial year to shareholders, debenture holders and anyone entitled to receive notice of general meetings (s 423), although in certain circumstances it may provide a strategic report instead of copies of the accounts (s 426 and Companies (Receipt of Accounts and Reports) Regulations 2013 (SI 2013/1973)). If it is a public company, it must then put the final accounts before the members in general meeting.

Companies normally have to have their accounts audited. Most small companies are exempt from this requirement (s 475). However, shareholders with at least 10% of the nominal issued share capital can always require the company to obtain an audit of its accounts for a financial year (s 476).

At the time of writing, the relevant provisions of the Economic Crime and Corporate Transparency Act 2023 are yet to be implemented. The Act is set to make a number of changes to the filing requirements for companies, including making the filing of accounts in digital format compulsory, making the filing of accounts compulsory for most companies irrespective of size and requiring companies claiming exemptions from filing/audit requirements to provide additional evidence.

7.4 ACCOUNTING PRINCIPLES

For many years company accounts have been subject to statutory regulation under successive Companies Acts. To supplement this statutory regulation, initially the professional bodies of the accounting profession issued recommendations of best practice to their members. By the 1970s it was felt that these to some extent ad hoc arrangements were no longer sufficient to meet the needs of the accounting world. A more formal and centralised system of setting standards and requirements was called for. The professional bodies therefore combined in producing uniform accounting principles to be followed.

7.4.1 UK regulation

The centralised regulation system created in the 1970s required accountants to follow generally accepted accounting principles (GAAP). These principles comprised a combination of statutory requirements, Financial Reporting Standards (FRSs) and a mixture of recommendations of best practice, called collectively 'UK GAAP'.

Over the years, UK GAAP expanded to the point where it was felt to be complex and unwieldy. In January 2015, the UK central regulator, the Financial Reporting Council, replaced UK GAAP with a new accounting regime, the key element of which is FRS 102 The Financial Reporting Standard applicable in the UK and Republic of Ireland. FRS 102 is a comprehensive statement of accounting practice applicable to the majority of UK companies. It is aimed at achieving consistency in the preparation of accounts and is subject to periodic review. FRS 102 addresses the accounting principles which must be adopted by, for example, specifying which method of calculation of depreciation should be used and how closing stock is to be valued, as well as dictating some of the detail which must appear on the face of the Profit and Loss Account and Balance Sheet, and specifying what additional documentation should be provided. FRS 102 (and its associated statutory requirements) is often referred to as 'UK GAAP' or 'New UK GAAP'.

7.4.2 International regulation

It will not surprise you to know that whilst the United Kingdom was developing its own system of accounting regulation, other countries were engaged in the same task. The system of regulation in this country was therefore referred to as UK GAAP in order to distinguish it from the systems of other jurisdictions, such as US GAAP or German GAAP.

The fact of different regulatory systems operating in different countries was of little practical significance until the 1990s when trade and commerce became increasingly international in nature. Individual countries having their own accounting systems was no longer sufficient to meet the needs of a global market. In 2001 the International Accounting Standards Board (IASB) was formed. The IASB issues its own International Financial Reporting Standards (IFRS) which are capable of being adopted in different jurisdictions. The IFRS cover the same aspects of accounts preparation and presentation as FRS 102, but have their own system of rules and regulations.

From 1 January 2021, group accounts of a parent company whose securities are admitted to trading on a UK regulated market must be prepared in accordance with UK Adopted International Accounting Standards (UK Adopted IAS). With that exception, an individual company can follow either FRS 102 or UK Adopted IAS in preparing its accounts.

7.4.3 Conclusion

The financial reporting rules change rapidly. However, in reality, business transactions are becoming increasingly complex, and accounting standards have to change to accommodate them. This book cannot even begin to address the detail and complexity of accounts regulation. Instead, we are going to focus on the results of this regulation, looking at how regulation affects some of the form and content of the accounts you will encounter in practice.

7.5 ACCOUNTS FORMATS

Section 395 of the CA 2006 requires companies to prepare either 'Companies Act Individual Accounts' or 'UK Adopted International Accounting Standards Individual Accounts'. Essentially, the format of Companies Act Individual Accounts complies with FRS 102 (see **7.5.1**), and that of International Accounting Standards Individual Accounts complies with UK Adopted IAS (see **7.5.2**).

Before we look at the differences between these two types of accounts formats, there is one presentation requirement that is common to both but which has been omitted from the examples that follow for the sake of simplicity. This is the requirement that the preceding year's figures must be shown alongside the equivalent figures for the current year. This is very helpful for anyone examining the accounts, as it enables direct year-on-year comparisons to be made, so that changes and trends in the company's performance may be identified.

7.5.1 Companies Act format

Section 395 of the CA 2006 provides that Companies Act Individual Accounts must be prepared 'in accordance with section 396'. Beyond stating that there must be a Profit and Loss Account and a Balance Sheet, s 396 does not give any indication of the format for the accounts. It does provide, however, that Companies Act Individual Accounts must comply with any relevant regulations. It is in these regulations that the detailed requirements for the format of the accounts may be found.

The main regulations dealing with company accounts formats are the Large and Medium-sized Companies and Groups (Accounts and Reports) Regulations 2008 (SI 2008/410) (and their equivalent for small companies, SI 2008/409). The Regulations contain a small number of format templates showing the way in which both Profit and Loss Accounts and Balance Sheets must be drawn up. These formats are not absolutely mandatory in the sense that some adaptation is permitted, and so you will encounter some variations in practice.

7.5.1.1 Profit and Loss Account

The following is a simple Profit and Loss Account (this may also be referred to as an Income Statement).

Example

Profit and Loss Account for the Year ended . . .

	£000	£000
TURNOVER	250,000	
Cost of Sales	100,000	
GROSS PROFIT		**150,000**
Distribution costs	15,000	
Administrative costs	20,000	
		(35,000)
OPERATING PROFIT		**115,000**
Interest Receivable		5,000
PROFIT BEFORE INTEREST		**120,000**
Interest Payable		(2,000)
PROFIT BEFORE TAXATION		**118,000**
Tax		(25,000)
PROFIT FOR THE FINANCIAL YEAR		**93,000**

You will notice immediately that the Profit and Loss Account for a company focuses on 'headline' figures such as 'Administration Expenses' rather than itemising each and every type of expense. This is because company accounts are usually accompanied by a set of Notes which will give a detailed breakdown and explanation of the figures, which avoids the Profit and Loss Account itself looking overly complicated. The way in which the items are grouped together is dictated by accounting standards. There are also some changes in terminology. For example, the sales figure is usually labelled 'Turnover'. You will also see the company's corporation tax liability at the end of the Profit and Loss Account.

The main difference in a company Profit and Loss Account is that it separates the income, expenses and profit from its operating activities from other items such as finance costs. A company's operating profit is simply the profit which it derives from its main trading activities.

With larger companies you will see additional items appearing on the accounts. For example, after the company's ordinary income and tax, you may see reference to 'extraordinary income', which would be a source of income unrelated to the usual business of the company's trade, such as damages received from litigation.

7.5.1.2 Balance Sheet

The following is a simple Balance Sheet (this may also be referred to as the Statement of Financial Position).

Example

Balance Sheet as at . . .

	£000	£000	£000
ASSETS			
FIXED ASSETS			
Tangible Assets			200,000
CURRENT ASSETS			
Stock	50,000		
Debtors	50,000		
Cash	45,000		
		145,000	
Amounts Falling Due within 1 Year			
Creditors	20,000		
Provision for Tax	25,000		
		(45,000)	
Net Current Assets			**100,000**
Total Assets less Current Liabilities			300,000
Amounts Falling Due after more than 1 year			
Bank Loan			(20,000)
NET ASSETS			**280,000**
CAPITAL AND RESERVES			
Share Capital			200,000
Profit and Loss Reserve			80,000
SHAREHOLDERS FUNDS			**280,000**

You will notice so far as the first section is concerned the heading is 'Assets' rather than the (by now familiar) employment of capital which appears on a sole trader/practitioner or partnership Balance Sheet. There are some cosmetic differences in that current and long-term liabilities are now labelled as amounts falling due within one year and more than one year respectively. You will also see that an additional figure is shown on the face of the accounts of 'Total Assets less Current Liabilities', which simply shows the value of the business before the long-term liabilities are accounted for. The only point of substance is that the company's liability for tax, which has usually not be paid at the date of the Balance Sheet, is shown.

7.5.2 International format

Accounts presented using an international format must comply with UK Adopted IAS. International standards tend to be less prescriptive in that, instead of providing templates to follow, they set out minimum requirements for the information which must appear on the face of the accounts.

7.5.2.1 Income Statement

The following is a simple Income Statement (Profit and Loss Account).

Example

Income Statement for the Year Ended . . .

	£000	£000
REVENUE	250,000	
Cost of sales	100,000	
GROSS PROFIT		**150,000**
Distribution expenses	15,000	
Administration expenses	20,000	
		(35,000)
OPERATING PROFIT		**115,000**
Finance Income		
Interest Receivable		5,000
Finance expenses		(2,000)
PROFIT BEFORE TAX		**118,000**
Tax		(25,000)
PROFIT FOR THE FINANCIAL YEAR		**93,000**

You will immediately notice that sales/turnover is now referred to as 'Revenue'. However, beyond that, the content and format are very similar to the Profit and Loss Account we considered earlier.

7.5.2.2 Statement of Financial Position

The following is a simple Statement of Financial Position (Balance Sheet).

Example

Statement of Financial Position as at . . .

	£000	£000	£000
ASSETS			
NON-CURRENT ASSETS			
Property, plant and equipment			200,000
CURRENT ASSETS			
Inventories	50,000		
Receivables	50,000		
Cash	45,000		
		145,000	
CURRENT LIABILITIES			
Payables	20,000		
Tax	25,000		
		(45,000)	
Net Current Assets			**100,000**
Total Assets less Current Liabilities			300,000
NON -CURRENT LIABILITIES			
Bank Loan			(20,000)
NET ASSETS			**280,000**
EQUITY			
Share Capital			200,000
Profit and Loss Reserve			80,000
TOTAL EQUITY			**280,000**

Cosmetically there are a number of differences between this style of presentation and the Balance Sheet which we considered earlier. However, the differences are essentially those of terminology. So, you will see that the term 'non-current assets' is used instead of 'fixed assets' and 'non-current liabilities' instead of 'long-term liabilities'. Similarly, 'debtors' and creditors' have become 'receivables' and 'payables' respectively. Closing stock is referred to as 'inventories', and 'debentures' as 'loan notes'. Once you allow for these simple changes in terminology, again the form and content are familiar. Incidentally, FRS 102 itself adopts this 'international' terminology.

7.6 ANNUAL REPORTS AND ACCOUNTS

Throughout this book we have focused on the Profit and Loss Account and the Balance Sheet produced by the business at the end of its accounting year. However, the CA 2006 and both FRS 102 and UK Adopted IAS require additional reports and financial statements to be produced. This collection of documents is often referred to as the 'Reports and Accounts'. The quantity of information will vary depending on the size and type of company.

When you are looking at the accounts of a company, particularly those of a company which is required to publish its accounts, in addition to the Profit and Loss Account (or Income Statement) and Balance Sheet (or Statement of Financial Position) you may encounter one or more of the following.

7.6.1 Statement of Cash Flows

As its title indicates, this Statement contains the details of all cash receipts (inflows) and payments (outflows) into and out of the company during the year. Cash can come into the business from a variety of sources: profits, capital, loans. Similarly, cash goes out of the business in a number of ways: dividends, buying fixed assets, loan repayments. In a statement of cash flows, the payments and receipts are grouped into various categories according to whether they are connected to the company's main trading activities, investments or something else.

The net profit figure which is calculated on the Profit and Loss Account is a key indicator of the company's performance. We have seen that when a company sells stock it generates income, which in turn increases the profits. However, if the company sells its stock mainly on credit, it will be generating income, and therefore a healthy profit, but it will not be bringing cash into the business. Cash is in many ways the lifeblood of the business. A company with insufficient levels of cash is likely to be in financial difficulties. In contrast to the profit calculated on the Profit and Loss Account, the Statement of Cash Flows highlights the incoming and outgoing of cash, and is therefore an important tool in assessing the performance of the business.

7.6.2 Statement of Comprehensive Income

This Statement is a FRS 102 requirement. It shows all gains and losses of whatever nature that have arisen during the company's accounting period. It is basically a summary of events which have occurred during the year which have had an immediate effect on the wealth of the business but which are not necessarily reflected in a conventional Profit and Loss Account, for example a revaluation of premises. This Statement can be combined with the Profit and Loss Account.

7.6.3 Statement of Changes in Equity

Once the post-tax profit of a company has been calculated, the directors will decide how much of the profit should be distributed to the shareholders as a dividend. This is an allocation of profit and could in theory be shown in an appropriation account in the same way as a partnership shows how its profit is allocated. However, for companies, in practice dividends are shown in a separate statement called a Statement of Changes in Equity. Dividends are not shown until they have been paid.

This Statement is not confined to dividends. It will also, for example, detail the issue of new shares.

7.6.4 Strategic Report

This is a statutory requirement under s 414A of the CA 2006 (small companies are exempt). It contains a review of the company's business designed to enable the performance of the company to be measured and assessed.

7.6.5 Chairman's Report

This is not a strict requirement, but a Chairman's Report is often produced by quoted companies. The Report usually sets the scene for the accounts, in terms of what has happened in the life of the company during the year. It should be read with a degree of care as the Chairman will inevitably put the best possible gloss on events of the past year.

7.6.6 Directors' Report

This is a statutory requirement under s 415 of the CA 2006. The contents of the Directors' Report are stipulated by the Act, but essentially it comprises factual information about the company and confirmation that the auditors have been supplied with all relevant information. Small companies are exempt from having to include some of the statutory information.

7.6.7 Auditors' Report

As the name suggests, this is a report given by the auditors. In the report the auditors are required to say whether in their opinion the accounts give a true and fair view of the financial state of the business. There has been criticism of auditors in recent years who have given an unqualified approval certificate to the accounts of companies which have then been revealed as having severe problems.

7.6.8 Notes

Both FRS 102 and UK Adopted IAS require the accounts to be accompanied by a set of explanatory notes. The notes often run to many pages, and they are usually the most informative part of the accounts as they expand on the information which appears in the Profit and Loss Account/Income Statement and Balance Sheet.

SUMMARY

(1) Company accounts are subject to statutory regulation under the CA 2006.

(2) Accountants follow generally accepted accounting principles (GAPP), which comprise standards, regulations and statements of good practice for the preparation and presentation of company accounts.

(3) There are two systems of accounting standards in the UK: FRS 102 and UK Adopted IAS.

(4) Those companies whose shares are traded on a regulated stock market in the EU must comply with the IFRS. Other companies may choose to follow either FRS 102 or the IFRS.

CHAPTER 8

ANALYSIS OF ACCOUNTS

8.1	Introduction	75
8.2	The purposes of analysing accounts	75
8.3	Who will want to analyse accounts and why?	75
8.4	The limitations of accounts	76
8.5	What information do you need?	76
8.6	Preliminary steps	77
8.7	Some general considerations	79
8.8	Trends and ratio analysis	80

LEARNING OUTCOMES

After reading this chapter you will be able to:

- interpret the basic information provided by a set of accounts
- explain the limitations of accounts
- employ a range of trends and ratios in order to assess the performance of a business.

8.1 INTRODUCTION

We have now seen how the financial information of a business is first collated and then presented as a set of Final Accounts. In this chapter we turn to the process of analysing those accounts. Through this process of analysis you will be able to assess the present state of any type of business and draw reasoned conclusions about its future.

8.2 THE PURPOSES OF ANALYSING ACCOUNTS

In broad terms, the purposes of analysing the accounts of a business are to assess the business's current performance and to predict its future prospects.

The analysis of accounts can help to answer any number of questions. For example:

- Is the present level of profitability satisfactory?
- Is the profitability likely to improve in the future?
- Can the business meet its current liabilities?
- Will the business be able to meet its liabilities in the future?
- Are investors receiving a satisfactory return on their investment?
- Will the business be doing better or worse in five years' time?

8.3 WHO WILL WANT TO ANALYSE ACCOUNTS AND WHY?

The following people are likely to be interested in reading accounts:

(a) *Investors* – to assess the level of risk and return.

(b) *Managers* – to make sure that the business is performing to its full potential.

(c) *Lenders* – to ensure that the debt will be repaid and that the business can pay interest.

(d) *HMRC* – to assess the profits for tax.

(e) *Potential purchasers* – to consider whether the business is worth buying.

(f) *Employees* – to negotiate terms and conditions of employment.

Not all of those interested will be able to get full information about the business they are assessing. Obviously, managers will be able to get all the necessary information, but how much an investor will be able to find out will depend largely on how much of an investment is involved – the larger the amount, the more influence a potential investor will have when demanding information.

8.4 THE LIMITATIONS OF ACCOUNTS

You must be able to understand what is in the accounts, but looking at accounts alone may provide a misleading picture of the state of a business. Accounts are produced only *after* events have occurred. This is an important limitation if you are trying to form a view of the likely performance of the business in the *future*.

Accounts can produce information of a financial nature only. A Balance Sheet is a helpful list of the assets and liabilities of the business; however, it will not indicate the health or otherwise of labour relations, despite the fact that many people would regard good staff relations as a very important asset. Similarly, a poor trade reputation would be regarded by many people as a liability, but it does not appear in the accounts.

The accounts of a business need to be seen in the wider context. There may be commercial or economic issues entirely beyond the control of management, such as a declining market for the firm's products or the general economic climate.

The accounts are an essential tool in the analysis of the position of a business, but they provide only part of the information needed.

8.5 WHAT INFORMATION DO YOU NEED?

It is important to be able to put the accounts that you are looking at in context by gaining a general picture of the business you are investigating:

(a) It is large or small?

(b) Is it growing or contracting?

(c) What is the nature of its business?

(d) Does it operate in an expanding or a declining market?

(e) Does it depend heavily on a particular product or products?

The questions you should ask depend on the circumstances and are largely a matter of common sense.

8.5.1 Public companies

We have looked at company accounts from the point of view of the company complying with its statutory obligation to provide certain information. However, for a public company the production of its Annual Report and Accounts gives the company an opportunity to promote itself, to its shareholders, to prospective investors and to analysts.

As you read any company's Annual Report and Accounts, be very aware of the need to question and check everything. If any of the figures in the accounts are unclear you will need to look for explanations, for example in the Notes or the Directors' Report. You may need to take a view on whether the Chairperson is expressing overly-optimistic hopes in their Statement. Those hopes may appear unreasonable in the light of the company's current financial position or the general economy.

It is unlikely, although not impossible, that you would find a direct lie in a company's Annual Report and Accounts, but you should always examine the information critically to see whether a particular proposal or intention appears to be justified.

Remember, when you are reading the Annual Report and Accounts, that there are other sources of information as well. Look for trustworthy newspaper reports, television news, online content etc.

8.5.2 Partnerships and sole trader/practitioners

There will be no published accounts for partnerships and sole traders/practitioners. Even so, you should obtain copies of the accounts they produce and study them.

You must gather as much information about the business as you can. Find out the following:

(a) Are its premises in a suitable area?

(b) Does it seem to be busy?

(c) Is it dealing in something which is going to provide an income in the long term?

(d) What sort of reputation does it have?

(e) What can you find out about the proprietors?

(f) What is its online presence?

You can then look at the accounts in the light of that information. When your analysis raises further questions, you can engage in detailed discussions of the problems with the proprietors or their advisers.

Obviously, the amount of information you can get will depend on what your relationship is, or is to be, with the business.

8.6 PRELIMINARY STEPS

As well as obtaining as much general information about the business as you can, there are a number of preliminary steps you should take before launching into a detailed analysis of the accounts. These involve, in part, checking the accuracy and reliability of the figures presented and, in part, building up a general picture of the business and the market in which it operates. This enables the information extracted to be considered in a proper context. What might be normal for a small business might be very unusual for a large one. A particular level of profitability may be commendable in a time of recession, but disappointing in a period when business generally is 'booming'.

Common preliminary steps are as follows:

(a) *Obtain the accounts for several years.*

If you are going to make a realistic assessment of a business, it is important that you obtain its accounts for several years rather than for the previous year alone. One year's accounts will reveal important information – the extent of borrowings, the value of fixed assets, the amount of unpaid bills, the value of closing stock – but it is difficult to reach reliable conclusions without making comparisons with earlier years.

(b) *Check the date of the Balance Sheet.*

A business can choose a Balance Sheet date to suit itself. If the business is seasonal then a Balance Sheet drawn up at one date could include figures which would show the business in a much more favourable light than a Balance Sheet drawn up at another date.

Example

A business manufactures Christmas decorations. It sells the decorations to department stores in September. A Balance Sheet drawn up in September would show a healthy cash balance and probably substantial debtors. By contrast, a Balance Sheet drawn up in July would show substantial closing stock, a high creditors figure and, probably, a large overdraft.

Always consider whether you have to take the date of the Balance Sheet into account when you are analysing the figures:

(i) Check the method of valuing fixed assets.

(ii) When were the assets last valued? Freehold premises purchased 20 years earlier for £250,000 may still be shown in the Balance Sheet at that value. Their current value will probably be quite different.

(iii) Has provision been made for depreciation? If so, what method has been used?

In the case of a company, you will be looking for the answers to these and other questions in the Notes and the Statement of accounting policies included in the company's published accounts. If you are dealing with a partnership or sole trader, you should ask for that information from the partners or proprietor.

Exercise 8A

What will be the effect on the Profit and Loss Account and on the Balance Sheet if values for fixed assets and depreciation are inaccurate?

(c) *Check how the closing stock is valued.*

The normal method is to value stock at the lower of cost or current market value. If you want to do the job thoroughly, you should inspect the stock. It may be that it includes items which are no longer readily saleable. For example, in the fashion trade, a business may have purchased items some months ago which are now out of fashion. They could still be appearing in the accounts under 'Closing stock' at cost price, when in fact their current market value is little or nothing.

Exercise 8B

How will the Profit and Loss Account and Balance Sheet be affected if the figure for stock is overstated?

(d) *Analyse the figure given for debtors.*

Will all the debtors actually pay? Has a provision been made for bad debts? It is quite possible for a business not to write off bad debts, so that the debtors figure appears larger than the amount of cash which the business can readily expect to receive.

Exercise 8C

Why might a business not write off bad debts?
What else is affected apart from the Balance Sheet?
Are there any dangers in a business having a large number of debtors?

(e) *Look for unusual or exceptional items or major changes.*

The picture given by the Profit and Loss Account and Balance Sheet for a particular year can sometimes be distorted because of some exceptional event or major change either in circumstances or in accounting policy.

Example

A business may have borrowed a substantial amount to invest in new plant or machinery. In the short term, profit may be reduced because there has been no time to use the new machinery to increase profits, yet interest charges will already have been incurred. However, in the long term, there may be prospects of rapid growth in future years.

Fixed assets such as land and buildings may have been revalued for the first time in many years. This will make the Balance Sheet look quite different, but in reality nothing has changed.

You will have to take all these matters into account, particularly if you are going to make comparisons with previous years.

8.7 SOME GENERAL CONSIDERATIONS

8.7.1 Profitability and ability to pay debts

The two main questions which people ask when reading the accounts of a business are:

(a) Is the business profitable?

(b) Can the business pay its debts as they fall due?

Profitability is not the same as solvency. The Profit and Loss Account shows whether the business has made a profit. The Balance Sheet shows whether it can pay its debts.

The fact that the accounts reveal that a profit has been made does not necessarily mean that there is money in the bank. The Trading and Profit and Loss Accounts of a business will record sales or levels of professional charges, which in turn will determine the amount of profit; but although the goods may have been sold or bills issued, payment may not yet have been received. Thus, although the Profit and Loss Account may show a large profit, the Balance Sheet may record a high figure under debtors and there may be no cash in the bank.

Alternatively, the business may have sold goods or issued bills and been paid; however, it may have purchased expensive new premises, paying cash. Again, the result is that while the Profit and Loss Account will show a profit, there is no money in the bank.

It is therefore a misconception to think that if a business is profitable, it must be able to pay its debts. This is not so. Obviously, a business which is unprofitable is not likely to be solvent for long, but just because a business is profitable does not necessarily mean that it is able to pay its debts at once.

Liquidity is an important issue for a business. A business can only use current assets to meet its liabilities if it is to continue in business. If it has to sell fixed assets to meet liabilities, it will eventually be unable to continue trading. It is therefore important that the business does not run short of current assets. Cash is the most liquid of current assets. Debts are also liquid as, even if they are not yet due for payment, the business can always turn them into cash quickly by selling them on to someone else to collect. Stock is less liquid as it may be difficult to sell quickly. Some items can only be sold at certain times of year.

Exercise 8D

The accounts of a business show that it has made a large profit but that it has no cash. In fact it has a large overdraft. How many possible factors can you think of to account for the lack of cash?

8.7.2 Treatment of bank overdrafts

It is relatively common for a business to have a bank overdraft. It is necessary to decide how to view the overdraft, particularly if this is substantial. An overdraft will normally appear in the Balance Sheet as a current liability because, in theory at least, it is repayable on demand. The reality may be quite different. The business may maintain a high overdraft indefinitely and finance its activities from it. Unless the business runs into difficulties, the bank will not take steps to call in the money owing.

As a current liability, the bank overdraft will be deducted from the current assets and will therefore reduce the net current assets figure. Ordinarily, a low net current assets figure would raise concerns about the ability of the business to pay its immediate debts. However, in reality the overdraft may be a source of long-term finance for the business, so a misleading picture may emerge if no distinction is made between the bank overdraft and ordinary trade creditors.

8.7.3 The impact of inflation

It is necessary to make allowance for the impact of inflation. If profits are increasing at the rate of 2% pa when inflation is running at 4% pa, in real terms profits are falling.

8.8 TRENDS AND RATIO ANALYSIS

8.8.1 Trends and ratios

Trends and ratios are a useful tool for measuring the performance of a business. In particular, trends and ratios make it easier to compare the figures from two or more sets of accounts, whether these are the accounts for different businesses or the accounts of one business for different years. The task is to calculate the appropriate trend or ratio and then use the result to draw conclusions about the performance of the business.

A trend is simply a comparison of figures from accounts for different years to see whether a pattern is established. For example, the net profit figures for successive years might appear as follows:

2021	2022	2023	2024
£50,000	£75,000	£90,000	£100,000

You will immediately see that the trend is for the net profit to increase year on year.

It can often be more helpful to look at the trend revealed when increases and decreases from year to year are expressed in percentage terms. The percentage change may be calculated using the following formula:

$$\frac{\text{figure for the later year} - \text{figure for the earlier year}}{\text{figure for the earlier year}} \times 100$$

Carrying out the calculation for the above net profit figures for 2020–2021 shows the following increase:

$$\frac{75{,}000 - 50{,}000}{50{,}000} \times 100 = 50\%$$

For the years 2022–2023 the increase is 20% and for the years 2023–2024 the increase is 11%. This shows us that whilst the trend is for the net profit figure to increase year on year, the rate at which net profits are increasing is slowing dramatically. This could be the result of, say, a successful marketing campaign which had a high impact on sales initially, but has now steadied into acceptable growth. Alternatively, it could be cause for concern indicating, perhaps, that whilst there is still demand for the product, interest is beginning to tail off.

Ratios are calculated using the figures from a single set of accounts. A ratio compares two figures by expressing the relationship of one to the other. The result can be expressed as a percentage or as a ratio. Once you have a percentage or ratio, it is also easy to compare the results of different years or of different businesses to establish the trends.

In reality, any two figures can be compared using a ratio and there is, therefore, any number of different ratios which may be used depending on which aspect of the business's performance you are considering. We shall look at a few of the more common ratios which you may encounter in practice.

8.8.2 Profitability ratios

Whether or not the business is making a profit is a key indicator of its success. Simply looking at the Profit and Loss Account will obviously show you whether the business is making a profit. However, using profitability ratios will help you to assess how effective the business is in generating profits and whether the level of profit is acceptable.

8.8.2.1 Return on capital employed

If you simply look at the net profit figure alone, it is difficult to make comparisons with how profitable the business is when compared with, say, its competitors. Comparisons may more easily be made by relating the profits of the business to the capital invested. This is referred to as the 'return on capital employed' (ROCE). It is normally expressed as a percentage:

$$\frac{\text{Net Profit}}{\text{Capital Employed}} \times 100$$

> **Example**
>
> The balance on the proprietor's capital account at the end of the accounting period is £200,000; net profit for the accounting period was £40,000. The return on capital is:
>
> $$\frac{40{,}000}{200{,}000} \times 100 = 20\%$$
>
> The proprietor may consider that this compares very favourably with putting the money in a bank or building society account.

The ROCE shows the profit being made on the resources available to the business. A business with a higher percentage is using its capital more efficiently. A business with a ROCE of, say, 40% is achieving a return of £40 of net profit for very £100 invested, compared with only £15 for a business with a ROCE of 15%.

For a company, the profit figure used in the calculation is usually the figure for operating profit, ie the profit before tax and interest are considered. This concentrates the calculation on the profits made by the company's main trading activity.

It is possible to calculate the return solely on the amount of capital the proprietor has invested. This allows the proprietor to judge whether the return on capital is satisfactory by reference to the return that could be obtained on other investments. As an alternative, long-term loans can be added to the capital employed in order to assess the return across all long-term funding of the business.

When calculating the return, you may choose to take the capital figure at the start of the year, at the end of the year or an average figure. It is normally easiest to take the figure at the end of the year, although arguably it is more accurate to take the figure at the start of the year as that was the amount invested during the relevant trading period.

8.8.2.2 Sales to capital employed

This is a similar calculation to ROCE, which we considered at **8.8.2.1**, in that it focuses on how well the business is using its net assets. However, rather than looking at the net profit generated, this ratio isolates one element of profit and shows the volume of sales produced by the net assets employed in the business.

The calculation is as follows:

$$\frac{\text{Sales}}{\text{Capital Employed}}$$

In simple terms, the more sales that the business is able to generate from its capital employed, the more profitable the business is likely to be. So, the higher the figure, the better.

Isolating the sales figure alone means that the ratio must be used with caution. For example, if the business decides to depreciate its fixed assets, this will have the effect of reducing the capital employed figure and thereby improving the ratio, and yet the business will not have improved its sales. Similarly, a business which owns its premises outright rather than renting them may have a low sales to capital employed ratio because its fixed assets will be high.

However, the business may be more profitable because the income which is produced from its sales is not being used up in paying rent.

8.8.2.3 Gross profit margin percentage

This is a useful ratio to use when assessing the profitability of a trading business. It relates the value of sales made to the gross profit made on them, the so-called 'profit margin'. It can be calculated as follows:

$$\frac{\text{Gross Profit}}{\text{Sales}} \times 100$$

The calculation demonstrates the profit being made on each item sold, so obviously a business is looking to achieve a high percentage figure. A gross profit margin of 35%, for example, shows that for every £1 of sales the business is making 35p in gross profit. This is a fairly basic measure: if a business is not selling its stock for more than it paid for the stock, then it is not going to be viable unless it either raises its prices or finds a cheaper supplier. However, a business with a low gross profit margin should be prompted to focus on its sale and purchase price in order to improve its profitability.

8.8.2.4 Net profit margin ratio

This is the same calculation as discussed in **8.7.2.3** above, but this time using the net profit figure (again, the calculation for a company would use the operating profit figure). The calculation is therefore a little more sophisticated, because it takes into account the effect of the other expenses of the business.

The calculation is as follows:

$$\frac{\text{Net Profit}}{\text{Sales}} \times 100$$

> **Example**
>
> A business has sales of £400,000 and a net profit of £40,000. The net profit percentage is:
>
> $$\frac{40{,}000}{400{,}000} \times 100 = 10\%$$
>
> This means that out of every £1 of sales, 90p goes in expenses and 10p is profit.

If the net profit margin is unfavourable, particularly compared to the gross profit margin, this helps the proprietor to identify the need to try to increase profitability by reducing expenses.

8.8.3 Liquidity ratios

Liquidity is concerned with whether the business has sufficient funds to pay its creditors on time. Liquidity ratios therefore help to identify whether the business is at risk of insolvency proceedings being initiated by those creditors who have not been paid.

8.8.3.1 Current ratio

The current ratio is a direct comparison of current assets with current liabilities. It is therefore a measure of the assets which can be turned into cash relatively readily in order to meet the liabilities which must be paid within 12 months. The result is normally expressed as a ratio:

$$\frac{\text{Current Assets}}{\text{Current Liabilities}} :1$$

So if the current assets are £40,000 and the current liabilities are £20,000, the current ratio will be:

$$\frac{40{,}000}{20{,}000} = 2:1$$

A ratio of 1:1 would mean that the business has exactly £1 of current assets with which to meet every £1 of current liabilities. Most businesses would expect to have a higher ratio, say 1.5:1. However, this depends on the type of business. Supermarkets, for example, will usually have current ratios which are much lower. This is because they buy goods on credit but sell mainly for cash. Each day, they know that large amounts of cash will be injected into the business. In general, therefore, they can meet liabilities due on a particular day from cash received on that day, and need only a small amount of additional available current assets.

8.8.3.2 Acid test

A potential problem with the current ratio is that it takes account of all the current assets. Closing stock, for example, may not be quickly saleable. Indeed, there may be doubt as to whether it is saleable at all. Changes in fashion and technology may make stock obsolete. In the same way, in a non-trading business there will be uncertainty as to how quickly work in progress may be turned into cash. The acid test is the ratio between current liabilities and current assets excluding stock (or work in progress in a non-trading business). The calculation is as follows:

$$\frac{\text{Current Assets} - \text{Closing Stock}}{\text{Current Liabilities}} :1$$

It is common also to exclude any prepayments from the current assets figure. As these represent amounts already paid by the business, their very nature means that they cannot usually be converted back into cash.

Example

The following is an extract from a Balance Sheet:

Current Assets		
Stock	65,000	
Debtors	50,000	
Cash	5,000	
		120,000
Current Liabilities		
Creditors	40,000	
Accruals	10,000	
		(50,000)
Net Current Assets		70,000

The acid test is: $\frac{120{,}000 - 65{,}000}{50{,}000} = 1.1:1$

An acid test of 1:1 means that the business has £1 of readily liquid assets for every £1 of current liabilities. The lower the ratio, the greater the risk of the business being unable to meet its debts as they fall due.

However, even a high ratio needs to be considered critically. The business may not be pursuing its debtors rigorously, or may not have written off sufficient bad debts. This would lead to an unrealistic current assets figure and consequently a high acid test ratio.

8.8.4 Efficiency ratios

Efficiency ratios assess how efficient the business is at using the assets available to it. (You should note that as they also deal with elements of liquidity, they are sometimes treated as liquidity ratios – see **8.8.3**.)

8.8.4.1 Stock turnover

This measures how efficient the business is at selling its stock. It is often expressed as a number of days:

$$\frac{\text{Closing Stock}}{\text{Cost of Goods Sold}} \text{ x } 365$$

Sometimes an 'Average' Closing Stock figure is used, which simply means an average of the stock held at the beginning and end of the year.

Generally speaking, a business will want to sell its stock quickly in order to generate income and will therefore be aiming at a short stock turnover period. If stock is taking too long to sell, this may be because it is being offered at too high a price or because there is simply no demand.

However, a low stock turnover period will not necessarily always be an indicator of efficiency. It could be a product of the business setting its stock levels too low with the result that it will not be able to respond to any increase in demand.

You must also consider the stock turnover figure in the context of the type of business you're dealing with. A supermarket, for example, would be expected to have a short stock turnover period. In contrast, a dealer in high value fine art would normally have a high stock turnover period.

8.8.4.2 Average settlement period for debtors

This shows the length of time it takes for debtors to pay. A business which is failing to collect its debts is losing out on the opportunity of having ready cash available and is not operating efficiently.

$$\frac{\text{Debtors}}{\text{Sales}} \text{ x } 365 = \text{Number of days it takes debtors to pay}$$

If a business is not converting its debtors into cash relatively quickly, it may indicate that its debt collection system is inefficient. It might also suggest that the business is being forced into selling too much on credit because it is not finding ready cash buyers. It could also act as a warning that a major customer is delaying payments because it is in financial difficulties.

An equivalent calculation can be done to see how quickly the business pays its creditors. The two figures may then be compared. A business which is quick to pay its own creditors but slow to secure payment from its debtors is being run inefficiently. It may experience cash flow problems as it is paying cash out faster than it is collecting money in. Such a business may need to improve its debt collection procedures and/or review the contractual terms on which it conducts its business. Conversely, a business which is collecting money from its debtors, but which still cannot pay its creditors promptly, has a cash shortage and may be heading for insolvency.

8.8.5 Gearing

Essentially, gearing is the relationship between the funding which a company derives as capital and the funding which it raises through borrowing. Looking at the how the business is financed in this way is helpful when considering the long-term prospects of the business. Borrowing in itself is not bad, and indeed most businesses will need to borrow money at times in order to fund expansion. However, a business which is too heavily reliant on borrowing may eventually run into difficulties if it cannot meet the loan repayments, perhaps as a result of interest rates rising.

There are many ways of looking at gearing, but at its simplest it may be calculated as follows:

$$\frac{\text{Long-term Liabilities}}{\text{Shareholders Funds}} \text{ x } 100$$

If the calculation produces a high percentage figure, the company is said to have high gearing, as it has a high proportion of borrowing compared to its capital. A low percentage figure, or low gearing, shows that the company has a low proportion of borrowing compared to capital.

For a shareholder, investment in a company with high gearing is in a sense more risky. This is because a company with high levels of borrowing will also have high interest payments. Every year the interest will have to be paid, regardless of the level of profit; this may leave little or nothing remaining which can be paid out to the shareholders as a dividend. Even a small reduction in the profits for one year could means that there is nothing left for the shareholders' dividend. If a company has low gearing, on the other hand, this means that the amount available for dividends is less susceptible to fluctuations in profit.

8.8.6 Investment ratios

Investment ratios are used by investors or potential investors to assess the performance of the business. The main investment ratio is the Earnings per Share figure. This is a figure which is arrived at by taking the profit figure after taxation for the year and dividing it by the number of shares in the company. The resulting figure is usually expressed as pence per share.

EXAMPLE

A company has profits of £150,000 and 200,000 issued shares; the earnings per share would be calculated as follows:

$$\frac{150,000}{200,000} = 0.75 \text{ or } 75\text{p per £1 share}$$

The figure shows the amount of profit being generated for each share in the company. In other words, it shows how much each shareholder would receive per share if all the profits for the year were to be paid out in dividends. However, it is important for the investor to remember that this is not the same as the dividend payment per share as a company would not, in practice, pay out all its profits in dividends. However, it is a useful tool for comparing the investment potential between different companies, or between shares and other types of investment.

SUMMARY

(1) It is preferable to look at several years' accounts to get a full picture.

(2) 'One off' events may distort the accounts.

(3) Profitability is not the same thing as an ability to pay debts.

(4) Analysis ratios are a useful tool in assessing the performance of a business in terms of:

- (a) profitability;
- (b) liquidity;
- (c) efficiency;
- (d) gearing;
- (e) investment.

SOLUTIONS

Exercise 8A

Effect on Profit and Loss Account

Depreciation is charged as an expense on the Profit and Loss Account. If the depreciation is understated, the profit will be artificially high.

The reverse will be true if the depreciation is overstated.

Effect on Balance Sheet

Depreciation

The figure for fixed assets will be unreliable if depreciation is inaccurate. The figure for capital owing to the proprietors will also be unreliable as it is increased by the profit calculated on the Profit and Loss Account.

Fixed assets

If assets are overstated, the Balance Sheet will appear healthier than it really is. Fixed assets and capital will both be higher than they should be.

If assets are understated, the business may appear to be producing a high profit from its capital, but since capital is understated this will be misleading.

Exercise 8B

Effect on Profit and Loss Account

Closing stock reduces the figure for cost of goods sold. If cost of goods sold is low, then gross and net profit will appear to be high.

Thus, an overstated closing figure increases profit figures.

Effect on Balance Sheet

Closing stock will be shown as a current asset. An inaccurate figure will improve the relationship between current assets and current liabilities.

Exercise 8C

A business may not write off bad debts because it is taking an unrealistic view of its debtors' ability to pay. Alternatively, it may be a deliberate ploy to give a misleading picture of the financial state of the business.

Debtors are shown in the Balance Sheet as current assets. A high debtors figure will increase the apparent value of the assets. It will affect the balance between current assets and current liabilities.

It is not only the Balance Sheet which will be affected by a failure to write off bad debts. Bad debts appear in the Profit and Loss as expenses. The profit figure will be overstated if insufficient debts are written off as bad.

Whilst a high debtors figure makes the position of the business appear better in the accounts, in practice there are dangers in the business having a large number of debtors. The business could have cash flow problems if the debtors do not pay. The business could be particularly vulnerable if a large proportion of the debts are owed by a single debtor, as that debtor may become insolvent and unable to pay.

Exercise 8D

You should have considered at least the following:

(a) excessive drawings by proprietors/dividends paid to shareholders;
(b) purchase of fixed assets out of cash received;
(c) failure to collect debts;
(d) excessive stock levels;
(e) dishonesty of staff.

PART II

SOLICITORS' ACCOUNTS

CHAPTER 9

The SRA Accounts Rules 2019

9.1	Introduction	89
9.2	Principles governing the Rules	90
9.3	Who is bound by the Rules?	91
9.4	Client money	92
9.5	Client bank account	93
9.6	Client bank account must not be used to provide banking facilities	93
9.7	Paying client money into the client bank account	99
9.8	Keeping client money separate from the firm's own money	100
9.9	Withdrawals of client money from the client bank account	105
9.10	Client accounting systems and controls	108
9.11	Paying interest to clients	110
9.12	Third party managed accounts	110
9.13	Dealings with other money belonging to clients or third parties	110
9.14	Obtaining and delivery of accountants' reports	111

LEARNING OUTCOMES

After reading this chapter you will be able to:

- explain the principles governing the SRA Accounts Rules and who is bound by them
- identify whether money is client money
- identify what money must or can pass through the client bank account
- identify the options available for dealing with money received in a bill
- identify the situations in which a client is entitled to interest and how that interest should be calculated
- recognise the records that a firm providing regulated services must maintain.

9.1 INTRODUCTION

A firm providing legal services is a business and must make a profit each year if it is to survive. Like any business, it requires day-to-day records of income, expenses, assets and liabilities, so that at the end of the year it can produce a Profit and Loss Account and Balance Sheet.

Unlike most other businesses, however, law firms frequently hold money that belongs to other people. For example, clients who are buying property or a business will normally give funds to their solicitor in advance of completion of the purchase.

The Solicitors Regulation Authority (the 'SRA') has strict rules about dealing with clients' money. The SRA Accounts Rules 2019 ('the Rules') are examined in some detail in this chapter, which is probably the most important chapter in this part of the book. You are unlikely ever to make entries in your firm's accounts, but you will have to understand the difference between client money and the firm's own money; and should you become a partner, you will be responsible (with your fellow partners) for ensuring that all SRA requirements are complied with. Hence you must understand what the Rules are designed to achieve.

It is, however, worth noting that the SRA launched a three-month consultation on 14 November 2024, 'Client money in legal services - safeguarding consumers and providing redress: The model of solicitors holding client money'. The consultation followed the collapse of the Axiom Ince Group which led to substantial losses for clients and a huge bill for the profession as a result of the way in which the compensation fund works.

Among the key issues explored in the consultation are:

> Whether in a digital age, and with feasible/credible alternatives becoming more available which may be better at safeguarding client's money, in the longer term is it still necessary or desirable for firms to hold client money as widely as currently the case, or at all.

It is fair to say that the proposed abolition of client bank accounts and replacement with third party managed accounts has met with significant criticism from the profession. The matter is discussed at more length in **Chapter 18** below.

This chapter deals with the principles which underpin the SRA Accounts Rules 2019 and with the Rules which impact most significantly on the way in which a firm providing regulated services is required to deal with client funds.

Historically, solicitors were subject to detailed and prescriptive Accounts Rules. However, in June 2017 the SRA announced that, in its view, the length and complexity of the Accounts Rules 2011 made it difficult for new entrants to the market to understand what was required of them, as well as for consumers to understand what to expect when a firm handled their money. Further, many firms found themselves in technical breach of the Accounts Rules 2011 in circumstances where there were no real risks to client money.

The SRA announced that it proposed to:

(a) *simplify the Accounts Rules:* by focusing on key principles and requirements for keeping client money safe, including:
  (i) keeping client money separate from the firm's own money;
  (ii) ensuring client money is returned promptly at the end of a matter;
  (iii) using client money only for its intended purpose;
  (iv) proportionate requirements for firms to obtain an annual accountant's report; and

(b) *support the Accounts Rules:* with an online toolkit consisting of guidance and case studies to aid compliance.

9.2 PRINCIPLES GOVERNING THE RULES

In the past the SRA regulated only solicitors. However, the arrival of alternative business structures in October 2011 means that legal services may now also be provided by multi-disciplinary practices and by firms owned by non-lawyers. The SRA hopes to regulate all those providing legal services and has rewritten its Accounts Rules and its Codes of Conduct so that they do not refer specifically to solicitors. Anyone who is regulated by the SRA will have to follow the same rules.

The Rules are designed to reduce the risk of accidental or deliberate misuse of client money, and to protect clients from the risks of accidental or deliberate mishandling of their money.

Those regulated by the SRA must follow seven pervasive Principles, which define the fundamental ethical and professional standards that the SRA expects of all firms and individuals (including non-lawyer owners) it regulates. These Principles apply to all aspects of practice covered in the SRA Handbook, including the regulation of Accounts. The Principles are as follows:

> You act:
>
> 1. in a way that upholds the constitutional principle of the rule of law, and the proper administration of justice.

2. in a way that upholds public trust and confidence in the solicitors' profession and in legal services provided by authorised persons.
3. with independence.
4. with honesty.
5. with integrity.
6. in a way that encourages equality, diversity and inclusion.
7. in the best interests of each client.

The SRA Handbook Glossary comprises a set of defined terms which are used in the SRA Handbook.

9.3 WHO IS BOUND BY THE RULES?

Rule 1.1 states that the Rules apply to authorised bodies, their managers and employees, and references to 'you' in the Rules should be read accordingly. An authorised body is one which provides reserved legal services such as the preparation of probate papers; the full list is set out in the Legal Services Act 2007, Sch 2.

A licensable body is one within which the managers/interest holders include both lawyers and non-lawyers.

The authorised body's managers are jointly and severally responsible for compliance with the Rules by the authorised body, its managers and employees (Rule 1.2).

Rule 1.3 provides that in relation to a licensed body, the rules apply only in respect of activities regulated by the SRA in accordance with the terms of its licence. A licensable body is one within which the managers/interest holders include both lawyers and non-lawyers. They vary widely with some being nearly entirely comprised of lawyers, and others being nearly entirely managed and/or owned by non-lawyers. In simple terms, they must have at least one lawyer manager and one non-lawyer manager or interest holder. They are also sometimes referred to as alternative business structures.

The case of *Weston v The Law Society* (1998) *The Times*, 15 July is a salutary reminder of how careful those responsible for compliance in a firm must be. The Court of Appeal confirmed that it was appropriate to strike off a solicitor despite the fact that no dishonesty was alleged against him. The solicitor in question was held to be liable for breaches of the Rules committed by his fellow partners even though he had been unaware of them. Lord Bingham of Cornhill referred to the 'duty of anyone holding anyone else's money to exercise a proper stewardship in relation to it'.

On 1 April 2023 *The Law Society Gazette* reported that one solicitor had been struck off for causing or allowing the transfer of £129,827.22 belonging to two clients to pay the stamp duty land tax owed by a third client. He later received £10,800 into his personal bank account from the third client when he knew, or ought to have known, that he was not entitled to receive it. His colleague and manager was ordered to pay a £7,501 fine for allowing the transfer without the clients' consent.

Mitigating factors for the manager were that no clients suffered any loss as he 'remediated the position once he was aware of the transfer' and the fine for the late payment of stamp duty was covered and paid by the firm's PI policy. The Solicitors Disciplinary Tribunal (SDT) said: 'The tribunal was satisfied that [the] misconduct fell within the range where a financial penalty was appropriate.'

On 3 January 2025, *The Law Society Gazette* reported that a solicitor had been given a suspension – suspended for two years if he complied with a two-year restriction order – after he failed to comply with a tribunal order and did not take 'adequate' steps to comply with accounts rules.

9.4 CLIENT MONEY

Rules 2–4 set out what an authorised body (referred to as 'a firm' in the rest of this chapter) must do with client money as defined in Rule 2.1.

Rule 4.1 requires client money to be kept separate from the money belonging to the firm (usually in a separate client bank account). Beyond that, no requirements are imposed on what the firm does with its own money. The firm will, of course, choose to operate one or more bank accounts for its own money, referred to as 'business' accounts.

A client is defined in the Glossary as 'the person for whom you act'. However, the definition of client money goes beyond holding money for a client. Rule 2.1 states that client money is money held or received by a firm:

(a) relating to regulated services delivered by you to a client;

(b) on behalf of a third party in relation to regulated services delivered by you (such as money held as agent, stakeholder or held to the sender's order);

(c) as a trustee or as the holder of a specified office or appointment, such as donee of a power of attorney, Court of Protection deputy or trustee of an occupational pension scheme;

(d) in respect of your fees and any unpaid disbursements if held or received prior to delivery of a bill for the same.

Rule 2.1(b) and (c) extends the meaning of client money significantly. Note particularly that money held to the sender's order is client money.

In *Challinor and Others v Juliet Bellis & Co and Another* [2013] EWHC 347 (Ch), Hildyard J made the point that a solicitor has a duty to clarify any ambiguity as to whom client money is held for.

'Fees' are defined in the Glossary as 'your own charges or profit costs (including any VAT element)'. 'Disbursements' are defined in the Glossary as 'any costs or expenses paid or to be paid to a third party on behalf of the client or trust (including any VAT element) save for office expenses such as postage and courier fees'. The word 'costs' is defined as 'fees and disbursements' and so covers both.

The effect of Rule 2.1(d) is that money received for all fees and future disbursements paid to the firm is considered client money unless and until billed. Such receipts must therefore be held in a client account (unless they are the only categories of client money held by the firm and the firm takes advantage of the exemption in Rule 2.2 – see below). Such money is often referred to as money received 'generally on account of costs'. Its use is dealt with under Rule 4.3. See below. However, broadly speaking, such money can be used for the purposes explained to the client.

The definition of client money does not include money received for disbursements which have already been paid, so where money is received in reimbursement of such a payment, it is a receipt of business money by the firm. Being business money it will be paid into a business bank account.

A firm might wish to send a bill to a client for its anticipated future fees and disbursements with a view to paying the money received in payment of that bill into the firm's business account, thus escaping the requirement that would apply under Rule 2.1 (d) to pay money received for unbilled fees and unpaid disbursements into the client bank account. This is permitted but there are reasons why firms should be cautious about billing for such future items. See **9.8.3** below.

Let us consider some scenarios:

- Firm receives £1,000 generally on account of costs.

  This is client money and must be held in the client bank account. It can be used to make payments on the client's behalf.

- Firm makes a payment of £100 from its business bank account for a client. The client gives the firm £100 in reimbursement.

  This is money received for a paid disbursement and must be held in the business account.
- Firm bills client for professional charges of £500 for future work plus £100 to cover a future disbursement. The client pays £600.

  This is all business money and will be held in the business bank account.

Exercise 9A

(a) Firm issues a bill to Client A for professional charges of £460. The client sends a cheque for £460.

Is the £460 client money?

(b) Firm asks Client B for £200 generally on account of costs. The client sends a cheque for £200.

Is the £200 client money?

(c) Firm pays a court fee of £100 for Client C using its own money and tells the client orally what has happened. The client reimburses the firm.

Is the £100 client money?

(d) Firm issues a bill to Client D for professional charges of £230 plus an unpaid disbursement of £100. The client sends a cheque for £330.

Is the £330 client money?

9.5 CLIENT BANK ACCOUNT

A client bank account is one opened by the firm in the name of the firm but used for client money. Rule 3.1 requires such an account to be at a bank or building society in England and Wales, and Rule 3.2 requires the account to include the word 'client' in its title to distinguish it from the firm's own business accounts. Including the word 'client' in the title has an added significance: section 85(2) of the Solicitors Act 1974 provides that a bank does not have any recourse or right against money in a client bank account in respect of any liability of the solicitor to the bank.

Rule 3.3 prohibits the use of a client bank account to provide banking facilities to clients or third parties. Payments into, and transfers or withdrawals from a client account must be in respect of the delivery of regulated services. This is such an important point that we will consider it separately at **9.6**.

9.6 CLIENT BANK ACCOUNT MUST NOT BE USED TO PROVIDE BANKING FACILITIES

9.6.1 The prohibition

Rule 3.3 provides that the client bank account must not be used to provide banking facilities for clients or third parties. Payments into, and transfers or withdrawals from, a client account must relate to the provision of regulated services. A similar prohibition was contained in Rule 14.5 of the previous Rules.

Rule 3.3 reflects decisions of the Solicitors Disciplinary Tribunal that it is not a proper part of a solicitor's everyday business or practice to operate a banking facility for third parties, whether they are clients of the firm or not. Concerns about the improper use of client accounts have been clearly and more broadly stated in case law, in particular in the three cases considered at **9.6.3** below.

A breach of Rule 3.3 is a serious matter in itself, but allowing a firm's client account to be used improperly may also result in a breach of the SRA Principles by failing to act:

- in a way that upholds the constitutional principle of the rule of law, and the proper administration of justice: Principle 1
- in a way that upholds public trust and confidence in the solicitors' profession and in legal services provided by authorised persons: Principle 2
- with independence: Principle 3
- with integrity: Principle 5.

It may also facilitate money laundering.

Money launderers who want to hide the illicit source of their funds will often try to pass money through a legitimate business. It is important to be alert to this danger.

EXAMPLE

You are working in your firm's property department. You have a client, Jack, who regularly instructs you to act on his behalf in property transactions which always fail to complete. He gives you large amounts to cover deposits and expenses which you pay into your client bank account and periodically return to him (less your moderate professional charges) using a firm cheque. He never queries your charges.

You should be suspicious of this pattern of behaviour and report the matter to your firm's money laundering officer.

The SRA takes breaches of anti-money laundering obligations very seriously. It has power to impose fines of up to £25,000, and during 2023 the SRA used those powers on a number of occasions even though the firms in question had not obtained a financial benefit from the breaches:

- On 18 January 2023 *The Law Society Gazette* reported that a two-partner firm was fined £20,000 for failing to put in place a compliant firm-wide risk assessment. The SRA said 'The conduct showed a disregard for statutory and regulatory obligations and had the potential to cause harm, by facilitating dubious transactions that could have led to money laundering (and/or terrorist financing). This could have been avoided had the firm established an adequate practice-wide (firm-wide) risk assessment.' The scale of the fine was chosen to create a 'credible deterrent' to other firms and signify the risk to the public and legal sector.
- On 27 November 2023 *The Law Society Gazette* reported that Ashfords LLP had been fined more than £100,000 by the Solicitors Regulation Authority for money laundering compliance failures reported by the firm itself. The fine, the fourth largest imposed by the SRA, was agreed despite the regulator stating that there was no suggestion that any money laundering or other financial crime took place. In published details of an agreed outcome, the SRA said that Ashfords had agreed to pay a penalty of £101,357 plus investigation costs of £1,350. The regulator said that it had identified areas of concern in relation to compliance with the 2017 Anti-Money Laundering (AML) Regulations and the SRA Principles and Code of Conduct.
- On 15 December 2023 *The Law Society Gazette* reported that two firms had been fined £7,900 and £3,120 respectively. The sums were based on the turnover of each business. One firm had lacked a compliant risk assessment for more than five years. The other firm admitted in a questionnaire to the SRA that it had been using a general risk assessment as its firm-wide AML assessment. This did not meet the requirements of the regulations as it was not tailored to the firm and did not address key risk factors. In neither case was there any evidence of harm to consumers or third parties, and nor did either firm benefit financially from the misconduct.

- On 24 January 2025, *The Law Society Gazette* reported that a London firm and its compliance officer had each been fined £25,000 after admitting multiple failings before a tribunal. Investigators reviewed AML documents provided by the firm on a total of 15 conveyancing matters and identified issues in 12 of those matters. Source of funds checks were found to be inadequate in certain matters and the firm did not have a compliant risk assessment in place. The compliance officer had made a declaration to the SRA in February 2020 that the firm had a fully compliant firm-wide risk assessment in place, as required by money laundering regulations. But this document was not drafted until February 2022. He admitted that he had realised a firm-wide risk assessment was required only after the SRA investigation had begun. The tribunal found that he acted recklessly in making a declaration without making sure that he understood exactly what a firm-wide risk assessment was.

9.6.2 SRA warning notice

On 18 December 2014 the SRA issued a warning notice to solicitors about the improper use of client accounts as a banking facility. The notice has been updated regularly, most recently on 1 March 2023. The notice is intended to help those regulated by the SRA to understand their obligations and how to comply with them. It states:

> Law firms, their managers and employees should not allow the firm's client account to be used to provide banking facilities to clients or third parties. You must also actively consider whether there are any risk factors suggesting that the transaction on which you are acting, even if it appears to be the normal work of a solicitor, is not genuine or is suspicious.

The warning notice explains that providing banking facilities through a client account is objectionable in itself. It says: 'You are not regulated as a bank to provide such facilities. If you do provide banking facilities for clients, you are trading on the trust and reputation from your status as a solicitor in doing so.'

It makes the point that the prohibition in Rule 3.3 – 'You must not use a client account to provide banking facilities to clients or third parties' – is simple and clear.

However, the second sentence of Rule 3.3 recognises that holding and moving money for clients may not be a breach where doing so is related to proper instructions regarding a transaction on which you are acting or in connection with the delivery of regulated services.

The warning notice states that the rule is not intended to prevent usual practice in traditional work undertaken by solicitors such as conveyancing, company acquisitions, the administration of estates or dealing with formal trusts. So, it does not affect a firm's ability to make usual and proper payments from client account when they are related to the transaction (such as the payment of estate agents' fees in a conveyancing transaction). The warning notice continues:

> Whether there is such a proper connection will depend on the facts of each case. The fact that you have a retainer with a client is insufficient to allow you to process funds freely through client account. You need to think carefully about whether there is any justification for money to pass through your client account when it could simply be paid directly between the clients.

Historically, some solicitors held funds for clients to enable them to pay the clients' routine outgoings. This was mainly for clients' convenience, such as where they were long-term private clients or based abroad. The SRA warning notice says:

> In view of technological change, such as the ease of internet and telephone banking, we consider that allowing client account to be used in this way is no longer justifiable and a breach of rule 3.3. Clients can now operate their bank accounts from their own homes or indeed from anywhere in the world. Allowing clients simply to hold money in a client account gives rise to significant risks and may evade sophisticated controls and risk analyses that banks apply to money held for their customers.

It continues:

> Factors you should bear in mind when considering such issues include:

- Throughout the retainer, you should question why you are being asked to receive funds and for what purpose. The further the details of the transaction are from the norm or from the usual legal or professional services a solicitor provides, the higher the risk that you may breach rule 3.3.
- You should always ask why you are being asked to make a payment or why the client cannot make or receive the payment directly themselves. The client's convenience is not a legitimate reason, nor is not having access to a bank account in the UK. Risk factors could involve the payment of substantial sums to others, including family members, or to corporate entities, particularly overseas, if there is no reason why the client could not receive the money into their own account and transfer it from there.
- You have a separate obligation to return client money to the client or third party promptly, as soon as there is no longer any proper reason for you to hold those funds (rule 2.5 of the Accounts Rules). If you retain funds in client account after completion of a transaction, there is risk (depending on how long you hold the money) of breaching both rule 2.5 and 3.3.

Rule 3.3 is to a large extent a preventative provision, intended to make it more difficult for people to use regulated businesses for improper purposes but also to deter law firms from helping such people. Any impropriety may be distant from the movement of money through a client account. In a classic laundering process, the movement through a client account may be the third or fourth stage of laundering the proceeds of a distant crime. But every stage contributes to the effectiveness of the laundering process.

It should also be noted that any exemption or exclusion under the Financial Services and Markets Act 2000 is likely to be lost if a deposit is taken in circumstances which do not form part of regulated services.

Although allowing a client account to be used as a banking facility can facilitate money laundering, Rule 3.3 exists independently of the anti-money laundering legislation and a breach of Rule 3.3 does not require there to be evidence of laundering. There are other dangers such as concealing the ownership of funds during a divorce or avoiding money being caught in an insolvency.

The SRA has published illustrative case studies (see www.sra.org.uk/solicitors/guidance/improper-use-client-account-banking-facility), including the following:

Unconnected payments from client account

A law firm acted for a property development company. The original retainer related to a redevelopment of a block of flats, the creation of separate leasehold interests and sale of the individual leases.

When the flats were sold, the client asked the firm to retain the proceeds in the firm's client account. The company then asked the firm to make a series of payments from client account, using the proceeds of sale from the first development to pay a building contractor, architect and council tax in relation to another development site, and to pay £56,000 to a consultant for his services as a sales agent.

The consultant then asked the firm to split the payment to him – paying £9,000 to a car dealership as a deposit on a new car and the balance to another firm of solicitors as a deposit on a property he was purchasing. The firm was not instructed to provide legal advice about the second development site. Its role was limited to making the requested payments.

The firm later found out that the consultant was in the process of going through a divorce.

Our view

There is a clear risk here that in making the payments the firm would be in breach of rule 3.3.

Making prompt payments on behalf of a client to third parties connected with a conveyancing transaction on which a law firm acted, such as to sales agents, is unlikely to breach rule 3.3. However, the less connected the payments are to the delivery of regulated services, the higher the risks are that the firm may breach rule 3.3.

Here, the payments relate to other transactions on which the law firm was not acting. Developers also frequently use different companies as special-purpose vehicles for each development and solicitors must be very wary of the risks in receiving funds that belong to Company A and paying them to Company B or to pay a liability of Company B.

> Firms should also ask themselves why the money cannot simply be paid to the client which can then make payments itself. Even if the liabilities are all the client's, it remains very risky to pay these when there is no reason the client cannot do so itself. The client's convenience is not a legitimate reason. We would expect the firm to be able to explain fully why the payments are being made and to have fully considered the risks involved – for example, involvement in money laundering, avoiding money being caught in an insolvency, or the hiding of assets.

9.6.3 The three judgments

The three judgments referred to at **9.6.1** (para 2) above are *Fuglers & Others v SRA* [2014] EWHC 179 (Admin); *Premji Naram Patel v SRA* [2012] EWHC 3373 (Admin); and *Attorney General of Zambia v Meer Care & Desai* [2008] EWCA Civ 1007.

Fuglers & Others v SRA

Fuglers acted for a Football Club. The Club's bank account was withdrawn after a winding-up petition was brought by HM Revenue & Customs (HMRC). The Club was insolvent. Over a four-month period, approximately £10 million of the Club's money passed through Fuglers' client account. The Solicitors Disciplinary Tribunal (SDT) fined the firm £50,000 and its two managers £5,000 and £20,000. The High Court dismissed an appeal and confirmed the seriousness of the misconduct that had been found by the SDT, setting out three reasons why client accounts must not be used as banking facilities for clients:

(1) *Objectionable in itself.* It is objectionable in itself for solicitors to be carrying out or facilitating banking activities because they are to that extent not acting as solicitors. If solicitors are providing banking activities which are not linked to an underlying transaction, they are engaged in carrying out or facilitating day-to-day commercial trading in the same way as bankers. This is objectionable because solicitors are qualified and regulated in relation to their activities as solicitors, and are held out by the profession as being regulated in relation to such activities. They are not qualified to act as bankers and are not regulated as bankers. If solicitors could operate a banking facility for clients which was divorced from any legal work being undertaken for them, they would in effect be trading on the trust and reputation which they acquired through their status as solicitors in circumstances where such trust would not be justified by the regulatory regimen.

(2) *Risk of money laundering.* Allowing a client bank account to be used as a banking facility, unrelated to any underlying transaction which the solicitor is carrying out, carries with it the obvious risk that the account may be used unscrupulously by the client for money laundering. Rule 14.5 (the predecessor to the existing Rule 3.3) was intended to reduce this risk.

(3) *Insolvency or risk of insolvency.* Allowing a client account to be used as a banking facility in an insolvency context allows the client to achieve what would normally be impossible as banks withdraw facilities upon notification that there has been a winding-up petition. The solicitor is therefore giving the client a commercial service which would otherwise be unavailable to it through the device of using a solicitor as if they were a bank. Secondly there is the risk of favouring one creditor over another. A third reason is the risk of the Insolvency Act 1986, s 127 applying so as to require creditors to reimburse payments from the client account in a subsequent liquidation. A solicitor who knowingly makes or facilitates such payments may be subject to a personal liability, quite apart from the liability of the payee to reimburse the amount transferred.

Premji Naram Patel v SRA

Mr Patel was a sole practitioner who acted for a company importing high value motor vehicles from Europe at a reduced price, to be sold in the UK for a substantial profit. Two significant investors were unwilling to pay funds directly to the company's owner because of past business failures. Instead investors paid money into the client account operated by Mr Patel. Mr Patel then transferred the relevant funds to the vehicle manufacturers directly.

The SDT imposed a fine of £7,500 on Mr Patel, who appealed to the High Court arguing that the second sentence of Rule 14.5 (the predecessor to the existing Rule 3.3) had to be read disjunctively: payments into and out of a client account have to relate to either (a) an underlying transaction, or (b) a service forming part of the firm's normal regulated activities. He submitted that the use of a client account is not in breach of the rule if its use relates to an underlying transaction, albeit not a legal transaction.

The court rejected that argument and upheld the fine imposed by the SDT, commenting that 'movements on client account must be in respect of instructions relating to an underlying transaction which is part of the accepted professional services of solicitors'. (Now the requirement would be that the movement on the client account related to an underlying transaction which is part of regulated services: see Rule 3.3 of the 2019 Rules.)

Attorney General of Zambia v Meer Care & Desai

In this case a fraudster paid enormous amounts of money belonging to the Zambian government into the client bank account of a firm of solicitors with two partners, Mr Meer and Mr Desai. The money was used on the instructions of the fraudster to make payments allegedly to meet debts of the government. Some money was used in that way but most of it was not. Very large sums were diverted away for the private purposes of the fraudster. At first instance Mr Meer was found guilty of dishonest assistance and conspiracy, and Mr Desai was held liable on the basis of vicarious responsibility, under s 10 of the Partnership Act 1890, for the acts of his partner. The convictions were quashed on appeal on the basis that Mr Meer had not acted dishonestly although he had clearly been naïve and gullible. He had not followed the guidance at the time which warned solicitors not to provide banking facilities to clients and to be aware of the risks of money laundering. As Lloyd LJ said at [234]:

> ... it is plain that he was providing the service of a bank account, albeit only in credit, or, as it was put in a graphic phrase in [the] skeleton argument for the appeals, a 'short-term money park', with almost none of the payments through the client account being related to any legal work done by the firm. It is equally plain that this was not a proper thing for a firm of solicitors to do.

Had Mr Meer refrained from providing banking services, he would not have found himself in the unenviable position of being cross-examined and convicted at first instance of criminal offences.

9.6.4 Deputies and use of client bank account

Rule 14.5 (the predecessor to Rule 3.3) was considered by the Office of the Public Guardian (OPG) in relation to solicitors who act as deputies for people who do not have capacity to manage their own property and financial affairs within the meaning of the Mental Capacity Act 2005. Such people are referred to as 'P' in the legislation.

The OPG was worried that solicitors acting as deputies who used the client bank account for P's funds might be infringing Rule 14.5. The SRA issued guidance in 2016 which indicated that this would not be the case.

However, the OPG then stated (in 'OPG's approach to solicitor client accounts', PG practice note 02/2016) that it had identified reasons of its own for not using the client bank account for P's money:

(1) The Mental Capacity Act Code of Practice suggests that P's funds should not be 'mixed' with those of other people. If P's funds are placed in the general client bank account, they will inevitably be mixed with funds belonging to the firm's clients. This problem would not arise if the deputy used a separate client bank account designated with P's name and used only for P's funds.

(2) The OPG needs to be satisfied that deputies have proper safeguards in place to protect deputyship funds. Deputies act under the authority of the court on behalf of vulnerable people, and extra care may need to be taken around who can authorise payments from deputyship funds. Setting up a separate bank account for a deputyship with named signatories may be simpler in practice.

(3) A deputy has a general duty to act in the incapacitated person's best interests, which can include managing their funds to gain the best return. There will be cases where large balances in a client account will not represent the best investment strategy for a client. In these cases, the OPG will question the appropriateness of keeping significant excess funds in this way.

The case studies accompanying the SRA Accounts Rules on improper use of the client bank account says this in relation to Rule 3.3 and attorneys:

> Where solicitors are acting as attorney under an LPA (or enduring power of attorney), they act on the instructions of the donor and in the specific circumstances set out in the power of attorney. In this situation, receiving or holding the donor's money into client account and making payments out of it, would not give rise to a breach of rule 3.3. You should always act in the best interests of your client (the donor) which may mean operating the client's own account as signatory or placing money in a designated deposit account.
>
> Solicitors must also comply with any other legal requirements. For example, for Court of Protection appointed deputies, the Office of the Public Guardian (OPG) has issued guidance which advises that law firms should not use client account to hold money and should instead use a designated deposit account or use the Court Funds Office account.

9.7 PAYING CLIENT MONEY INTO THE CLIENT BANK ACCOUNT

The normal rule contained in Rule 2.3 is that client money must be paid 'promptly' into a client bank account.

However, Rule 2.3 contains the following exceptions to the general rule:

(a) where client money falls within Rule 2.1(c) (money held as a trustee or holder of a specified office or appointment) and paying it into a client bank account would conflict with obligations relating to the specified office or appointment;

(b) the client money represents payments received from the Legal Aid Agency (LAA) for the firm's costs (see below); or

(c) the firm agrees an alternative arrangement in writing with the client, or the third party, for whom the money is held.

The exception in (b) for legal aid payments means that firms can receive these payments into their own business accounts. The payment will often include advance payments for parties (such as counsel) providing professional services to the client. There is no requirement for such professionals to be paid within a specified time or for such sums to be transferred to the client account bank if the party providing the professional services is not paid within the specified time.

The lack of such a requirement does not mean that firms will be able to hold payments from the LAA in their business account indefinitely. If, for example, a firm does not pay an expert's fee (because the firm retains the money in its account to avoid increasing its overdraft) and thereby delays a client's matter, this would constitute a breach of the rule requiring payments to be made promptly. It is also likely that this would be a breach of the SRA Code of Conduct. The firm would almost certainly be breaching Principle 5 (acting with integrity) and Principle 7 (acting in best interests of client).

There is a further limited exception in Rule 2.2 which applies where the only client money a firm receives or holds falls within Rule 2.1(d) (money for fees and unpaid disbursements received prior to delivery of a bill) and the firm is liable for the disbursements and does not have a client bank account for any other reason. If these conditions are fulfilled, the money can be held outside a client bank account, but the firm must inform the client in advance of where and how the money will be held.

An example of an unpaid disbursement for which the firm would be liable is where a firm has an account at the Land Registry and pays monthly for searches or where the firm has instructed counsel on behalf of a client.

Note that the Rule 2.2 exception cannot apply if the firm receives any other types of client money, for example funds to complete the purchase of property or funds held for the beneficiaries of a trust or an estate.

For firms that do fall within the Rule 2.2 exception, there are significant benefits. The ability to dispense with a client bank account results in potential cost savings in areas such as professional indemnity insurance and compliance, as no accountant's report will be required.

For those firms with a client account, the definition of client money in Rule 2.1(d) means that money received by the firm in advance of the issue of a bill for fees and unpaid disbursements is client money and, therefore, must be paid into client account.

Rule 2.4 requires firms to ensure that client money is available on demand unless an alternative arrangement is agreed in writing with the client or the third party for whom the money is held. This requirement means that firms should not tie up client money in deposit accounts which require extended notice periods.

Rule 2.5 requires client money to be returned promptly to the client or the third party for whom the money is held as soon as there is no longer any proper reason to hold those funds.

Notice that the Rules do not stipulate any particular time limits, and there is no guidance as to the meaning of 'promptly'. Firms will have to make their own decisions as to how quickly money should be paid in or returned. However, the use of the word 'promptly' signals that the SRA does not expect firms to be dilatory. The SRA has produced guidance, 'Planning for and completing an accountant's report', for accountants reporting on the treatment of client money and compliance with the Rules. The guidance suggests (at 3.2) that significant delay in the banking of client money into the client bank account is something that should lead to a qualification on the report but does not indicate what is significant.

9.8 KEEPING CLIENT MONEY SEPARATE FROM THE FIRM'S OWN MONEY

Rule 4.1 requires client money to be kept separate from the firm's own money.

9.8.1 Dealing with mixed receipts

When, as is often the case, a firm receives a mixed payment containing, for example, client money plus money to pay the firm's bill, Rule 4.2 states that the firm must allocate funds 'promptly' to the correct bank account.

Example

A firm sends a bill for its fees and disbursements to a client, together with a completion statement showing the balance due to complete the client's flat purchase. The client sends £300,000 (required to complete the flat purchase) plus £360 for the firm's professional charges plus £100 for disbursements the firm has paid and £1,000 for future disbursements.

The money for completion (£300,000) is client money. The money for the fees and billed disbursements (£1,460) is the firm's own money.

Ideally, the receipt should be split between bank accounts so that £300,000 is paid immediately into the client bank account and £1,460 into the firm's own business account. However, this will rarely be practicable.

> If the client pays by cheque, some banks will allow the cheque to be split between two accounts, but this is unusual. Normally the whole cheque will have to be paid into one account and funds moved promptly to the other account.
>
> Similarly, if the client is making an online transfer, the money will usually be paid into one bank account and the firm will need to transfer funds out promptly.

Unlike the old Rules, the 2019 Rules allow the firm to choose whether a mixed receipt is paid initially into the firm's client or business bank account. The SRA said in its Consultation on changes to the Rules (June 2016) that it wanted to replace the existing prescriptive requirements that mixed payments had to be paid into the client account with a broader requirement requiring mixed payments to be allocated promptly to the correct account. Rule 4.2 does this. The focus is on where the money ends up and not into which account it was originally paid. Many of those who responded to the SRA Consultation were unhappy with this, fearing that client money might be used to prop up business account shortfalls. However, the SRA declined to amend the draft rule, content that the application of other rules, such as acting with honesty and integrity, would result in compliance. In its Response to the Consultation, the SRA said (at para 72):

> If a firm were to use client money to manipulate their cash position, it is likely they would find themselves in breach of our rules. Firms will still be required to move money between accounts promptly and comply with all our other rules. This includes the requirement to act in a client's best interest, to not retain funds for longer than necessary and to act with honesty and integrity.

Firms will need a policy on what is meant by 'promptly', and respondents requested that the SRA issue guidance accordingly. Under the previous Rules, transfers were required to be made within 14 days, so this will presumably be a safe period. In Annex 1.5 to the Response to its Consultation, the SRA gave an example of 'prompt', which involved payment two weeks after the event. It said:

> 'Promptly' is not a defined term and will depend on all the circumstances of the matter, the nature of the firm and the instructions received – underpinned by the obligation in the SRA Code of Conduct for Solicitors and Firms to ensure that money and assets are safeguarded and the SRA Principles including that they act in the client's best interests.

9.8.2 Moving money from client to business bank account for fees and disbursements

Firms will normally request money generally on account of costs: the money requested will be intended to cover the firm's fees for its professional services and its future disbursements on behalf of the client. Until a bill is issued, such money is client money and must be paid into the client bank account. Rule 4.3 deals with withdrawing such money and provides:

> Where you are holding client money and some or all of that money will be used to pay your costs:
>
> (a) you must give a bill of costs, or other written notification, to the client or the paying party;
>
> (b) this must be done before you transfer any client money from a client account to make the payment; and
>
> (c) any such payment must be for the specific sum identified in the bill of costs or other written notification, and covered by the amount held for the particular client or third party.

Where a firm is holding money in the client bank account generally on account of costs and issues a bill, or other written notification of costs, it should transfer the money promptly. However, sometimes, the bill will include an item for a future disbursement which has not yet been paid. For example, in a property transaction the firm might issue a bill before completion which would include the amount required for stamp duty land tax and Land Registry fees. It would be tiresome for the firm to have to transfer the money for those items to the business account and would incur a risk to the client, if for example the firm became insolvent (see **9.8.3** below). Fortunately, the SRA has published guidance, 'Taking money for your firm's costs' (published 20 September 2020), which deals with this (and other matters relating to transferring funds from the client to the business account). The guidance says:

> Where the bill does include anticipated disbursements which have not yet been incurred, you will not be considered to be in breach of rule 4.3 by leaving the money associated with those billed anticipated disbursements in the client bank account until such time as they are paid.

9.8.3 Billing for anticipated fees and disbursements

Under the 2011 version of the Rules (Rule 20(3)), money for the firm's professional charges could only be withdrawn from the client bank account when the money was 'properly' required. The use of the word 'properly' prevented a firm from transferring funds from the client bank account for costs where a bill had been sent to the client but the work covered by the bill had not yet been completed. The word 'properly' does not appear in Rule 4(3) of the 2019 Rules. It is therefore permissible under the 2019 Rules to transfer money from the client bank account if a bill has been given to the client for work to be undertaken in the future.

However, although the SRA guidance, 'Taking money for your firm's costs' (published 14 September 2020), accepts that Rule 4.3 permits billing for future work and disbursements and paying the money received into the firm's business account, it highlights the following risks:

- If the client decides to terminate the retainer and asks for the money to be repaid, can the money be paid back immediately?
- If the matter does not proceed, for example the other side pulls out of a transaction, can the money be paid back immediately?
- Following the incapacity or death of a sole practitioner, can the money be paid back immediately?
- If the firm becomes subject to an insolvency event, and the client's money is not held in a ringfenced client account, how will the client be able to progress their matter or pay any disbursements due if they have already paid in advance for these and the insolvency practitioner refuses to repay the client's money because it is held in the firm's business account?

The guidance continues:

> You have an ongoing duty to safeguard money and assets that have been entrusted to you and not prefer your own interests, for example in maintaining cashflow, over those of your clients. The obligation to safeguard money entrusted to you is not limited to only that money which is held in a client account.
>
> You will need to think very carefully about the reasons why you are billing for these sums in advance and the risks to your client in your paying these monies into your firm's business account. It is important to remember that the sending of a bill in these circumstances does not mean that this money is no longer a client's money and it does not need to be safeguarded because it does not sit in a client account.
>
> In all cases, you will therefore need to think carefully about whether your broader obligations properly allow you to bill for such payments and receive money into your business account.
>
> We would not expect firms to bill for advance disbursements that the client will remain liable to pay for such as Stamp Duty Land Tax, and to receive such money into the firm's business account. In our view, this would be improper and a breach of our Standards and Regulations. Until the disbursement is paid the client remains liable for it, and this may be for a significant sum. Therefore, any risk to your firm's business account could result in the transaction failing or the client having to pay twice. Billing to receive money in these circumstances is likely to fail to meet obligations to act in the best interests of your client, safeguard their money or possibly act with integrity.
>
> In all cases where you may be considering billing for such advance payments, you will therefore need to think carefully about whether your broader obligations properly allow you to do this.
>
> If you do consider it is proper, you will need to make sure that your client is fully informed of the risks around their money being received into your firm's business account. How you explain the risks to clients may depend on the nature of your client and any vulnerability they may have.

> Knowing these risks, your client might only be prepared to pay a bill sent for work that has been done and disbursements for which you are liable and have been incurred by you.

Reporting Accountants are also likely to qualify a report if their view is such that money belonging to the client is, has been or may be, placed at risk.

In December 2022 the SRA issued a Consultation on 'Minor Amendments' to the SRA Standards and Regulations. Law firms complained that, despite the SRA's guidance, there was still a lack of clarity as to the circumstances in which it is appropriate to transfer money from the client bank account to the business account for anticipated costs. The SRA announced that it was proposing to amend the Rules to only allow money to be transferred for fees and disbursements that have already been incurred. However, on 5 December 2023 the SRA announced that, because it was undertaking more extensive regulatory reviews, it would postpone the Accounts Rules changes. It said:

> In light of recent events, including Axiom and a general increase in the number and size of interventions, we have decided that it is necessary to review our consumer protection arrangements. This includes reviewing risks to client money and the effectiveness of our current arrangements for protecting against them. We have reflected carefully and do not feel that it is the right time to make minor changes to the Accounts Rules while we are reviewing these wider issues.
>
> If we do not change our policy on our Accounts Rules following this review, we then plan to seek approval for these minor changes.

In the SRA consultation launched on14 November 2024, 'Client money in legal services - safeguarding consumers and providing redress: The model of solicitors holding client money', the SRA announced that it was pressing ahead with the amendment to Rule 2.1(d).

Rule 2.1(d) will be amended to make it clear that money received for unpaid disbursements remains client money despite the delivery of a bill or other written notification of costs until the disbursement is paid.

9.8.4 Transferring money for paid disbursements

Another significant change from the previous Rules is that the obligation contained in Rule 4(3) to send or give a bill to the client prior to transferring sums from the client bank account now applies to the firm's 'costs' rather than just to the firm's 'fees'. Critically, the definition of 'costs' comprises the firm's profit costs *and disbursements*, whereas the definition of 'fees', which was used in the equivalent provision of the previous Rules, was purely the profit cost element of the bill.

Therefore, the 2019 Rules appeared to make it impossible for a firm to transfer funds held in a client bank account to cover disbursements paid out of its own money on behalf of the client prior to giving a bill to the client.

However, the SRA guidance, 'Taking money for your firm's costs', referred to above, addressed this in response to queries from firms. The firms were worried that they would have to issue a bill, or other written notification of costs, if they wanted to move money from the client account to reimburse themselves for disbursements which have already been paid on behalf of the client, for example, where the firm has paid for a Land Registry search or court fee using its own money (often by a direct debit from the firm's business account).

The guidance states that Rule 5 (dealt with at **9.9** below) permits money to be withdrawn from the client bank account '*for the purpose for which it is being held*'. Provided the firm has made it clear to the client that the client money in question may be used to reimburse the firm for payments made, this will be permitted without issuing a bill, or other written notification of costs, under Rule 5. The explanation may be made in a client care letter, the firm's terms of engagement or in other communication with the client.

In the SRA Consultation referred to above on 'Minor Amendments' to the Rules, the SRA proposed to make a change to the wording of Rule 4 to make it clear that withdrawing money for paid disbursements is permissible without a bill. It proposed a new Rule 4.4 to say that the obligation to deliver a bill contained in Rule 4.3 does not apply where '*you withdraw client money from a client account in full or partial reimbursement of money spent by you on behalf of the client, or the third party for whom the money is held*'. This would remain subject to the limitation contained in Rule 5.1 that money can only be withdrawn for the purpose for which it is held. Hence firms would still need to explain to clients how their money can be used. As with the proposed amendment limiting transfers to those for fees and disbursements that have already been incurred (see **9.8.3** above), this amendment has been deferred pending the SRA's wider review of regulation.

In the SRA Consultation launched on 14 November 2024, 'Client money in legal services - safeguarding consumers and providing redress: The model of solicitors holding client money', the SRA announced that it was pressing ahead with the amendments to Rule 4.

A new Rule 4.4 will state:

> Rule 4.3 does not apply where you withdraw client money from a client account in full or partial reimbursement of money spent by you on behalf of the client, or the third party for whom the money is held.

Rule 5 does not permit a transfer where disbursements have not yet been incurred or have not been paid by the firm.

Let us consider some scenarios:

- You receive from a client a bank transfer of £500,960 made up of: £500,000 for completion of a purchase plus billed items of £360 for your professional charges and VAT, and £600 for paid disbursements.

  This is a mixed receipt. The money received for the billed items is all business money. The money for completion is client money.

  It does not matter which bank account the money is paid into initially, but a transfer must be made promptly to ensure that the firm ends up with £500,000 in the client bank account and £960 in the business bank account.

- You receive £1,000 from a client generally on account of costs. You pay a disbursement of £700 and a further disbursement of £500.

  The receipt of £1,000 is client money and must be paid into the client bank account. You can then use client money to pay the disbursement of £700. You do not have enough money to pay the second disbursement from the client bank account so will have to pay it from your business bank account. You can transfer the £300 remaining in your client bank account to your business bank account without issuing a bill or other written notification to your client provided you have made it clear to the client that the money paid on account may be used in this way.

Exercise 9B

A firm has a client bank account and a bank account for its own business money. It receives the following receipts. Are they receipts of client money, the firm's own business money or a mixture?

(a) Arshad sends £300 on account of costs.

(b) Following receipt of a bill, Bhopal sends £300 to cover the firm's fees and VAT.

(c) Following receipt of a bill, Chris sends £300 to cover the firm's fees and VAT together with £250,000 to complete the purchase of a flat.

(d) Following receipt of a bill, Danuta sends £300 to cover the firm's fees and VAT together with £3,000 to meet counsel's fees as yet unpaid.

> **Exercise 9C**
>
> Following receipt of the money requested from the clients in Exercise 9B, your firm pays a disbursement of £100. In which, if any, of (a)–(d) can £100 be transferred from the client to the business account without issuing a bill or other written notification of costs?

9.9 WITHDRAWALS OF CLIENT MONEY FROM THE CLIENT BANK ACCOUNT

9.9.1 Circumstances in which money can be withdrawn

Client money can only be withdrawn in one of the following circumstances (Rule 5.1):

(a) for the purpose for which it is being held; or

(b) following receipt of instructions from the client or the third party for whom the money is held; or

(c) on the SRA's prior written authorisation or in prescribed circumstances.

Rule 5.2 requires all withdrawals to be appropriately authorised and supervised.

Rule 5.3 is particularly important: withdrawals can only be made from the client bank account for a client if sufficient funds are held in the account for that client. If more is taken for one client than is held for them, the balance represents money held for other clients. Errors must be corrected promptly upon discovery and any money improperly withdrawn must be immediately replaced (Rule 6).

A firm must be careful if it is holding client money generally on account of costs and a disbursement needs to be paid. If the disbursement exceeds the amount of client money held, the firm must not make the payment from the client bank account. Options are as follows:

(a) The payment can be made from the firm's business bank account. Money cannot be transferred from the client bank account to partially reimburse the firm unless a bill is issued or the firm made the client aware that it would be used in this way (see **9.8.4** above and the SRA guidance, 'Taking money for your firm's costs').

(b) Under the previous SRA Accounts Rules, there was a specific Rule (Rule 14.2(c)) which allowed a firm to advance its own money to a client in such cases. The advance became client money and subject to the Rules applying to client money. There is nothing specific in the 2019 Rules authorising an advance but there seems nothing to prevent a firm making such an advance. It is useful where there is almost enough client money to make the payment.

> **Example**
>
> A firm is holding £1,900 for a client and needs to pay a disbursement of £2,000. It could advance £100, adding it to the money held for the client in the client bank account. The payment can then be made from the client bank account. The client will owe the firm £100.

9.9.2 Residual client account balances

Rule 2.5 requires client money to be returned promptly to the client, or the third party for whom the money is held, as soon as there is no longer any proper reason to hold those funds. A residual client account balance arises where money was not returned to the client at the end of a retainer and cannot now be returned as the client cannot be identified or traced. Firms should, therefore, very rarely be holding residual client account balances. However, many firms have historic balances which they have to deal with.

Left-over client account balances may seem a small matter. However, an SRA investigation completed in 2017 illustrates that this is far from the case. During 2013 and 2014, the SRA had been in correspondence with a City firm regarding concerns over the existence of residual client ledger balances. A subsequent inspection of the firm's accounts by the SRA's Forensic Investigation team concluded that there were no less than 2,007 client matters with a client ledger balance totalling £15,230,900 where there had been no movement on the relevant client ledger for a period of at least one year. Subsequent analysis by the firm identified that, of this amount, £7,324,276 related to inactive matters whilst further client ledger balances totalling £1,609,648 remained under review.

In May 2013 the firm circulated its written policy on clearing residual client ledger balances to all of the firm's UK members. A course of action was agreed between the firm and the SRA. An action plan setting out the process and deadlines for clearing the residual balances was approved by the SRA in January 2014.

One partner who became his department's risk manager with responsibility for implementing the action plan failed to do so correctly. Instead, the dormant balances held on the client bank account for his department were transferred to the firm's own business bank account after being applied against invoices that had been raised improperly on those matters. In one instance, the partner had transferred time on an unconnected matter, which could not be recovered and was destined to be written off by the firm, to one of the inactive matters before raising an invoice and transferring funds from client to business bank account.

Dishonesty was not alleged by the SRA, and the tribunal, in its published judgment, noted as follows:

> He had been instructed to clear residual balances; that was his motivation, but he had gone about it in the wrong way. He should have made more enquiries about how to carry out his instructions in accordance with the accounts rules. His actions were not planned in terms of committing misconduct. However, the Respondent was quite an experienced solicitor having been admitted in 2004. The Tribunal considered that there had been harm to the reputation of the profession as a result of what the Respondent had done because he was not treating client money properly. He had been cavalier in his approach to the residual balances. The resulting harm to the profession's reputation was reasonably foreseeable as a result of the Respondent's conduct.

The partner was suspended from practice for a period of three months from 20 November 2017. Additionally, he agreed to pay the SRA costs of almost £18,000 and faced strict controls on his return to practice for a period of two years, including not being able to act as a sole practitioner, partner, member or director of a firm. He was not allowed to hold client money or operate a client or business bank account or to authorise payments from a client bank account. Finally, he was not permitted to act as either a COLP or a COFA for the same period of two years.

Rule 5.1(c) allows client money to be withdrawn from the client bank account on the SRA's prior written authorisation or 'in prescribed circumstances'. The Rule itself does not set out the prescribed circumstances, but the SRA has issued the following:

> **Prescribed circumstances under Rule 5.1 (c)**
>
> You may withdraw residual client balances of £500 or less on any one client matter from a client account provided:
>
> 1. the balance is paid to a charity of your choice
> 2. you have taken reasonable steps to return the money to the rightful owner. The reasonableness of such steps will depend on:
>   - i the age of the residual balance;
>   - ii the amount of the residual balance;
>   - iii if you have access to the client's most up to date contact details;
>   - iv if not, the costs associated with tracing your client.
>
> We expect you to make more intensive efforts to locate the rightful owner for larger or more recent residual balances or for balances where more details are held about the client.

> 3. you record the steps taken to return the money to the rightful owner and retain those records, together with all relevant documentation for at least six years;
> 4. you keep appropriate accounting records, including:
>   i a central register which records the name of the rightful owner on whose behalf the money was held, the amount, name of the recipient charity (and their charity number) and the date of the payment; and
>   ii all receipts from the charity and confirmation of any indemnity provided against any legitimate claim subsequently made for the sum they have received.
> 5. you do not deduct from the residual balance any costs incurred in attempting to trace or communicate with the rightful owner.
>
> The records referred to in points 3 and 4 above may be requested by your reporting accountant who will look at whether you have followed these prescribed circumstances.
>
> For amounts over £500 you will need our authority before removing this money from the client account. Please use our application form.

There is separate SRA guidance, 'Granting authority to withdraw residual client balances', updated 8 October 2020, which deals with the matters the SRA takes into account when dealing with requests to withdraw amounts in excess of £500. This says:

> We will look at whether the applicant firm has made adequate attempts to trace and repay the rightful owner
>
> We will assess the application having regard to:
>
> - the amount of money and the length of time it has been held by the firm
> - the steps taken to trace the owner of the money
> - the costs involved in making further enquiries
> - the likelihood of success of tracing the client or third party given the information held
> - the proposed use to be made of the money, for example to be paid to charity or transferred to the firm's business account.
>
> We require the firm to provide evidence of the steps already taken to locate the client. We will then review what has been done and the result of those actions to decide whether adequate steps have been taken.
>
> **What are 'adequate steps' to trace and repay the owner?**
>
> Adequate steps will differ according to circumstances. We will consider whether the reasonable costs of taking steps to trace the client or third party are proportionate in relation to the amount of money held. Therefore, the larger the sum involved, the greater attempts we would expect to be made.
>
> We would expect firms to make use of social media, newspapers or tracing services and, where appropriate, make a search of Companies House and/or the Probate Registry.
>
> In most cases we would expect firms, as a minimum, to make use of the Department of Work and Pensions' (DWP) letter forwarding service, in addition to undertaking any free searches on the internet. It is likely that adequate steps would include placing an advert in an appropriate publication, if proportionate in view of the amount of money. This may be a local or national newspaper, depending on the circumstances.
>
> Other adequate steps may mean employing a tracing agent or investigator to help trace the client. If the cost is proportionate to the amount of money held and we are of the view that, in the particular circumstances, it may be successful in tracing the client, we are likely to recommend firms do this before we make a decision

There is a special form, 'Withdrawal of residual client balances'.

The SRA in its three-month consultation started on 14 November 2024, 'Client money in legal services - safeguarding consumers and providing redress: The model of solicitors holding client money', said:

> Through our inspection and investigations work, we have seen examples of firms who are not returning client money promptly at the end of a case, leading to high residual balances. We have heard from some compliance experts that this is not always treated as a priority by firms and their employees.

9.10 CLIENT ACCOUNTING SYSTEMS AND CONTROLS

The client bank account will contain client money held for many different clients, so it is necessary for firms to maintain accurate records, showing for each client:

- all receipts and payments of client money;
- all payments made on behalf of the client from the firm's own money; and
- bills issued to the client.

Rule 8.1(a) requires firms to maintain a client ledger account for each client identified by their name and an appropriate description of the matter. The client ledger account must show all receipts and payments of client money. It must also record any payments made by the firm from its own money on behalf of the client, the issue of bills to the client and any receipts of money in payment of such bills.

Rule 8.1(c) requires firms to have a separate cash book which shows all transactions through client bank accounts.

There is no requirement to maintain a cash book to show dealings with the firm's own money but firms will obviously choose to do so.

Rule 8.2 requires firms to obtain bank statements for all client bank accounts and for the firm's own business bank accounts at least every five weeks, and Rule 8.3 requires them to prepare bank reconciliation statements for the client bank accounts at least every five weeks. Any discrepancies revealed by the reconciliation must be investigated promptly.

Rule 8.4 requires a central record of bills and other written notifications of costs to be kept in a readily accessible form.

Firms that do not operate a client account do not need to comply with the record keeping requirements in Rule 8.1(b) and (c), but they must keep the readily accessible central record of bills or written notifications of costs given as required by Rule 8.4.

There is SRA guidance on accounting systems, 'Helping you keep accurate client accounting records' (updated 25 November 2019). It advises that accounts should be maintained on the double-entry principle. It says that firms should have clear procedures for ensuring that all withdrawals from client accounts are properly authorised:

> Good compliance can be achieved by making sure you have:
>
> - established clear systems and controls for ensuring that persons permitted to authorise the withdrawal of client money from a client account have an appropriate understanding of the requirements of the Accounts Rules and sufficient seniority within the firm.
> - persons nominated to authorise payments. That person should ensure that there is evidence which supports the reason for each payment, and that this is recorded together with the date of the payment.
> - procedures for ensuring that sufficient money is held for a particular client before any withdrawals are made for that client. Your controls should be adequate to prevent a debit balance arising but if one does, the controls should make sure that it is identified and rectified promptly.
> - systems for the transfer of costs from a client to a business account. Normally transfers should be made only after issuing a bill or other written notification of costs. Rule 8.4 requires you to keep a readily accessible central record of all bills or other written notifications of costs given by you.
> - systems which help to control and record accurately any transfers between different clients of the firm. Where these arise as a result of loans between clients, the written authority of both the lender and borrower should be obtained and retained on the file.
> - checks and controls to make sure client files are closed promptly, and the prompt payments back to clients of any residual balances.

- systems which make sure clients (or other people on whose behalf money is held) are kept regularly informed when funds are retained for a specified reason (which should be in respect of the delivery by you of regulated services) at the end of a matter or the substantial conclusion of a matter. This should help ensure that your client account is not being used as a banking facility when there is no need for you to hold onto monies.

On 20 June 2024, the SRA issued a Warning Notice, 'Money missing from client account'. The notice is aimed at all those regulated by the SRA but is particularly relevant to managers of firms or a firm's COFA or COLP.

The Notice makes the point that any deficiency on client account exposes clients and others to a risk of financial loss and damage to public confidence. Missing money must be replaced with extreme urgency. There must be proper systems and controls in compliance with the accounts rules, and it is for a firm's principals to ensure that this is the case.

The Notice sets out relevant case law which holds that client money is sacrosanct and that proper stewardship of it is vital.

In *Bolton v The Law Society* [1993] EWCA Civ 32, Lord Bingham said:

> People trust solicitors and firms to look after their money. Failing to keep their money safe has wider consequences for clients and the reputation of the profession. A loss of client money could affect anyone who places their money in a client account. The client account of a solicitor is sacrosanct.

In *Levy v SRA* [2011] EWHC 740 (Admin) (at [30]), Cranston J said:

> ... Client money is sacrosanct, and a proper stewardship in relation to it is vital. Client money can only be used for that client's matters. There must be proper systems and controls to ensure compliance with the account rules and it is for a firm's principals to ensure that. Errors must be promptly remedied. Transfers from the client account to the office account can only be made when properly required for payment of the solicitors' costs, the firm first notifying the client that payment is to be made from moneys held for the client. No transfer should ever be made from the client account unless a solicitor is satisfied that there are funds to meet it. Each of these simple rules is not merely good practice but is critical to the lawful operation of the client account by any solicitor.

The Notice includes the following warnings:

- A shortage on client account impacts all clients of the firm. A firm that continues to transact with a shortage on its client account risks using other clients' funds to facilitate those transactions.
- Ultimately, a deficient client account is likely to be distributed pro rata.
- You may well breach your duty to act in the best interests of clients if you pay client money into an already deficient account without fully informed consent – it is highly unlikely a properly advised client would pay funds into a deficient account with the risk of only receiving a proportion back. Failing to inform clients exposes them to a risk of loss.
- Until missing money is replaced, you should not take costs from the client account – you cannot 'properly' require payment of your fees from money held in a client account in such circumstances. It is not in the best interests of the firm's clients to do so and risks using other clients' money to subsidise a client's costs. Any money taken for costs in these circumstances is serious misconduct which may give rise to disciplinary action.
- If you or your insurers do not replace the money promptly, you are at serious risk of intervention by the SRA. Even if the money is replaced there is a risk of intervention if there is reason to suspect dishonesty and/or serious breaches of the Accounts Rules.
- There may be circumstances where a shortage has occurred due to circumstances beyond the firm's control. This includes a theft or a cyber-attack. In these situations, there is still an obligation on the firm and its managers to replace the shortage.
- Offences under the Fraud Act 2006 may be committed once you are on notice that money is missing if you do not act properly and honestly.

9.11 PAYING INTEREST TO CLIENTS

Rule 7.1 requires firms to account to clients or third parties for a fair sum of interest on any client money held on their behalf.

Rule 7.2 allows firms to agree otherwise with clients or third parties, but the agreement must be in writing and the firm must provide sufficient information to enable clients and third parties to give informed consent.

In the SRA's consultation on client money started on 14 November 2024, one of the topics considered is whether the rules on interest earned on client accounts need changing so they better serve clients' interests. This matter is considered further in **Chapter 15** below.

9.12 THIRD PARTY MANAGED ACCOUNTS

Rule 11 allows firms to enter into arrangements with a client to use a third party managed account (TPMA) for the purpose of receiving payments from or on behalf of, or making payments to or on behalf of, the client in respect of regulated services delivered by the firm in the following circumstances:

(a) use of the account must not result in you receiving or holding the client's money; and

(b) you take reasonable steps to ensure, before accepting instructions, that the client is informed of and understands:

 (i) the terms of the contractual arrangements relating to the use of the TPMA, and in particular how any fees for use of the TPMA will be paid and who will bear them; and

 (ii) the client's right to terminate the agreement and dispute payment requests made by you.

Rule 11.2 requires the firm to obtain regular statements from the provider of the TPMA and ensure that these accurately reflect all transactions on the account.

These accounts will offer an alternative to operating a client bank account which will be attractive to some firms, particularly smaller firms that do not handle large amounts of client money. However, many firms will not find them a viable option due to uncertainty surrounding timings of payment and discomfort with control over client funds resting with a third party.

Money held in a TPMA is not held by the solicitor or firm but by the TPMA provider. It does not meet the definition of client money as set out in Rule 2.1. This means that the provisions in the Accounts Rules relating to holding client money do not apply to monies in a TPMA.

Regulation will be by the FCA and not by the SRA. The firm will not be responsible for the monies in the TPMA, as these are held by the TPMA provider and are not under the firm's direct control. However, firms using TPMAs will have to ensure that they comply with the standards in the Code of Conduct, including the duty to act in clients' best interests and safeguard money and assets belonging to clients. The SRA says it would expect that this would include an assessment of the suitability of the product in the particular circumstances and for the particular client.

Firms using a TPMA must notify the SRA that they are doing so by filling out a TPMA form (available on the SRA website) and emailing it to the SRA.

9.13 DEALINGS WITH OTHER MONEY BELONGING TO CLIENTS OR THIRD PARTIES

Rules 9 states that firms may open a joint account with a client or third party. Rules 2–8 do not apply to such money save for:

(a) obtaining statements from banks and building societies and other financial institutions at least every five weeks (Rule 8.2); and

(b) keeping a readily accessible central record of bills and other notifications of costs (Rule 8.4).

If the firm operates the client's own bank account as a signatory, again, Rule 10.1 provides that Rules 2–8 do not apply save for Rule 8.2 and Rule 8.4 and, in addition, Rule 8.3, which requires reconciliations of the account at least every five weeks.

In its Consultation on 'Minor Amendments' to the Standards and Regulations, the SRA reported that firms operating a client's own account have reported difficulty in implementing the requirements to reconcile client accounts every five weeks and obtain bank statements. Many firms reported that it is often not possible to access monthly bank statements to an account belonging to a client which they control. The SRA therefore proposed to amend Rule 10 in order to make the arrangements workable so that firms must:

- undertake reconciliation every 16 weeks;
- maintain a central register of clients' own accounts under control of the firm;
- keep records of transactions carried out by the firm on behalf of the client and record bills and other notification of costs relating to the client's matter.

The proposal adds a new Rule 10.2 requiring the reconciliation to be signed off by the COFA or a manager of the firm at least every 16 weeks. However, like the other proposed amendments, there is a delay pending further review.

9.14 OBTAINING AND DELIVERY OF ACCOUNTANTS' REPORTS

Rule 12 requires firms which have, at any time during an accounting period, held or received client money, or operated a joint account or a client's own account as signatory, to:

(a) obtain an accountant's report for that accounting period within six months of the end of the period; and

(b) deliver it to the SRA within six months of the end of the accounting period if the accountant's report is qualified to show a failure to comply with the rules, such that money belonging to clients or third parties is, or has been, or is likely to be placed, at risk.

Reports must be prepared and signed by an accountant who is a member of one of the chartered accountancy bodies and who is, or works for, a registered auditor.

It used to be necessary for all accountants' reports to be submitted to the SRA, not just those with qualifications. Many commentators are critical of the change. The Law Society in its response to the SRA's consultation on client money in legal services called for the reintroduction of a mandatory accountant's report submission for all firms holding client money (see www.lawsociety.org.uk/campaigns/consultation-responses/sra-consultation-on-client-money-in-legal-services).

Firms are not required to obtain an accountant's report if:

(a) all of the client money held or received during an accounting period is money received from the Legal Aid Agency; or

(b) in the accounting period, the statement or passbook balance of client money held or received does not exceed:

   (i) an average of £10,000; and

   (ii) a maximum of £250,000,

   or the equivalent in foreign currency.

The SRA has published guidance, 'Accountant's report and the exemption to obtain one' (updated 25 November 2019), which includes the following:

> The exemption applies to a single accounting period which could span over 12 months. There may be circumstances where in one calendar year you are exempt but in the second year, the level of client account balances held means that you cannot rely on the exemption. It is your firm's responsibility in all cases to make sure that the rules are complied with and if an accountant's report is required, that the report is obtained.

Under Rule 12.4 the SRA has the right to require a report where a firm ceases to operate as an authorised body and to hold or operate a client account, or it considers that it is otherwise in the public interest to do so.

SUMMARY

(1) A firm must keep client money separate from the firm's own money (Rule 4).

(2) Subject to exceptions, client money must be paid into a client bank account promptly and must be kept separate from the firm's own money.

(3) Funds from mixed payments must be allocated promptly to the correct bank account.

(4) Firms must never withdraw more client money for a client than is held in the client bank account for that client (Rule 5.3).

(5) Clients are usually – though not always – entitled to interest on client money held for them by solicitors (Rule 7).

(6) All dealings with client money must be recorded (Rule 8).

SOLUTIONS

Exercise 9A

(a) Not client money. It is a specific payment of a bill.

(b) Client money. It is generally on account of costs.

(c) Not client money. It is received specifically for a paid disbursement.

(d) Not client money. It is received in payment of a bill.

Exercise 9B

(a) This is a receipt of client money because it is *on account of* costs, ie no bill has been issued.

(b) This is a receipt of money belonging to the firm because it is for fees and a bill has been issued.

(c) This is a mixed receipt. The money for fees belongs to the firm because a bill has been issued. The money for completion is held for the client and is client money.

(d) This is a receipt of money belonging to the firm because it is for fees and a disbursement and a bill has been issued.

Exercise 9C

(a) £100 can be transferred provided it was made clear to the client that the money received might be used in this way.

(b) There is no money in the client account to be moved. The firm must bill the client for a further £100.

(c) Although there is money in the client bank account, it was given only to cover the purchase price and cannot be withdrawn for other purposes without the client's express consent.

(d) All the money received was for billed items and is business money. Hence, there is no money in the client account to be moved. The firm must bill the client for a further £100.

CHAPTER 10

Entries for Recording Simple Client Transactions

10.1	Introduction	113
10.2	The two sets of accounting records	113
10.3	The format of the accounts	114
10.4	Dealing with receipts of money	115
10.5	Dealing with payments of money	116
10.6	Recording the firm's professional charges	118

LEARNING OUTCOMES

After reading this chapter you will be able to:

- explain why a firm providing regulated services needs two separate sets of accounts
- explain what those accounts look like
- deal appropriately with receipts and payments of both business and client money
- make appropriate entries to deal with professional charges and VAT when issuing a bill.

10.1 INTRODUCTION

The SRA Accounts Rules are primarily concerned with keeping client money safe and ensuring that proper records are kept to allow errors and discrepancies to be picked up on inspection by reporting accountants and the SRA. There are, therefore, rules relating to the handling of money during client transactions and its recording. This chapter looks at the Rules relating to recording a simple client transaction.

10.2 THE TWO SETS OF ACCOUNTING RECORDS

In order to control dealings with client money, a more sophisticated set of day-to-day accounts is needed for a firm providing regulated services than for most other businesses. It is essential that all the records of 'client money' dealings are clearly separated from the records of the ordinary business dealings of the firm. Rule 8 sets out the recording requirements of the Rules.

One way of understanding the system is to think of a law firm as carrying on two separate businesses with two separate sets of accounts. Thus, the law firm would need one set (Set A) for the first business – say the business which handles client money – and another set (Set B) for the second – say the firm's ordinary business accounts. This explains the reason for one of the fundamental bookkeeping rules for firms providing legal services. The two sets of accounts are entirely separate. Thus, you cannot enter a debit on one set of accounts (Set A) and a credit on the other set (Set B).

10.3 THE FORMAT OF THE ACCOUNTS

10.3.1 Requirements as to formats

Law firms may choose any of the various systems on the market which enable the recording requirements of Rule 8 to be satisfied. They all have one thing in common – they are based on the principles of double entry bookkeeping.

Guidance issued by the SRA, 'Helping you keep accurate client accounting records', includes the following:

- your books should be maintained on the double-entry principle. This means that every transaction relating to client money should be recorded in at least the client cash book and the client ledger.
- your books should be legible, up to date and contain narratives alongside the entries which identify and provide adequate information about the transaction. The current balance, if not shown on the client ledger account, should be readily ascertainable. In accordance with Rule 8, entries should be made in chronological order and record the date of the underlying transaction.
- ledger accounts should include the name of the client or other person or trust for whom the money is held and contain a heading which provides a description of the matter or transaction, for example, Client: Mr A Nother: Matter: sale of 1 Property Road, London. This will help you link the money held or received with those for whom it is held.
- business account entries (which reflect, for example, money due to your firm for costs) in relation to each client or trust matter are kept up to date as well as the client account entries. This is because it is important to make sure that any credit balances on the business side of the client ledger in respect of client or trust matters are reviewed on a regular basis. For example, at the same time you carry out client account reconciliations, and fully investigated in case of any impact on the client or trust matter and the monies you hold for them.
- you keep a separate contemporaneous and chronological record of any inter-ledger transfers.

10.3.2 The dual cash account

Anyone running a business will need a cash account to record dealings with each bank account. A law firm is *required* by Rule 8.1(c) to keep a cash account for dealings with the client bank account. The Rules do not require firms to have a cash account to record dealings with its own money, but obviously no business can function without a record of cash received and spent. Thus, the law firm will need (at least) two separate cash accounts. To ease the administrative burden of actually moving from a cash account in one place to another cash account in a different place and back again, the normal format is to have the two individual cash accounts on the same page next to one another. One set of columns for 'Date' and 'Details' will do for both accounts. Traditionally the firm's own money was referred to as 'office' money, but the 2019 Rules use the term 'business' account for the account(s) holding the firm's own money.

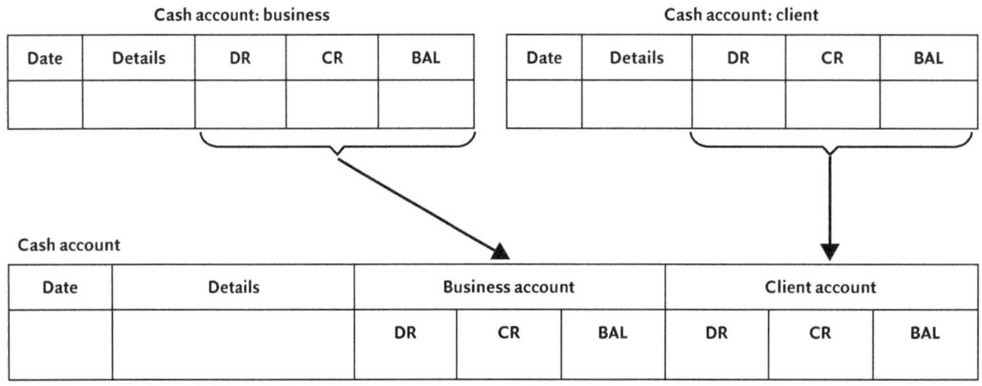

10.3.3 The dual ledger account for each client

Rule 8.1 requires dealings with client money on behalf of a client to be recorded. It also requires the issue of bills to a client, payments of the firm's own money on behalf of clients and receipts in payment of bills to be recorded. This requires two separate ledger accounts although, as with the two cash accounts, it is usual to combine the two ledger accounts to show them side by side.

Client ledger account: business

Date	Details	DR	CR	BAL

Client ledger account: client

Date	Details	DR	CR	BAL

Client ledger account

Date	Details	Business account			Client account		
		DR	CR	BAL	DR	CR	BAL

10.4 DEALING WITH RECEIPTS OF MONEY

First decide whether you are receiving business money or client money. The receipt can then be recorded in the correct section.

The entry in the cash account for a receipt is a DR entry.

The corresponding CR entry is in the ledger account of the client from whom, or on whose behalf, the money is received.

Receipts of client money will be held for the relevant client in the client bank account.

Receipts of business money will reduce the indebtedness of the relevant client to the firm.

Note: In the examples that follow the running balances on the cash accounts are not completed. The amount of the balance on a cash account depends on the total funds held in the bank account at the time. A receipt will increase the balance, and a payment will reduce it. The balance on the cash account is not referable to any one client.

Example

Client Jones owes your firm £100 following the issue of a bill. (This means there is a DR balance of £100 on the business columns of Jones's ledger account.) You receive £20 from client Jones to reduce his debt. This is a receipt of business money. It reduces the amount Jones owes the firm.

DR Cash account
CR Jones ledger } Business section

Client: Jones
Matter:

Date	Details	Business account			Client account		
		DR	CR	BAL	DR	CR	BAL
	Balance			100DR			
	Cash		20	80DR			

Cash account							
Date	Details	Business account			Client account		
		DR	CR	BAL	DR	CR	BAL
	Balance			XXX			XXX
	Jones	20		XXX			

Example

You receive £300 from client Brown on account of costs. This is a receipt of client money. The firm will hold the money for Brown in its client bank account.

DR Cash account
CR Brown ledger } Client section

Client: Brown Matter:							
Date	Details	Business account			Client account		
		DR	CR	BAL	DR	CR	BAL
	Cash					300	300CR

Cash account							
Date	Details	Business account			Client account		
		DR	CR	BAL	DR	CR	BAL
	Balance						XXX
	Brown				300		XXX

10.5 DEALING WITH PAYMENTS OF MONEY

First, decide whether you are making the payment from the firm's own business bank account or from its client bank account so that the payment can be recorded in the appropriate cash account.

The entry on the cash account for a payment is a CR entry.

The corresponding double entry is a DR in the ledger account of the client on whose behalf the payment is made.

If the payment is made from the business bank account, the resulting DR balance on the business columns of the client ledger will show that the client owes the firm money, ie, is *a debtor*. If the payment is made from the client bank account, it will reduce the amount held for the client (ie, it will reduce the CR balance on the client columns of the client ledger).

Remember that, under Rule 5.3, a payment must not be made from a client bank account unless the firm is holding sufficient funds in its client bank account for that client.

Example

You pay court fees of £40 on behalf of client Black. You hold no client money for Black so must make the payment using business money:

CR Cash account
DR Black ledger } Business section

Client: Black
Matter:

Date	Details	Business account			Client account		
		DR	**CR**	**BAL**	**DR**	**CR**	**BAL**
	Cash	**40**		40DR			

Cash account

Date	Details	Business account			Client account		
		DR	**CR**	**BAL**	**DR**	**CR**	**BAL**
	Balance			xxx			
	Black		**40**	xxx			

Example

You are holding client money of £500 for client White generally on account of costs. You make a payment of £400 for client White.

You hold sufficient client money for White to be able to make the payment using client money.

CR Cash account } Client section
DR White ledger }

Client: White
Matter:

Date	Details	Business account			Client account		
		DR	**CR**	**BAL**	**DR**	**CR**	**BAL**
	Balance						500CR
	Cash				**400**		100CR

Cash account

Date	Details	Business account			Client account		
		DR	**CR**	**BAL**	**DR**	**CR**	**BAL**
	Balance						xxx
	White					**400**	xxx

Exercise 10A

You act for Smith. Record the following events on Smith's ledger account and on the cash account.

Note: Assume that the balances on the cash account are: business £2,000 DR, client £20,000 DR. Assume the balances on Smith's ledger account are zero.

June

1 Smith sends £1,000 generally on account of costs.

Note: This is a receipt of client money because it is not in payment of a bill.

2 Firm pays £100 on Smith's behalf.

Note: This can be paid from the client bank account since sufficient funds are available and the money was received generally on account of costs.

4 Firm pays £900 on Smith's behalf.

Note: This can be paid from the client bank account since sufficient funds are available.

6 Firm pays £200 on Smith's behalf.

	Note: This must be paid from the business bank account since no funds are held for Smith.
8	Firm pays £400 on Smith's behalf.
	Note: This must be paid from the business bank account since no funds are held for Smith.

10.6 RECORDING THE FIRM'S PROFESSIONAL CHARGES

When the firm issues a bill to the client, it will include an item for its professional charges and VAT on those charges. The solicitor will want to make entries in the accounts to show that:

(1) the client owes the firm the charges and VAT.

At this stage, there is no movement of cash, so no entry is made in the cash account.

On the client ledger account, the bookkeeper must make DR entries for professional charges and VAT in the business section. The entries must be made in the business section. This is because the purpose of the DR entries is to show that the client owes money to the firm. You are not yet recording the receipt of cash;

(2) the firm has earned income in the form of professional charges and owes HMRC money in VAT.

The corresponding CR entries are made on an income ledger account and an account in the name of HMRC respectively.

The income ledger account could be called 'professional charges' or 'professional fees'. Traditionally it has been called 'profit costs' and we will use that name.

At the end of the year, the balance on the profit costs account will show the amount the firm has billed for professional charges.

The HMRC ledger account shows how much the firm owes HMRC in VAT (see **Chapter 12** for a discussion of the way in which firms account to HMRC for VAT charged to clients).

Example

Firm issues a bill for £400 profit costs plus £80 VAT to client Smith.

DR Smith ledger account £400 } business section
DR Smith ledger account £80 }

CR Profit costs account £400
CR HMRC account £80
(See **Chapter 12** for details of VAT.)

Client: Smith
Matter:

Date	Details	Business account			Client account		
		DR	CR	BAL	DR	CR	BAL
	Profit costs	400		400DR			
	VAT	80		480DR			

Profit costs

Date	Details	DR	CR	BAL
	Smith		400	400CR

HMRC

Date	Details	DR	CR	BAL
	Smith		80	80CR

Note that when the firm sends a bill, it will include details of disbursements already paid on the client's behalf and disbursements to be paid in the future. As clients will normally have provided money on account of costs, it is usual to provide an accompanying statement setting out how much of the client's money has been used already, and whether further funds are required from the client to meet the firm's professional charges and future disbursements or whether there is a balance to be returned to the client.

No entries are made on the accounts in relation to disbursements when the bill is sent. Disbursements are recorded as and when they are paid.

Exercise 10B

Prepare the cash account and client ledger account for Rex to record the following events.

You act for Rex in a litigation matter. The balances on the cash account are business £1,000DR, client £1,000DR. The balances on Rex's ledger account are zero.

June

1 Rex sends you £200 generally on account of costs.

Note: This is a receipt of client money because it is not in payment of a bill.

2 You pay court fees £20.

Note: This can be paid from the client bank account since sufficient funds are available.

5 You pay expert witness £180.

Note: This can be paid from the client bank account since sufficient funds are available.

7 You pay another expert witness £150.

Note: There is no client money available. The payment must be made from the business bank account.

10 The matter is settled. You receive a cheque from the defendant for £5,000 in full and final settlement. This cheque is made out to the firm.

Note: The firm has received client money and should pay it into the client bank account. (Had the cheque been made out to the client, the firm would simply have forwarded it to the client. It would not have been possible to pay the cheque into a bank account in the firm's name.)

12 You send client a cheque for £5,000.

Note: This is a payment of client money.

14 You send Rex a bill. Profit costs £200. VAT £40. The bill includes a section showing the disbursements paid from the money sent on account of costs and the disbursement paid from the firm's own business bank account. The accompanying statement will set out the amount required from the client (£240 + £150 = £390).

16 Rex sends you the £390 requested on 14 June.

Note: This will be a receipt of business money. It should be paid into the business bank account.

SUMMARY

(1) A law firm will have two cash accounts: one for business money and one for client money. They are frequently shown side by side.

(2) A law firm will have two client ledger accounts: one for business money dealings and one for client money dealings. They are frequently shown side by side.

(3) When dealing with cash receipts or payments, decide first whether it involves business money or client money, then record the receipt or payment in the appropriate section of the accounts.

(4) The entries for a receipt are:

- CR on client ledger
- DR on cash account

in the business or client section as appropriate.

The entries for a payment are:

- DR on client ledger
- CR on cash account

in the business or client section as appropriate.

(5) When a bill is sent, entries are made:

(a) to record professional charges with a DR entry in the business section of the client ledger and a CR entry in the profit costs account;

(b) to record VAT with a DR entry in the business section of the client ledger and a CR entry in the HMRC account.

No entries are made in relation to disbursements when a bill is sent. Disbursements are recorded when they are paid.

SOLUTIONS

Exercise 10A

Client: Smith
Matter:

Date	Details	Business account			Client account		
		DR	CR	BAL	DR	CR	BAL
June							
1	Cash. On a/c costs					1,000	1,000CR
2	Cash				100		900CR
4	Cash				900		–
6	Cash	200		200DR			
8	Cash	400		600DR			

Cash account

Date	Details	Business account			Client account		
		DR	CR	BAL	DR	CR	BAL
June	Balances			2,000DR			20,000DR
1	Smith. On a/c costs				1,000		21,000DR
2	Smith					100	20,900DR
4	Smith					900	20,000DR
6	Smith		200	1,800DR			
8	Smith		400	1,400DR			

Exercise 10B

Client: Rex
Matter: Litigation

Date	Details	Business account			Client account		
		DR	CR	BAL	DR	CR	BAL
June							
1	Cash. On a/c costs					200	200CR
2	Cash. Court fees				20		180CR
5	Cash. Expert witness				180		–
7	Cash. Expert witness	150		150DR			
10	Cash. Settlement					5,000	5,000CR
12	Cash. To client				5,000		–
14	Costs	200					
	VAT	40		390DR			
16	Cash. Amount due		390	–			

Cash account

Date	Details	Business account			Client account		
		DR	CR	BAL	DR	CR	BAL
June	Balance			1,000DR			1,000DR
1	Rex. On a/c costs				200		1,200DR
2	Rex. Court fees					20	1,180DR
5	Rex. Expert witness					180	1,000DR
7	Rex. Expert witness		150	850DR			
10	Rex. Settlement				5,000		6,000DR
12	Rex. Amount sent					5,000	1,000DR
16	Rex. Amount requested	390		1,240DR			

Note: There will be credit entries on the profit costs account and HMRC account to record the fact that the client was charged £200 profit costs and £40 VAT.

CHAPTER 11

TRANSFERS

11.1	Introduction	123
11.2	Cash transfers	123
11.3	Inter-client transfers	126

LEARNING OUTCOMES

After reading this chapter you will be able to:

- explain the difference between cash transfers and inter-client transfers
- make appropriate entries to record each kind of transfer.

11.1 INTRODUCTION

Rules 8.1(a) of the Rules requires firms to record on each client's ledger account all client and business money receipts and payments made for that client on the client and business section of the accounts, as appropriate. Hence if a client's money is withdrawn from the client bank account and paid into the business bank account, for example to pay the firm's charges, this must be recorded. This type of transfer is called a cash transfer.

A firm must keep a running total of the amount owed to each client, so if a firm is holding money in the client bank account for one client and stops holding the money to the order of the first client and starts holding it to the order of a second client, the change in ownership of the money must be recorded. This type of transfer is called an inter-client transfer.

In this chapter you will study the entries required to record cash transfers and inter-client transfers.

11.2 CASH TRANSFERS

11.2.1 Why might such a transfer occur?

11.2.1.1 Payment of firm's professional fees and disbursements

Once a bill (or other written notification) has been issued, a firm can transfer money from the client bank account to the business bank account for its own professional fees, including any VAT element, and any disbursements included on the bill.

As we saw at **9.8.4**, a firm can also withdraw money from the client bank account in reimbursement of paid disbursements provided this was within the purpose for which the money was being held (Rule 5).

11.2.1.2 Other reasons for cash transfers

Other reasons include:

(a) to advance money to a client or trust where the solicitor needs to make a payment on behalf of the client or trust and insufficient client money is available (once advanced, the money becomes client money);

(b) to replace money withdrawn in breach of Rule 5.3;

(c) to allow the client a sum in lieu of interest.

11.2.2 Recording a transfer from client to business bank account

This is done in two parts, as follows:

(1) Record the payment of money from the client bank account:

CR cash account
DR client's ledger account } Client section

(2) Record the receipt of money into the business bank account:

DR cash account
CR client's ledger account } Business section

Example

You act for Green. On 10 April, you receive £800 from Green on account of costs to be incurred. On 26 April, you send Green a bill for £400 plus £80 VAT. On 28 April, you transfer £480 from the client bank account to the business bank account.

Entries are as follows.

(1) The £800 is client money. It will be paid into the client bank account and recorded in Green's ledger account and in the cash account.

Client: Green
Matter: Miscellaneous

Date	Details	Business account			Client account		
		DR	CR	BAL	DR	CR	BAL
Apr 10	Cash: From Green. On account					**800**	800CR

Cash account

Date	Details	Business account			Client account		
		DR	CR	BAL	DR	CR	BAL
Apr							xxx
10	Green				**800**		

(2) When the bill is issued, the entries for profit costs and VAT will be DR entries on Green's ledger account (remember that entries for profit costs and VAT on the issue of a bill are always debited in the *business* section to show that the client owes the firm money).

The CR entries will be on the profit costs and HMRC account which we have not shown.

Client: Green
Matter: Miscellaneous

Date	Details	Business account			Client account		
		DR	CR	BAL	DR	CR	BAL
Apr							
10	Cash: From Green. On account					800	800CR
26	Profit costs	**400**		400DR			
	VAT	**80**		**480**DR			

Cash account

Date	Details	Business account			Client account		
		DR	CR	BAL	DR	CR	BAL
Apr							xxx
10	Green				800		

(3) The payment from client account will look like this:

DR Green's ledger } Client section
CR Cash

Client: Green
Matter: Miscellaneous

Date	Details	Business account			Client account		
		DR	**CR**	**BAL**	**DR**	**CR**	**BAL**
Apr							
10	Cash: From Green. On account					800	800CR
26	Profit costs	400		400DR			
	VAT	80		480DR			
28	Cash. Transfer from client account				**480**		320CR

Cash account

Date	Details	Business account			Client account		
		DR	**CR**	**BAL**	**DR**	**CR**	**BAL**
Apr							xxx
10	Green				800		
28	Green					**480**	

(4) The receipt into business account will look like this:

CR Green's ledger } Business section
DR Cash

Client: Green
Matter: Miscellaneous

Date	Details	Business account			Client account		
		DR	**CR**	**BAL**	**DR**	**CR**	**BAL**
Apr							
10	Cash: From Green. On account					800	800CR
26	Profit costs	400		400DR			
	VAT	80		480DR			
28	Cash. Transfer from client account				480		320CR
	Cash. Transfer to business account		**480**	-			

Cash account

Date	Details	Business account			Client account		
		DR	**CR**	**BAL**	**DR**	**CR**	**BAL**
Apr							xxx
10	Green				800		
28	Green					480	
	Green	**480**					

Note: For the sake of convenience, the payment from the client bank account and the receipt into the business bank account are often shown on the same line as set out below:

Client: Green
Matter: Miscellaneous

Date	Details	Business account			Client account		
		DR	**CR**	**BAL**	**DR**	**CR**	**BAL**
Apr							
10	Cash: From Green. On account					800	800CR
26	Profit costs	400		400DR			
	VAT	80		480DR			
28	Cash. Transfer from client account to business account		**480**	-	**480**		320CR

Cash account							
Date	Details	Business account			Client account		
		DR	CR	BAL	DR	CR	BAL
Apr							xxx
10	Green				800		
10	Green. Transfer from client to business account	**480**				**480**	

The residual client balance must be returned promptly to the client (Rule 2.5).

11.3 INTER-CLIENT TRANSFERS

11.3.1 What is happening?

Sometimes, a firm which is holding money in the client bank account for Client A stops holding that money for Client A and starts holding it for Client B. An example would be where A owes B money and asks the firm to hold the money for B. No money is taken out of the client bank account. However, the firm must make changes to the firm's internal accounts to record the change in whom the money is held for. This is necessary to comply with the obligation to show receipts and payments made for each client. This type of transfer is sometimes referred to as a 'paper' transfer or an 'inter-client' transfer.

11.3.2 How to record

No entries are made on the cash account as no money is moving in or out of a bank account. Instead a DR entry is made in the client section of the ledger account of the client for whom the money was originally held, and a CR entry is made in the client section of the ledger account of the client for whom the money is now held. So:

DR Client ledger account of first client
CR Client ledger account of second client

Example

You are instructed by Anne Brown to collect a debt of £10,000 from White & Co. You write to White & Co requesting payment. On 7 August, you receive a cheque from White & Co for £10,000 in payment of the debt.

You already act for Anne's sister, Jane Brown, who is buying a flat. On 9 August, Anne tells you that she is making a gift of £1,000 to Jane and asks you to hold £1,000 of her money to the order of Jane. You make the necessary inter-client transfer.

Entries are as follows.

(1) When the £10,000 is received, it is client money held to the order of Anne. It will be recorded like this:

Cash account							
Date	Details	Business account			Client account		
		DR	CR	BAL	DR	CR	BAL
Aug							xxx
7	Anne Brown				**10,000**		

Client: Anne Brown Matter: Debt collection							
Date	**Details**	**Business account**			**Client account**		
		DR	**CR**	**BAL**	**DR**	**CR**	**BAL**
Aug							
7	Cash. From White & Co. Debt					**10,000**	10,000CR

(2) When Anne instructs you to hold £1,000 to the order of Jane, there will be no entry on the cash account. There will be the following entries on the ledger accounts of Anne and Jane:

Client: Anne Brown Matter: Debt collection							
Date	**Details**	**Business account**			**Client account**		
		DR	**CR**	**BAL**	**DR**	**CR**	**BAL**
Aug							
7	Cash. From White & Co. Debt					10,000	10,000CR
9	Jane Brown. Transfer				**1,000**		9,000CR

Client: Jane Brown Matter: Litigation							
Date	**Details**	**Business account**			**Client account**		
		DR	**CR**	**BAL**	**DR**	**CR**	**BAL**
Aug							
9	Anne Brown. Transfer					**1,000**	1,000CR

In the details column of each ledger account, it is essential to give the name of the ledger account where the other part of the double entry is made.

Exercise 11A

The following events occur:

February

1 You receive £800 generally on account of costs from your client, Dean.

4 You pay a court fee of £100 (no VAT) on behalf of your client, Wade.

5 You receive £7,000 on behalf of your client, Will. It is a debt collected.

8 You agree to act for Simon. You ask for £300 generally on account of costs. Dean tells you that he is prepared to lend Simon the money for this. Dean and Simon instruct you in writing to make the necessary transfer.

11 You issue a bill to Will. Your costs are £400 plus £80 VAT. You transfer the costs from the client bank account to the business bank account.

13 You issue a bill to Wade for £200 plus £40 VAT. Will, who is Wade's uncle, instructs you to transfer an amount sufficient to pay Wade's indebtedness to you from the amount you are holding for Will. It is a gift from Will to Wade.

14 You issue Dean a bill for £600 plus £120 VAT. You transfer the remaining money held for him in the client bank account to the business bank account in part payment of the bill.

Prepare the clients' ledger accounts and the cash account.

SUMMARY

(1) Cash transfers from one bank account to another involve a cash payment from one bank account and a cash receipt into the other.

(2) One pair of entries records the payment; one pair of entries records the receipt.

(3) Inter-client transfers do not involved the movement of cash. The cash remains in the client bank account.

(4) To record an inter-client transfer there is a DR entry in the client section of the transferor's ledger account and a CR entry in the client section of the transferee's ledger account.

SOLUTIONS

Exercise 11A

1 February — The money is client money. You must pay it into the client bank account (Rule 2.3).

4 February — You are holding no money for Wade, so you must pay the money out of the business bank account (Rule 5.3).

5 February — The money is client money. You must pay it into the client bank account (Rule 2.3).

8 February — This is an inter-client transfer.

11 February — **The bill** DR Will's ledger account business section with profit costs and VAT. CR profit costs account and HMRC ledger account respectively.

The transfer For the payment from the client bank account, CR cash; DR Will – client section. For the receipt into the business bank account, DR cash; CR Will – business section. This is permitted under Rule 4.3.

13 February — **The bill** DR Wade's ledger account business section with profit costs and VAT. CR profit costs account and HMRC ledger account respectively.

The transfer This is not an inter-client transfer. The money could be withdrawn from the client bank account on Will's instructions, but it is being received specifically in payment of your bill. It is a receipt of business money and, as such, should be paid into the business bank account. You must therefore record a cash payment from the client bank account on behalf of Will (CR cash; DR Will – client section) and a cash receipt into the business bank account on behalf of Wade (DR cash; CR Wade – business section).

14 February — **The bill** Entries as above.

The transfer The entries are the same as those on 11 February.

Note: When Dean pays the balance, the money received will be business money and will be paid straight into the business bank account.

The accounts are shown below.

Client: Dean
Matter: Miscellaneous

Date	Details	Business account			Client account		
		DR	CR	BAL	DR	CR	BAL
Feb							
1	Cash. From Dean. Generally on account.					800	800CR
8	Simon. Transfer				300		500CR
14	Profit costs	600		600DR			
	VAT	120		720DR			
	Cash. Transfer from client to business account		500	220DR	500		–

Client: Wade
Matter: Miscellaneous

Date	Details	Business account			Client account		
		DR	CR	BAL	DR	CR	BAL
Feb							
4	Cash. Court fee	100		100DR			
13	Profit costs	200		300DR			
	VAT	40		340DR			
	Cash: Transfer from Will		340	–			

Client: Will
Matter: Miscellaneous

Date	Details	Business account			Client account		
		DR	CR	BAL	DR	CR	BAL
Feb							
5	Cash. Debt collected					7,000	7,000CR
11	Profit costs	400		400DR			
	VAT	80		480DR			
	Cash. Transfer costs from client to business account		**480**	–	480		6,520CR
13	Cash. From client to business account for Wade				340		6,180CR

Client: Simon
Matter: Miscellaneous

Date	Details	Business account			Client account		
		DR	CR	BAL	DR	CR	BAL
Feb							
8	Dean. Transfer					300	300CR

Cash account

Date	Details	Business account			Client account		
		DR	CR	BAL	DR	CR	BAL
Feb				xxx			xxx
1	Dean				800		
4	Wade		100				
5	Will				7,000		
11	Will	480				480	
13	Will					340	
	Wade	340					
14	Dean	500				500	

CHAPTER 12

VALUE ADDED TAX

12.1	Introduction	131
12.2	General principles	131
12.3	VAT and firms providing legal services	135

LEARNING OUTCOMES

After reading this chapter you will be able to:

- explain in outline the general principles of VAT
- explain how, in relation to firms providing regulated services, VAT applies to professional charges and disbursements.

12.1 INTRODUCTION

This chapter deals with VAT in so far as it affects firms providing legal services. We begin with a brief outline of the way in which VAT works. We then look at the particular issues that arise in relation to firms providing services.

Value added tax is relevant both to the firm's professional charges and to some disbursements paid by the firm on behalf of clients.

12.2 GENERAL PRINCIPLES

Value added tax involves two distinct aspects: output tax (charged by a business to its customers) and input tax (charged to the business by its suppliers). A business registered for VAT charges its customers output tax for which it must then account to HMRC. In other words, it acts as an unpaid tax collector.

It will normally be possible for such a business to deduct input tax charged to the business from the amount accounted for to HMRC. See **12.2.2**.

The standard rate of VAT has been 20% since 4 January 2011. There is also a zero rate and a reduced rate which apply to some goods and services. Some goods and services are exempt from VAT. See **12.2.1.3**.

12.2.1 Output tax

Value added tax is chargeable on the supply of goods or services where the supply is a taxable supply and is made by a taxable person in the course or furtherance of a business carried on by them (Value Added Tax Act (VATA) 1994, s 4(1)). Each element of this definition will be considered further below.

The person making the supply is liable to account to the Government for the amount of tax which they charge.

12.2.1.1 Supply of goods

This comprises all forms of supply whereby the whole property in goods is transferred, including a gift of goods.

12.2.1.2 Supply of services

This is anything which is not a supply of goods, but is done for a consideration. Note that a gratuitous supply of services is not a supply for VAT purposes, in contrast to a gift of goods.

12.2.1.3 Taxable supply

This means any supply of goods or services other than an exempt supply. Exempt supplies are listed in Sch 9 to the VATA 1994 and include supplies of land (except for new commercial sales and leases of commercial property where the supplier has opted to be taxable), insurance, some postal services, finance, health services, and burial and cremation.

Taxable supplies may be divided into two main categories:

(a) those which are chargeable at the standard rate; and

(b) those which are chargeable at a zero rate. Zero-rated supplies are listed in Sch 8 to the VATA 1994 and include supplies of food, water, books, international services and transport.

A reduced rate of 5% applies, inter alia, to mobility aids, domestic fuel, installation of energy-saving materials, smoking cessation products such as nicotine patches and gum, renovation and alteration of certain dwellings and residential conversions, children's car seats and carrycots with restraint straps.

Zero-rated and exempt supplies are similar in that no VAT is actually charged in either case by the supplier to their customer.

However, they must be carefully distinguished, since only a person who makes taxable supplies is able to recover input tax, ie, the VAT charged to them by their suppliers.

A firm supplying legal services will be making a standard-rated supply. Legal services include professional charges and *some* payments made for clients (see below). A solicitor supplying insurance will be making an exempt supply.

12.2.1.4 Taxable person

A person is a taxable person if they *are* or *are required to be* registered under the Act. A person must register if, broadly, the value of taxable supplies (*not* profit) in the preceding 12 months exceeded a figure specified in each year's Budget (currently £90,000). A firm of solicitors will virtually always have to be registered.

Notice that voluntary registration is permitted. A person may register voluntarily in order to recover input tax charged.

12.2.1.5 Business

Value added tax is chargeable by a taxable person only on taxable supplies made in the course or furtherance of a business carried on by them.

'Business' includes any trade, profession or vocation, but the term is not limited to these activities since it also covers, for example, the provision by certain clubs and associations of facilities to members.

Furthermore, although the services of an employee are not generally taxable, the Act provides that, where a person, in the course of carrying on a trade, profession or vocation, accepts any office, any services supplied by them as holder of the office shall be treated as supplied in the course of a business carried on by them and are therefore chargeable with VAT.

A firm supplying legal services which is a taxable person must charge VAT not only on its supplies of legal services but also on any other supplies it makes in the course of its business, eg, the sale of redundant office equipment.

12.2.2 Input tax

Where a taxable person is charged VAT on the supply of goods or services for the purposes of their business, they may deduct the tax charged to them from the amount of output tax which they account for to HMRC (s 25(2)). Since input tax charged to a taxable person is recoverable, it follows that VAT is not an expense of a person who makes only taxable supplies, whether at the standard or zero rate.

A person who makes only exempt supplies is not a taxable person and so is unable to recover any input tax.

Example

A, an undertaker, and B, a bookseller, each buy stationery for £200 + £40 VAT. The bookseller supplies zero rated goods and so can recover the VAT; therefore, the expense to be charged to the Profit and Loss Account is only £200. The undertaker supplies exempt services and so cannot recover the VAT; therefore, the expense to be charged to the Profit and Loss Account is £240.

Where a taxable person makes both taxable and exempt supplies, they are then partly exempt and may recover only a proportion of the input tax charged to them. A solicitor who supplies insurance may find themselves in this position.

Where the exempt supplies made by a taxable person fall within certain de minimis limits, they can be ignored, with the result that all input tax is recoverable.

12.2.3 Value of supply

Where a supply is fully taxable, VAT at the standard rate (20%) is payable on the value of the supply. If the consideration is in money, the value of the supply is such amount as, with the addition of the total tax payable, is equal to the consideration (s 19(2)).

If a price or fee is agreed, this will be deemed to include VAT unless expressly stated to be tax exclusive.

It is important to remember to quote for a fee *plus* VAT. If VAT is not stated to be extra, the customer will only pay the fee quoted; the business will have to pay the VAT from the quoted fee and will end up with less money than it expected.

For example, if a business registered for VAT, and making standard-rated supplies, quotes a fee of £100 and does not stipulate that VAT is extra, the £100 received is deemed to be made up of the fee and VAT at 20%. The total receipt is 120% of the fee so 100/120 will be fee and 20/120 will be VAT.

Exercise 12A

A firm agrees to provide a legal service for client X for £240. How much will be recorded on the profit costs account and how much as VAT?

12.2.4 Time of supply

The importance of the time of supply (or tax point) is that it decides the quarter at the end of which a taxable person becomes liable to account for output tax on a particular supply. It also determines the quarter in which a taxable person can claim input tax on a taxable supply made to them. The basic tax points are as follows:

(a) *Goods* When the goods are removed or made available to the purchaser (s 6(2)).

(b) *Services* When the services are completed (s 6(3)).

These basic tax points will be varied in the following cases:

(a) If, within 14 days after the basic tax point, the supplier issues a tax invoice, the date of the invoice will become the tax point unless a longer period has been agreed with HMRC (s 6(5) and (6)). In the case of solicitors, there is a general extension of the 14-day period to three months, so that, provided solicitors deliver their bills within three months of completion of their services, the date of each bill will be the tax point.

(b) If, before a basic tax point arises, the supplier issues a tax invoice or receives payment, the supply will, to the extent covered by the invoice or payment, be treated as taking place at the date of the invoice or payment (s 6(4)).

12.2.5 Tax invoices

Such invoices are of vital importance to a taxable person since they are evidence of their right to recover the input tax on a supply made to them, ie, without such an invoice, they will generally be unable to claim an input credit, irrespective of whether or not they have made payment to the supplier.

A taxable person making a taxable supply to another taxable person must, within 30 days after the time of supply (or within such longer period as HMRC allows), provide them with a tax invoice, which must state the following particulars:

(a) an identifying number;
(b) the date of the supply, ie, the tax point;
(c) the supplier's name, address and VAT registration number;
(d) the name and address of the person to whom the supply is made;
(e) the type of supply, eg, sale, loan, hire;
(f) the description of the goods or services supplied;
(g) the quantity of goods or the extent of the services and the amount (excluding VAT) payable for each description;
(h) the total amount payable (excluding VAT);
(i) the rate of cash discount;
(j) the rate and amount of tax charged.

12.2.6 Collection and accounts

Accounting for VAT will generally be by reference to quarterly accounting periods. Within one month after the end of each quarter, a taxable person must submit a completed return form to HMRC, together with a remittance for the tax due. The amount payable, ie total output tax charged less deductible input tax, is obtained from a statutory VAT account, which is required to be kept by every taxable person for each tax period. Apart from these details of the tax due, the return form must also contain a list of the tax exclusive value of all outputs, and also the total of all inputs exclusive of tax.

Example

(a) During an accounting period, a firm providing legal services sends bills charging total professional charges of £200,000 plus output tax of £40,000. In the same period, the firm buys office equipment for £40,000 plus input tax of £8,000.

The firm accounts to HMRC as follows:

	£
Output tax charged	40,000
less input tax suffered	(8,000)
Payable to HMRC	32,000

The firm has to account for the £32,000 due irrespective of whether or not the customers have yet paid the firm the cash. This can sometimes cause a cashflow problem.

(b) During an accounting period, a retailer sells food for £50,000 plus output VAT at the zero rate. In the same period, the retailer buys equipment for £10,000 plus input tax of £2,000.

The retailer accounts to HMRC as follows:

	£
Output tax charged	0
less input tax suffered	(2,000)
Recoverable from HMRC	2,000

Note: In both these examples, the supplier can recover the input tax paid because the supplier is making taxable supplies, even though, in the case of the retailer, they are at the zero rate.

(c) A funeral director sends bills for burial and cremation totalling £150,000. No VAT is charged as these are exempt supplies. During the same period, the funeral director buys equipment for £15,000 plus input tax of £3,000.

The funeral director is not a taxable person and so does not account to HMRC. Therefore, the funeral director cannot recover the input tax paid. The cost of the equipment to the business is £18,000.

12.3 VAT AND FIRMS PROVIDING LEGAL SERVICES

12.3.1 Professional charges

Firms providing legal services must charge VAT on their supply of services.

Example

Bill	£
Professional charges	200.00
VAT @ 20%	40.00
Total	240.00

Entries: The firm will need a ledger account in the name of HMRC as well as a profit costs account and a ledger account in the name of the client.

CR Profit costs account with professional charges

CR HMRC with VAT

DR Client ledger account (business section) with professional charges and VAT as two separate figures

Client:
Matter:

Date	Details	Business account			Client account		
		DR	CR	BAL	DR	CR	BAL
	Profit costs	200		200DR			
	VAT	40		240			

Profit costs account

Date	Details	Business account		
		DR	CR	BAL
	Client		200	xxx

HMRC account					
Date	Details	Business account			
		DR	CR	BAL	
	Client		40	xxx	

12.3.2 What are disbursements for VAT purposes?

As a matter of convenience for the client, firms providing legal services frequently pay expenses (eg, court fees) on behalf of the client. Such expenses are often referred to as 'disbursements'. HMRC does not regard 'disbursements' as part of the supply of legal services and so the firm does not have to charge VAT on them. However, to qualify as a disbursement for this purpose, an item must fulfil certain conditions. Not all items paid on behalf of a client are regarded by HMRC as disbursements. Generally, it is only advantageous to treat a payment as a disbursement for VAT purposes (as opposed to part of the supply of legal services) where no VAT is chargeable on the supply by the third party, or where the client is not entitled to reclaim it as input tax.

12.3.2.1 HMRC's view of disbursements

HMRC's view of what constitutes a disbursement is set out in para 25.1.1 of HMRC VAT Notice 700 (see also HMRC's VAT Taxable Person Manual at VTAXPER39000). The crucial point is that if costs are incurred by suppliers in the course of making their own supply to their clients, then they must be included in the value of those supplies when VAT is calculated. If the payment to third parties is made purely as the agent of the client then it is a disbursement for VAT purposes, and is not included in the amount on which VAT is charged.

To be a disbursement, the Notice says that all the following conditions must be met:

- you acted as the agent of your client when you paid the third party;
- your client actually received and used the goods or services provided by the third party (this condition usually prevents the agent's own travelling and subsistence expenses, telephone bills, postage, and other costs being treated as disbursements for VAT purposes);
- your client was responsible for paying the third party (examples include estate duty and stamp duty payable by your client on a contract to be made by the client);
- your client authorised you to make the payment on their behalf;
- your client knew that the goods or services you paid for would be provided by a third party;
- your outlay will be separately itemised when you invoice your client; you recover only the exact amount which you paid to the third party; and
- the goods or services, which you paid for, are clearly additional to the supplies which you make to your client on your own account.

HMRC's view is that all the conditions set out above must be satisfied before a payment can be treated as a disbursement for VAT purposes.

The House of Lords decision in *Nell Gwynn House Maintenance Fund Trustees v C&E Commissioners* [1999] STC 79 confirmed that VAT law draws a clear distinction in principle between:

(i) expenses paid to a third party that have been incurred by you in the course of making your own supply of services to your client and which are part of the whole of the services rendered by you to your client; and

(ii) expenses for specific services that have been supplied by the third party to your client and you have merely acted as your client's known and authorised representative in paying the third party.

Only in case (ii) can the amounts of the payments to the third party qualify for treatment as disbursements for VAT purposes.

Examples of disbursements are items where the client is responsible for paying the third party, such as:

- inheritance tax;
- capital gains tax;
- stamp duty and stamp duty land tax;
- estate agents' fees.

Counsel's fees are disbursements as the service is supplied to the client (even though the solicitor is responsible for ensuring payment). The Law Society's Practice Note, 'VAT treatment of disbursements and expenses', says that Land Registry fees for registration of title are disbursements (the position of searches and official copies is different – see **12.3.2.2** below). HMRC's VAT Manual says at VTAXPER46000 that the following can be treated as disbursements:

- statutory charges such as court fees, estate duty, incorporation fees, land charge and land registry fees, probate fees, stamp duty;
- charges for the professional services of a third party. For example, the sale of a property is usually organised by a solicitor, who will present a bill to the vendor for both the solicitor's own services and the commission payable to the estate agent. The supply of the estate agent's services is to the vendor, not the solicitor, and so the solicitor may treat this as a disbursement for VAT purposes. The fees of notaries, surveyors, or witnesses, and charges for police and medical reports may also fall into this category.

The paragraph says that telegraphic transfer fees or CHAPS which represent a charge by the bank to the solicitor for the service of transferring money out of the solicitor's bank account cannot be treated as a disbursement and nor can general expenses borne by the solicitor including travel, accommodation and telephone charges. There is judicial authority for both of these propositions.

In the tribunal case of *Shuttleworth & Co v Commissioners of Customs and Excise* (LON/94/986A), it was held that the transfer of funds by a solicitor was part of the overall conveyancing service provided by a solicitor to their client. Therefore, a CHAPS fee paid by a solicitor to the bank could not, for VAT purposes, be treated as a disbursement in the solicitor's invoice to their client. In *Rowe and Maw* [1975] STC 340, the High Court ruled that travelling costs incurred by a solicitor in the course of their duties for their client and recovered from the client at cost could not be treated as a disbursement. The supply of travel was to the solicitor and therefore formed part of their onward supply of legal services to the client.

12.3.2.2 So what items are not disbursements?

Items which do not qualify as disbursements are those which are a necessary part of the service supplied to the client, for example, telephone charges, postage and photocopying charges; these are overheads of the business, and HMRC requires the firm to charge VAT on them. The SRA considers that it is not normally appropriate to make a separate charge for such items, although there may be exceptional cases where it is permissible, eg when unusual amounts of photocopying are involved. Firms normally increase their professional charges to cover these items.

Travelling expenses incurred by a solicitor are not disbursements and must be included as part of the overall charge. This view was upheld in the case of *Rowe & Maw (A Firm) v Customs and Excise Commissioners* [1975] 1 WLR 1291. The court held that the cost of fares incurred by a solicitor was incurred for the solicitor, not for the client.

Any expenses incurred by a firm in order for it to complete its supply of professional services will not be a disbursement.

Until 1 December 2020 there was some uncertainty as to whether or not search fees could be treated as disbursements. This was because of a concession agreed informally between HMRC and the legal profession in 1991 which allowed solicitors and conveyancers to treat fees for property searches conducted by post as disbursements, even though not meeting all the disbursement conditions set out in section 25.1.1 of HMRC's VAT Notice 700. Increasingly such searches came to be carried out electronically by specialist online search agencies engaged by solicitors. In *Brabners LLP v HMRC* [2017] UKFTT 0666 (TC) it was held that an electronic search fee could not be treated as a disbursement as it did not fulfil the criteria. The result produced inconsistency so HMRC withdrew the concession for postal searches as from 1 December 2020. See Revenue and Customs Brief 6 (2020): 'VAT treatment of property search fees charged by solicitors and conveyancers'.

HMRC's view, as set out in full in its internal manual 'VAT Taxable Person Manual' (VTAXPER47000), is that whether a fee for a search is to be treated as a disbursement will depend on how the information obtained in the search is used. If it is passed on to the client without comment or analysis, the fee may be treated as a disbursement – it would be relatively unusual for this to be the case. More commonly, the firm will use the information to provide advice or a report, and here the fee for the search will form part of the charges for its services and will be subject to VAT.

HMRC said in Revenue and Customs Brief 6 (2020) that revised guidance on VAT disbursements would be published '*to ensure consistency and provide clarity*'. Further guidance is required as there is a lack of clarity in the case law as to what can and cannot be regarded as a disbursement. The decision in *Barratt, Goff and Tomlinson (a firm) v HMRC (Law Society Intervening)* [2011] UKFTT 71 (TC) differs from the *Brabners* decision. In *Barratt* the tribunal allowed fees paid by solicitors for medical records and reports obtained in connection with personal injury claims to be treated as disbursements. The justification for the difference between the two decisions appears to be that solicitors can only obtain access to patient records with the client's consent. The records are otherwise confidential and are not matters of public record. The client is the subject matter of the records and (at least for certain purposes) could be regarded as the 'owner' of the records and reports. In these circumstances, the solicitor is, arguably, merely an intermediary used to facilitate the obtaining of the service. There is, therefore, an arguable difference from the position in relation to property searches where anyone can commission searches.

The Court of Appeal recently indicated that it thought there was a strong case for a position that disbursement treatment should not be available where a solicitor acts as 'more than a postbox'. That was in the context of a case about medical reports and records obtained by a solicitor for use in a client's personal injury claim (*British Airways plc v Prosser* [2019] EWCA Civ 547). Newey LJ said at [37] that in a typical case in which a solicitor commissions a reporting agency to obtain a medical report or records, the report/records will be 'supplied to the solicitor ... to enable him effectively to perform the service supplied to his client' (in the words of Bridge J in the *Rowe & Maw* case).

In the *Barratt* case, there was no commissioning from a reporting agency. Barratt obtained medical reports and records itself. Newey J said at [38]:

> That distinction could potentially affect the contractual analysis: it is easier to conceive of a solicitor who obtains reports and records direct acting merely as his client's agent, although there is plainly scope for argument to the contrary. I can see a strong case for saying that, whatever the true contractual position, as a matter of economic and commercial reality a solicitor who is more than a postbox does not incur the cost of the reports/records 'in the name of and on behalf of' his client. The point was not, however, squarely before us and I prefer not to express a final view on it.

The same item may amount to a disbursement in one situation and not in another. For example, a solicitor dealing with the administration of an estate might pay a valuer's fee on a particular asset. This would be a disbursement if the personal representative, who was also a beneficiary and entitled to the asset to be valued, had requested the valuation to assist in the decision as to whether or not to sell the asset but would not be if the solicitor had requested it in order to calculate the inheritance tax payable on the estate.

The Law Society Practice Note, 'VAT treatment of disbursements and expenses', says that fees for Official Copy entries obtained on the sale of a property are unlikely to fulfil the criteria for a disbursement.

It is worth noting that HMRC does still say in its internal manual, 'VAT Taxable Person Manual' at VTAXPER47000, that when a vendor's solicitor obtains an office copy entry and recharges the fee to their client, they may treat it as a disbursement and outside the scope of VAT. However the Law Society Practice Note suggests being cautious in treating items as disbursements. If the seller's solicitor uses the official copies as part of their advice (for example, to obtain the title number to insert in the transfer or to ascertain what restrictions are on title), then the solicitor will have made use of the official copies to provide advice. This would mean that the supply of the information is a supply to the solicitor, and therefore the cost must be treated as part of the overall legal services subject to VAT at the standard rate, rather than treated as a disbursement.

12.3.3 The treatment of 'non-disbursements' in the firm's accounts

'Non-disbursements' are payments made to third parties by the firm which do not come within the narrow definition of disbursements. HMRC sometimes refers to them in its guidance as 'recharges'. Firms have to treat these items as part of their taxable supply. It is important that firms do not mis-classify these items as disbursements. If they fail to charge VAT on these items, they are understating their VAT outputs. They will become liable for the underpayment of VAT with interest and penalties.

Firms do not usually make a separate charge for items such as postage, fares and telephone calls which are really just overheads of the business. They simply make sure that the amount they charge for professional fees is sufficient to cover the overheads.

Search fees could be dealt with similarly by recording the payment using a searches account:

Entries:

CR Cash – Business section with the amount paid

If the search fee bears VAT (as most do), the VAT exclusive amount and the VAT will be entered as separate items.

DR Searches account

Plus, if the search is taxable:

DR HMRC account with the VAT charged to the firm

However, firms will normally want a record of searches incurred for each client so that they are shown separately from professional charges on the bill. It will therefore be necessary to enter them on the client ledger account so that they will not be overlooked when a bill is sent. The easiest course is to debit them to the client ledger when they are paid and include a note in the details column that they are part of the firm's taxable supply.

Entries:

CR Cash – Business section

If the search fee bears VAT (as most do), the VAT exclusive amount and the VAT will be entered as separate items.

DR Client ledger – Business section with the VAT exclusive amount and make a note in the details column that the payment is part of the firm's taxable supply

Plus, if the search is taxable:

DR HMRC account with the VAT input tax charged to the firm

When the bill is issued, VAT output tax will be charged on the professional charges and the search.

Example

You act for Bartok who is buying a house.

May

1 You pay a mining search fee of £10 + VAT of £2. This is not a disbursement for VAT purposes, although you will want to show it separately on your bill.

2 You pay a local land charge search fee of £10 which again is not a disbursement for VAT but will be shown separately on the bill.

30 You issue a bill. Your professional charges are £300 + VAT of £60 but you will increase your VAT by £4. Your bill will show the two search fees separately from your professional charges.

Client: Bartok
Matter: Purchase

Date	Details	Business account			Client account		
		DR	CR	BAL	DR	CR	BAL
May							
1	Mining search (VAT £2 paid)	10		10DR			
2	Local land charge search (VAT £2 paid)	10		20DR			
30	Profit costs	300		320DR			
	VAT on £320	64		384DR			

HMRC

Date	Details	Business account		
		DR	CR	BAL
May				
1	Cash. Bartok. Mining search	2		
2	Cash. Bartok. Local land charge search	2		
30	Profit costs		64	

The Bill will appear as follows

Professional charges	£300
Taxable search fees:	
Mining search	£10
Local land charges search	£10
	£320
VAT @ 20%	£64

Where items paid for by solicitors do not fulfil the criteria for disbursements and are included in the supply of legal services, the result is that the client pays VAT on the combined figure.

This only has a financial impact on the client if the supplier of the search did not charge VAT. Including the cost in the solicitor's supply of services means that the client pays additional VAT. Of course, if the client is registered for VAT, the VAT paid is input tax and will reduce the amount of output tax they pay.

Where the original supplier charged VAT, the solicitor will treat that VAT as input tax. The VAT exclusive amount will be added to the supply and the solicitor will charge output tax. There is no effect on the amount paid by the client. However, where the client is not registered for VAT, they cannot recover the tax paid.

12.3.4 The treatment of disbursements in the firm's accounts

The firm simply passes on the cost to the client. The payment may be for an item which is non-taxable or which includes its own VAT element.

12.3.4.1 Non-taxable disbursements

These are payments for something not subject to VAT, such as exempt supplies and supplies not in the course of business, for example court fees, stamp duty land tax, Land Registry fees, etc.

The firm can pay these out of the client bank account if there is sufficient money in the client bank account. Otherwise, they are paid out of the business bank account.

In neither case does the firm pay VAT to the supplier or charge the client VAT when obtaining reimbursement.

12.3.4.2 Disbursements including a VAT element

These are payments made by the firm to a taxable person in respect of taxable supplies (eg, counsel, surveyor, accountant, estate agent, etc). The payment made by the firm will include a VAT element. That VAT element is passed on to the client. The firm does not charge the client any additional VAT.

The difficulty with passing on VAT is that clients who are registered for VAT will want to recover it from HMRC and can do so only if they have a VAT invoice addressed to them. When a firm pays a disbursement that includes VAT on behalf of a client, the supplier may have addressed the invoice to the client or to the firm making the payment.

If the invoice is addressed to the client, life is simple. The '*agency*' method is used and the VAT inclusive amount is simply passed on to the client.

It is rather more complicated if the invoice is addressed to the firm. The '*principal*' method must be used which requires the solicitor to resupply the service to the client and provide a new VAT invoice.

(1) *Agency method*

If the invoice is addressed to the client, the supply is treated as made to the client. The firm simply acts as the agent, handing over the money on behalf of the client. If there is sufficient client money standing to the credit of the client, the payment can be made from the client bank account; otherwise, it must be made from the business bank account.

The firm does not separate the supplier's fee and VAT in the firm's accounting records; it simply records the total paid.

The firm must, if asked, send the supplier's tax invoice to the client. If the client is registered for VAT and the supply is in the course or furtherance of a business, the client will use the invoice to recover the input tax.

Example

You pay a surveyor's bill on behalf of a client, ABC Co Ltd. The bill is for £1,000 plus £200 VAT. The invoice is addressed to the client and is paid using the agency method.

You simply pay the total sum of £1,200 and do not distinguish between the fee and the VAT. Whether the payment is made out of business money or client money, you will charge the client £1,200, again without distinguishing between fee and VAT.

Assume that you are holding £2,000 on account of costs and so are able to make the payment from the client bank account. The entries will be as follows:

Client: ABC Co Ltd
Matter: Contract Dispute

Date	Details	Business account			Client account		
		DR	CR	BAL	DR	CR	BAL
							2,000 CR
	Cash – surveyor				1,200		800 CR

Cash account

Date	Details	Business account			Client account		
		DR	CR	BAL	DR	CR	BAL
							xxx
	ABC Co Ltd – surveyor					1,200	xxx

No entries are made on the firm's HMRC ledger account in relation to the payment.

If the client is registered for VAT, and therefore wants the invoice, you must send the client the surveyor's original invoice. The invoice is addressed to the client, and so the client can claim an input.

(2) *Principal method*

If the invoice is addressed to the firm, the supply is treated as made to the firm in the first instance. The firm can claim the supply as an input. The firm, therefore, must use business money to pay the supplier's fees, together with the input tax.

The firm then resupplies the item to the client at the same price.

The firm will charge the client output tax on both the firm's professional charges *and* the disbursement.

If the client is entitled to a tax invoice, the firm will provide one invoice to cover both the disbursement and the firm's own professional charges.

Example

You receive a surveyor's invoice for £200 plus £40 VAT. You pay:

	£
Surveyor's fee	200
plus input tax	40
	240

You record the fee and the VAT as separate items on the cash account.

The VAT is recorded on the HMRC account. The tax exclusive amount is recorded on the client ledger account.

When you later charge the client your own professional charges of £400, the bill will include:

	£
Surveyor's fee	200
Professional charges	400
plus output tax (£40 + £80)	120

The surveyor's fee and the VAT are separate items on the bill.

Note: A disbursement paid on the principal method must be paid out of the business bank account, even if there is client money available. This is because the supply is treated as made to the firm and not to the client.

So, if we take the same example that we used at (1) above for the agency method, the firm will have to pay the disbursement from the business bank account even though client money is held for the client. The entries will be as follows:

Client: ABC Co Ltd
Matter: Contract Dispute

Date	Details	Business account			Client account		
		DR	CR	BAL	DR	CR	BAL
							2,000 CR
	Cash – surveyor (VAT £200 paid)	1,000		1,000 DR			

HMRC account

Date	Details	Business account		
		DR	CR	BAL
	Cash – surveyor	200		XXX

Cash account

Date	Details	Business account			Client account		
		DR	CR	BAL	DR	CR	BAL
	ABC Co Ltd – surveyor		1,000	XXX			XXX
	– VAT		200	XXX			XXX

When you charge the client for the work done, the VAT on the profit costs is increased by the VAT on the disbursement. Assume you charge profit costs of £600.

Client: ABC Co Ltd
Matter: Contract Dispute

Date	Details	Business account			Client account		
		DR	CR	BAL	DR	CR	BAL
							2,000 CR
	Cash – surveyor (VAT £200 paid)	1,000		1,000 DR			
	Profit costs	600		1,600 DR			
	VAT (£200 + £120)	320		1,920 DR			

HMRC account

Date	Details	Business account		
		DR	CR	BAL
	Cash – surveyor	200		XXX
	Client		320	XXX

Profit costs

Date	Details	Business account		
		DR	CR	BAL
	Client		600	XXX

HELP ON PRINCIPAL METHOD

Students generally find principal method disbursements difficult to deal with. The following summary may be helpful:

(1) Identify that the disbursement is to be treated on the principal basis – if the invoice is addressed to the firm, it will be treated on the principal basis.

(2) CR the disbursement and the VAT on it to cash account business section – it is common, but not essential, to show the two elements separately.

(3) DR VAT to HMRC ledger.
DR VAT exclusive amount to client ledger business section.
Make a memorandum note in the 'Details' column of the client ledger of the amount of VAT which must be added to the VAT charged to the client when an invoice is issued.

(4) When a bill is issued, add the VAT on the principal method disbursement to the VAT on the professional charges and make the normal entries for delivery of a bill.
DR client ledger business section, with VAT and costs as two separate amounts.
CR the profit costs account with costs.
CR HMRC account with total VAT charged.

12.3.4.3 Counsel's fees – concessionary treatment

Normally, counsel's fee notes are addressed to the firm and therefore would have to be treated on the principal basis. However, a concessionary treatment for counsel's fees was agreed between HMRC, The Law Society and the Bar when VAT was first introduced, and was published in the *Law Society Gazette*, 4 April 1973. The concession is not set out in any HMRC manual or VAT notice.

The firm is allowed to alter the fee note so that it is addressed to the client. It is then treated on the agency basis. The firm must give the fee note to the client so that the client can reclaim the input tax. The firm should keep a photocopy of the amended receipted fee note in case the fee note needs to be dealt with in an assessment of costs.

On 31 August 2021, the Law Society announced that HMRC had recently confirmed that the concession still stands but that it is reviewing the concession to consider whether it should be withdrawn. See 'Confirmation and review of VAT concessionary treatment for counsel's fees – share your experiences'.

Exercise 12B

You act for Barton in connection with a tax dispute. The following events occur:

July

8 You receive £1,000 from Barton on account of costs to be incurred.

10 You pay a court fee of £100 out of client money.

22 You pay an accountant's fee of £400 plus £80 VAT. The invoice was addressed to you. The payment is a disbursement

29 You pay counsel's fee of £600 plus £120 VAT. The invoice was addressed to you but you add Barton's name.

August

7 You send Barton a bill and VAT invoice. Your profit costs are £800 plus appropriate VAT.

9 You transfer the £180 remaining in the client bank account to the business bank account in part payment of your costs.

11 You receive from Barton a cheque for the balance of the costs outstanding.

Prepare the cash account and client ledger account for Barton, together with the relevant entries on the ledger account for HMRC.

Exercise 12C

You act for Avis in a boundary dispute. The following events occur:

November

5	You pay a court fee of £100 on Avis's behalf.
7	You receive a cheque from Avis for £1,200 in payment of the £100 court fee and an additional £1,100 generally on account of costs. You do not split the cheque.
9	You pay counsel's fee of £400 plus VAT on behalf of Avis. The invoice was addressed to you, but you add the name and address of Avis.
11	You pay a surveyor's fee of £200 plus VAT. The invoice was addressed to you. The payment is a disbursement.
13	You send Avis a bill. Your profit costs are £600 plus VAT.
15	You transfer the £620 remaining in the client bank account in part payment of your bill. You receive a cheque from Avis for the balance of £340.

Comment on the application of the SRA Accounts Rules 2019, and explain what steps you will take to deal with the VAT elements involved in this transaction.

Prepare the cash account and client ledger account for Avis, together with the relevant entries on the ledger account for HMRC.

SUMMARY

(1) Persons who are registered for VAT must charge their customers/clients VAT at zero, standard or reduced rate on all taxable supplies of goods and services made in the course or furtherance of the business, and can recover any VAT charged to the business. A solicitor's taxable supply will be increased by payments made to third parties which do not qualify as disbursements.

(2) Persons who make only exempt supplies do not charge VAT to their customers/clients, but neither can they recover VAT charged to the business.

(3) Firms must charge VAT on their supply of legal services but do not charge VAT on disbursements paid on behalf of their clients as these are not part of the supply of legal services. However, to qualify as a disbursement, the supply must be for the client's use and not for the solicitor. If the payment is for an item required by the solicitor to provide legal services, the item is not a disbursement. It is part of the solicitor's fee for providing the service. The solicitor must charge VAT on the item.

(4) The cost of a disbursement is simply passed on to the client.

(5) If the disbursement includes an element of VAT charged by the original supplier, the firm will treat the disbursement either on the agency basis or on the principal basis. The choice of basis is governed by to whom the invoice is addressed.

(6) If the invoice is addressed to the client, the firm treats the disbursement on the agency basis:

(a) the whole payment is recorded on the cash account and client ledger without distinguishing the VAT;

(b) the firm can use client money to make the payment if there is sufficient available: if not, the firm uses its own money;

(c) the firm must give the client the original supplier's invoice if the client is registered for VAT.

(7) If the invoice is addressed to the firm, the firm treats the disbursement on the principal basis:

(a) the whole payment is recorded on the cash account, the VAT is recorded on the HMRC account and the VAT exclusive amount is recorded on the client's ledger account;

(b) the VAT will be charged to the client when the firm bills the client;

(c) the firm must use its own money to pay the disbursement even if client money is available;

(d) the firm must give the client a VAT invoice covering both the professional charges of the firm and the VAT on the disbursement;

(e) in the case of counsel's fee note, the firm is allowed to cross out the firm's name and add the client's; the invoice can then be dealt with on the agency basis.

SOLUTIONS

Exercise 12A

The fee is inclusive of VAT. If the professional charges are regarded as 100%, the solicitor may be said to have received 100% plus 20% (profit costs plus VAT). To calculate the amount to be treated as professional charges, it is therefore necessary to divide by 120 to give 1% of the receipt and to multiply by 100 to give 100% of the receipt.

$$\text{Receipt} \times \frac{100}{120}$$

$$£240 \times \frac{100}{120} = £200$$

$$\text{VAT} = £40$$

Exercise 12B

Notes

July

8 The money is client money. It should paid into the client bank account promptly pursuant to Rule 2.3.

10 Rule 5.1 permits the payment out of the client bank account. The court fees are exempt from VAT.

22 The invoice was addressed to you, so the disbursement must be paid using the principal method out of the firm's own money. Remember that you are responsible for paying the input tax.

At this stage, you only debit the fee, not the VAT, to the client. The cash account records the fee and the total paid, ie the VAT. You debit the VAT to the HMRC ledger account.

[*Note*: You will see a note in the details column of Barton's ledger account that the solicitor has paid input tax. This is a reminder to charge the client output tax later.]

29 Adding the client's name to the invoice, as permitted under the concession, means you can treat the payment on the agency basis.

There is sufficient money in the client bank account, and it is sensible to make the payment out of client's money as permitted by Rule 5.1.

August

7 You debit Barton's ledger account, business section, with your professional charges and VAT. You must consider carefully how much output tax to charge.

You must charge output tax at the standard rate on the value of the legal services, ie:

(1) the value of the professional charges of £800; plus
(2) the value of any general disbursements – there are none in this case; plus
(3) the value of any taxable disbursements paid on the principal method – in this case the accountant's fee of £400.

Therefore, you must charge VAT on £800 professional charges plus £400 accountant's fee, which makes a total of £1,200. VAT @ 20% is £240.

The double entries for professional charges and VAT will be in the profit costs ledger account (not shown) and HMRC ledger account respectively.

[*Note*: There is no entry in the cash account at this point as no movement of money is involved.]

August

9 Rule 4.3 permits the withdrawal from the client bank account for payment of costs because a bill or other written notification of costs has been issued.

11 This money is received from Barton specifically in payment of the outstanding professional charges and expenses. The money should be paid straight into the firm's business bank account.

The accounts will look like this:

Client: Barton
Matter: Tax dispute

Date	Details	Business account			Client account		
		DR	CR	BAL	DR	CR	BAL
Jul							
8	Cash. On account					1,000	1,000CR
10	Cash. Court fee				100		900CR
22	Cash. Accountant's fee [VAT £80 paid]	400		400DR			
29	Cash. Counsel's fee				720		180CR
Aug							
7	Profit costs	800		1,200DR			
	VAT (£80 + £160)	240		1,440DR			
9	Cash. Transfer from client to business		180	1,260DR	180		–
11	Cash. From Barton. Balance due		1,260	–			

Cash account

Date	Details	Business account			Client account		
		DR	CR	BAL	DR	CR	BAL
Jul	Balance			XXX			XXX
8	Barton				1,000		
10	Barton					100	
22	Barton		400				
	VAT		80				
29	Barton					720	
Aug							
9	Barton	**180**				180	
11	Barton	**1,260**					

HMRC account

Date	Details	Business account		
		DR	CR	BAL
Jul				
22	Cash. Re Barton	**80**		80DR
Aug				
7	Barton		**240**	160CR

The CR balance shown on HMRC ledger account represents the amount of VAT owed to HMRC.

Exercise 12C

(1) 5 November You are not holding any money for Avis. Therefore, Rule 5.3 applies and the money cannot be paid out of the client account. The payment is made out of the business account.

Entries:

DR Avis ledger account
CR Cash account
} Business section

7 November	The receipt is a mixture of business and client money. Rule 4.2 requires you to allocate promptly any funds from mixed payments to the correct bank account. If the funds are paid into the client bank account initially, then £100 must be transferred to the business bank account promptly. *Entries:* CR Avis ledger account £1,200 / DR Cash account £1,200 } Client section DR Avis ledger account £100 / CR Cash account £100 } Client section CR Avis ledger account £100 / DR Cash £100 } Business section
9 November	The payment is now treated as addressed to Avis. You pay an inclusive sum of £480 with no separate record of VAT. There is sufficient money in the client bank account, so make the payment out of the client bank account – Rule 5.1. *Entries:* DR Avis ledger account / CR Cash account } Client section
11 November	This invoice was addressed to you, so you must pay it using the principal method. You record the fee and VAT separately. You DR the fee to Avis and the VAT to HMRC. Even though there is enough money in the client bank account, you must make a payment on the principal method out of the business bank account. *Entries:* Fee: DR Avis ledger account / CR Cash account } Business section VAT: DR HMRC ledger account / CR Cash account } Business section
13 November	You make entries for professional charges and VAT separately. The DR entry in the client's ledger account is in the business section. You calculate VAT on the total of profit costs, general disbursements (none in this case) and taxable disbursements paid on the principal method. The surveyor's fee was paid on the principal method. VAT is therefore charged on £600 profit costs plus £200 surveyor's fee, making a total of £800. VAT will be £160.

Entries:

Professional charges	DR Avis ledger account CR Profit costs account	Business section
VAT	DR Avis ledger account CR HMRC account	Business section

15 November You have £620 remaining in the client bank account. Avis owes you £960. You will transfer the £620 and receive a cheque for £340 from Avis.

Rule 4.3 allows you to withdraw money from the client bank account to pay your professional charges provided you have given the client a bill or other written notification of costs. You cannot withdraw more than you are holding for the client (Rule 5.3) so are limited to a transfer of £620.

When the client sends the balance of £340, this is a receipt of business money. You must keep client and business money separate (Rule 4.1), so you should pay the money into your business account.

Entries:

For transfer

Withdrawal from client account

DR Avis ledger account
CR Cash account } Client section

Receipt into business account

CR Avis ledger account
DR Cash account } Business section

For receipt of money from Avis into business account

CR Avis ledger account
DR Cash account } Business section

Client: Avis
Matter: Boundary dispute

Date	Details	Business account			Client account		
		DR	CR	BAL	DR	CR	BAL
Nov							
5	Cash. Court fee	100		100DR			
7	Cash. From Avis. On account of costs					1,200	1,200CR
7	Cash. Repayment court fee		100	–	100		1,100CR
9	Cash. Counsel's fee				480		620CR
11	Cash. Surveyor's fee [VAT £40 paid]	200		200DR			
13	Profit costs	600		800DR			
	VAT (£120 + £40)	160		960DR			
15	Cash. Transfer from client to business account		620	340DR	620		–
	Cash. From Avis. Balance due		340	–			

Cash account							
Date	**Details**	**Business account**			**Client account**		
		DR	**CR**	**BAL**	**DR**	**CR**	**BAL**
Nov	Balance			xxx			xxx
5	Avis		100				
7	Avis				1,200		
7	Avis	100				100	
9	Avis					480	
11	Avis		200				
	C&E		40				
15	Avis	620				620	
	Avis	340					

HMRC account				
Date	**Details**	**Business account**		
		DR	**CR**	**BAL**
Nov				
11	Cash. Re Avis	40		40DR
13	Avis. VAT		160	120CR

CHAPTER 13

Splitting Cheques, Mixed Receipts and Dealing With Bills

13.1	Introduction	153
13.2	Receipts partly of business and partly of client money	153
13.3	Dealing with bills	155
13.4	Revision of material in Chapters 9–13	155

LEARNING OUTCOMES

After reading this chapter you will be able to:

- deal with receipts that are a mixture of business and client money
- select the appropriate option to deal with money received in payment of a bill.

13.1 INTRODUCTION

Those providing legal services often receive funds from clients that are a mixture of business and client money. Rule 4.2 of the Accounts Rules requires you to allocate funds promptly to the correct bank account.

13.2 RECEIPTS PARTLY OF BUSINESS AND PARTLY OF CLIENT MONEY

You may receive a cheque which is made up partly of business money and partly of client money.

Example

You act for Carollo Ltd. You paid £40 out of the business bank account on its behalf on 1 February. In response to a request by you, it sends a cheque for £100 on 10 February, partly to pay back the £40 and partly on account of costs. The £40 is business money because it is received for a paid disbursement, and the £60 is client money.

13.2.1 Split cheques

If your bank allows it, you can 'split' the cheque. This means paying the different parts of the cheque into different bank accounts. Thus, you would pay the £40 into the business bank account and the £60 into the client bank account.

On splitting the cheque the entries are:

DR Business portion to Cash account – Business section
DR Client portion to Cash account – Client section

CR Business portion to Client ledger – Business section
CR Client portion to Client ledger – Client section

13.2.2 Unsplit cheques and direct transfers

Banks are usually unwilling to split cheques in practice as it creates administrative problems for them, so paying the money into one bank account and transferring money is more common. Rule 4.2 provides that money received as a mixed payment must be allocated 'promptly' to the correct account. When a cheque is received which is a mixed receipt the firm can choose whether to pay it initially into the client or business bank account. Firms will have different policies. Some may adopt a fixed rule that all mixed receipts are paid initially into the client bank account. Others may have a more flexible policy, allocating a mixed receipt in accordance with the make-up of the mixed receipt. For example, a firm operating a flexible policy would pay a receipt which is 90% client money, 10% business money into the client bank account but would pay a receipt that was 10% client money, 90% business money into the business bank account.

There is no guidance on the meaning of promptly but under the old Rules transfers had to be made within 14 days so firms may use this as a guide.

Rather than paying by cheque, most clients will pay by bank transfer. It is cumbersome to give clients details of both the client bank account and the business bank account. Firms are probably most likely to give clients details of the client bank account so that all money will be received into that account. The firm will then transfer business money to a business account.

Entries are:

DR whole amount to Cash account
CR whole amount to Client ledger } Client section

When later transferring business portion:

CR Cash account
DR Client ledger } Client section

DR Cash account
CR Client ledger } Business section

Entries (if cheque split):

Client: Carollo Ltd
Matter:

Date	Details	Business account			Client account		
Feb		DR	CR	BAL	DR	CR	BAL
1	Cash	40		40DR			
10	Cash		**40**	–		**60**	60CR

Cash account

Date	Details	Business account			Client account		
Feb		DR	CR	BAL	DR	CR	BAL
							XXX
1	Carollo		40				
10	Carollo	**40**			**60**		

Entries (if whole amount received into client bank account and a transfer is later made of the business money element):

Client: Carollo Ltd
Matter:

Date	Details	Business account			Client account		
Feb		**DR**	**CR**	**BAL**	**DR**	**CR**	**BAL**
1	Cash	40		40DR			
10	Cash					**100**	100CR
	Cash transfer		**40**	–	**40**		60CR

Cash account

Date	Details	Business account			Client account		
Feb		**DR**	**CR**	**BAL**	**DR**	**CR**	**BAL**
				xxx			xxx
1	Carollo		40				
10	Carollo				**100**		
	Carollo transfer	**40**				**40**	

Exercise 13A

You act for Brian. Complete the ledger accounts to record the following events.

March

7	Pay £30 by cheque on Brian's behalf.
15	You send him a written notification that you have paid £30 on his behalf and ask him to give you another £70 on account of costs. He gives you a cheque for £100.
21	Pay £50 by cheque on Brian's behalf.
31	Brian instructs you to hold the balance on behalf of Christine.

13.3 DEALING WITH BILLS

(a) When a bill has been issued for professional charges and paid and/or unpaid disbursements, money received in payment of the bill will be the firm's own money and must be paid into the business bank account.

(b) Where the firm is holding client money in the client bank account and issues a bill for professional charges and paid and/or unpaid disbursements, the whole amount billed can be transferred to the business bank account.

(c) Where the firm is holding client money in the client bank account, money due to the firm for disbursements paid with the firm's own money cannot be transferred unless a bill has been issued or the firm made it clear when the money was received that it would be used in this way.

Remember that even if a bill (or other written notification) has not been issued, money received for a paid disbursement is the firm's money not client money.

Remember too that billing for unpaid disbursements can cause risks to client money. See **9.8.3**.

13.4 REVISION OF MATERIAL IN CHAPTERS 9–13

Exercise 13B

(1) **Which one of the following items received by a solicitors' partnership is entirely business money?**

   (a) Money received from a client on account of costs.

   (b) Money received for billed professional charges and disbursements.

(c) Money received for billed professional charges and additional funds to complete the purchase of the client's house purchase.
(d) None of the above.

(2) **Client X sends a solicitor a cheque for £100,240 in satisfaction of the solicitor's bill for professional charges of £240 and £100,000 to complete the purchase of a property for the client. Which one of the following statements is correct?**
(a) The cheque is client money and must be paid into the client bank account.
(b) The cheque is a mixture of business and client money and must be paid into the client bank account.
(c) The cheque is a mixture of business and client money and must not be paid into the client bank account.
(d) The cheque is a mixture of business and client money and can be paid into the client bank account.

(3) **A solicitor is holding £1,000 for Client A. Client A instructs the solicitor to hold £300 of that money to the order of Client B, to whom A owes money. Which one of the following statements is correct?**
(a) A client bank account cheque for £300 must be sent to B.
(b) No entries need be made.
(c) A client bank account cheque for £300 must be drawn, and then the cheque must be paid into the client bank account on B's behalf.
(d) Entries must be made on the client ledger accounts of A and B.

(4) **Brown is a bookseller. He sells only books. He does not charge his customers VAT. Is this because:**
(a) His turnover does not exceed the limit for compulsory registration?
(b) He makes only exempt supplies?
(c) He is not carrying on a 'business' for the purposes of the VATA 1994?
(d) He makes only zero-rated supplies?

(5) **A solicitor (registered for VAT) agrees to draft a will for Client X for £100. Which of the following statements is correct?**
(a) He must charge £20 VAT on top of the fee.
(b) He must not charge VAT.
(c) The client will pay him £100 plus VAT.
(d) The client will pay him £100.

(6) **A solicitor completes the administration of an estate on 31 March and sends a bill on 2 April. When is the tax point?**
(a) 31 March.
(b) 2 April.
(c) 14 April.
(d) 30 June.

(7) **A solicitor receives an invoice from a builder for £200 + £40 VAT in respect of a property transaction being conducted for Client X. The invoice is addressed to the solicitor's firm and the payment is a disbursement. The solicitor holds £1,000 in the client bank account for X generally on account of costs. Which one of the following statements is correct?**
(a) The solicitor can pay the invoice from the client bank account.
(b) The solicitor must pay the invoice from the business bank account.
(c) The solicitor must debit the client ledger account immediately with £240.
(d) All of the above statements are incorrect.

(8) **On which one or more of the following must a solicitor charge VAT?**
(a) Postage, fares, telephone.
(b) Land Registry fee for registration of title.
(c) Land Registry searches supplied without comment or analysis to the client.
(d) Land Registry searches used as the basis of a report to the client.
(e) Court fees.
(f) Fees for medical reports.

(9) **Which of the following statements are true and which are false?**
(a) All firms regulated by the SRA must have a client bank account.
(b) Client money must always be paid into the client bank account.
(c) Business money must never be paid into the client bank account.
(d) If a firm holds money on account of costs in the client bank account and pays a disbursement from its own business account, it cannot transfer money to reimburse itself without issuing a bill.
(e) Where a firm receives an amount which is a mixture of business and client money, it can choose which bank account to pay the money into.

(10) **A firm holds £1,500 on account of costs. It gives the client the following bill:**

Professional charges	£600
VAT	£120
Paid disbursements	£200
Unpaid disbursements	£300
Total	£1,220

The firm wishes to transfer as much as possible to the business bank account. The firm can transfer which of the following?
(a) £720
(b) £920
(c) £1,020
(d) £1,220

SUMMARY

(1) A cheque received from a client which is a mixture of business and client money can be split between the business and client bank account, or paid into either the client or business bank account.
(2) If it is all paid into the client bank account, the business money must be transferred to the business bank account promptly. If it is all paid into the business bank account, the client money must be transferred to the client bank account promptly.

SOLUTIONS

Exercise 13A

Notes

7 March No client money, so business money must be used.

15 March This cheque includes business and client money, so can be split if your bank permits. If split, you must record two separate receipts, one for client money and one for business money. If not split, the cheque can be paid into either business or client bank account but the money must be allocated promptly to the correct bank account. In our example we have split the cheque.

21 March Client money is available and can be used.
31 March This is an inter-client transfer. No entry is made on the cash account

DR Brian ledger } Client section
CR Christine ledger

Client: Brian
Matter:

Date	Details	Business account			Client account		
		DR	CR	BAL	DR	CR	BAL
March							XXX
7	Cash. Payment	30		30DR			
15	Cash. From you		30	–		70	70CR
21	Cash. Payment				50		20
31	Christine. Transfer				20		–

Client: Christine
Matter:

Date	Details	Business account			Client account		
		DR	CR	BAL	DR	CR	BAL
March							
31	Brian. Transfer					20	20CR

Cash account

Date	Details	Business account			Client account		
		DR	CR	BAL	DR	CR	BAL
March				XXX			XXX
7	Brian. Payment		30				
15	Brian. Amount from Brian	30			70		
21	Brian. Payment					50	

Exercise 13B

(1) (b) Once billed, money received for professional charges and disbursements is outside the definition of client money (see Rule 2.1(d)).

(2) (d) The cheque is a mixture of business and client money. Rule 4.2 only requires you to allocate the funds 'promptly' to the correct account, so it can all be paid into either bank account initially.

(3) (d) Rule 8.1 requires you to record all receipts and payments of client money for each client.

(4) (d) Books are zero rated.

(5) (d) The solicitor must apportion the fee between the VAT and the VAT exclusive element.

(6) (b) The tax point is the date the bill is issued.

(7) (b) The disbursement must be treated on the principal basis and, therefore, must be paid from the business bank account.

(8) (a) and (d) A solicitor must charge VAT on the supply of legal services but not on items which are additional to the supply and which are supplied to the client and simply paid on behalf of the client by the solicitor. Items (a) and (d) are part of the supply of legal services and so are subject to VAT. Items (b), (c) and (e) are disbursements, so the solicitor simply passes on the cost to the client without charging VAT. There is case law authority suggesting that (f) is a disbursement but it is not entirely clear whether HMRC accepts this.

(9) (a) False. A firm does not need a client bank account if the requirements of Rule 2.2 are met (this is where the only client money received is for fees and unpaid disbursements prior to delivery of a bill).

(b) and (c) False. Under Rule 4.2 mixed receipts can be paid initially into either bank account provided money is allocated 'promptly' to the correct account.

(d) False. Although Rule 4.3 requires a bill to be delivered before money is transferred from the client bank account in payment of costs, which includes disbursements as well as professional charges, Rule 5 permits money to be withdrawn from the client bank account 'for the purpose for which it is being held'. Provided the firm has made it clear to the client that money paid generally on account of costs may be used to reimburse the firm for payments made, this will be permitted without issuing a bill, or other written notification of costs, under Rule 5. See SRA guidance, 'Taking money for your firm's costs' (published 20 September 2020).

(e) True. Rule 4.2 merely requires that funds from mixed payments are allocated promptly to the correct client account or business account.

(10) (d) Once a bill is issued, professional charges, paid and unpaid disbursements can be transferred to the business account. Note that this will be changed if the SRA makes its proposed amendment which will only allow transfers for fees and disbursements which have already been incurred. See **9.8.3** above.

CHAPTER 14

MISCELLANEOUS MATTERS

14.1	Introduction	161
14.2	Receipt of a cheque made out to the client or a third party	161
14.3	Dishonoured cheques	162
14.4	Abatements	164
14.5	Bad debts	165
14.6	Petty cash	166
14.7	Insurance commission	167

LEARNING OUTCOMES

After reading this chapter you will be able to deal with the following miscellaneous transactions:

- receipt of a cheque made out to a client or third party
- dishonoured cheques
- abatements
- bad debts
- petty cash
- insurance commission.

14.1 INTRODUCTION

So far you have looked at the treatment of those basic transactions a firm providing legal services will carry out every day. More transactions may occur from time to time, and this chapter considers how to deal with them.

14.2 RECEIPT OF A CHEQUE MADE OUT TO THE CLIENT OR A THIRD PARTY

If you receive a cheque made out not to the firm but to the client (or a third party), you *cannot* pay that cheque into a firm bank account. The firm is not the payee.

Your only obligation is to forward the cheque to the payee without delay. You have not received client money because the cheque is not 'money' as far as you are concerned; it is a piece of paper which you cannot turn into cash. As you have not received *client money*, there is no obligation under Rule 8.1(a) to record the event on the client ledger account and cash account. However, you will want to keep a written record on the correspondence file.

As a precaution, many firms will have a special control account where all cheques received by the firm will be recorded irrespective of the payee. This is not required by the Rules but helps to prevent cheques being overlooked. The SRA guidance, 'Helping you keep accurate client accounting records', says:

> We expect you to have systems and controls in place for identifying client money, including cash, when received in the firm, and for promptly recording the receipt of the money in, for example, a cash diary.

14.3 DISHONOURED CHEQUES

There is nothing in the rules to prevent a firm drawing against a cheque which has been paid into the client bank account but which has not yet been cleared. However, if that cheque is then dishonoured, there will be a breach of Rule 5.3. More money will have been taken from the client bank account than is held for the particular client. Money belonging to other clients will, therefore, have been used to make the payment. Under Rule 6.1 any breaches of the rules must be corrected promptly upon discovery, and any money improperly withdrawn from a client account must be immediately replaced. Hence, the firm will have to make good the shortfall by transferring its own money to the client bank account.

Example

On 1 March, you receive a cheque for £500 on account of costs from your client, Smith.

On 2 March, you pay a court fee of £100 out of the client bank account on behalf of Smith.

On 4 March, the bank informs the solicitor that Smith's cheque for £500 has been dishonoured.

First you must make entries to reverse the apparent receipt on 1 March. Then you must deal with the consequences of the payment from the client bank account.

Because it turns out that you had no money for Smith when you made the £100 payment, you must have used £100 belonging to another client for the benefit of Smith. You must, therefore, transfer £100 from the business bank account to the client bank account to remedy your breach of the rules.

On 7 March, Smith tells you that there are now sufficient funds to meet the cheque. He asks you to re-present it. You do so on 7 March and it is met.

When you re-present the cheque, the client now owes you £100. So the receipt is a mixture of business and client money. This means you can either split the cheque, or pay the whole amount into one account and transfer funds to the other account promptly (Rule 4.2). If you pay the whole £500 into the client bank account, you must transfer the £100 to the business bank account promptly.

Notes:

March

1 The money is client money (Rule 2.1) and is paid into the client bank account (Rule 2.3).

Entries:

CR Smith ledger account
DR Cash account } Client section

2 You make the payment from the client bank account even though the cheque from Smith has not yet been cleared.

Entries:

DR Smith ledger account
CR Cash account } Client section

4 To record the dishonouring, you must make entries reversing those made when you received the cheque.

Entries:

DR Smith ledger account
CR Cash account } Client section

This results in a DR balance of £100 on Smith's ledger account and you are in breach of Rule 5.3. Effectively, you have used client money on behalf of a client for whom you were not holding any.

4 You must make an *immediate* transfer of £100 from the business bank account to the client bank account to rectify the breach.

Entries:

Withdrawal from business account

DR Smith ledger account
CR Cash account
} Business section

Receipt into client account

CR Smith ledger account
DR Cash account
} Client section

7 When the cheque is re-presented you can, under Rule 4.2, either pay the whole amount into one bank account, or, as in this example, split it so that £100 goes into the business bank account and £400 into the client bank account.

Entries if split:

£100 Business money

CR Smith ledger account
DR Cash account
} Business section

£400 Client money

CR Smith ledger account
DR Cash account
} Client section

The accounts look like this:

Client: Smith
Matter: Miscellaneous

Date	Details	Business account			Client account		
		DR	CR	BAL	DR	CR	BAL
March							
1	Cash. From Smith On account					500	500CR
2	Cash. Court fee				100		400CR
4	Cash. Smith's cheque – returned				500		100DR
	Cash. Transfer from business account to rectify breach	100		100DR		100	–
7	Cash. Smith's cheque re-presented		100	–		400	400CR

Cash account

Date	Details	Business account			Client account		
		DR	CR	BAL	DR	CR	BAL
March							XXX
1	Smith				500		
2	Smith					100	
4	Smith					500	
	Smith		100		100		
7	Smith	100			400		

A well-run firm will operate a system which makes it impossible to draw against a client bank cheque before it has cleared.

14.4 ABATEMENTS

Clients may complain that the amount of their bill is too high. Sometimes, the firm may decide to reduce, or abate, the costs. HMRC allows the output tax charged on the bill to be reduced proportionately.

In order to record the abatement, you reverse the entries made on the profit costs and HMRC account when the bill was sent to the extent of the abatement. You also send the client a VAT credit note.

Entries:

DR Profit costs account
DR HMRC account
} with the reduction

CR Client ledger account (business section) with the reduction in your professional charges and VAT.

Example

You send your client Jones a bill for £600 plus VAT on 4 May. On 6 May, after discussion with Jones, you agree to reduce the bill by £100 plus VAT.

The accounts will look like this:

Client: Jones
Matter: Miscellaneous

Date	Details	Business account			Client account		
		DR	CR	BAL	DR	CR	BAL
May							
4	Profit costs	600		600DR			
	VAT	120		720DR			
6	Profit costs – Abatement		100	620DR			
	VAT – Abatement		20	600DR			

Profit costs account

Date	Details	Business account		
		DR	CR	BAL
May				
4	Jones		600	600CR
6	Jones. Abatement	100		500CR

HMRC account

Date	Details	Business account		
		DR	CR	BAL
May				
4	Jones		120	120CR
6	Jones	**20**		100CR

If preferred, the firm may debit abatements to a separate abatements account. If this is done, the debit balance on the abatements account is transferred to the debit side of the costs account at the end of the accounting period.

14.5 BAD DEBTS

14.5.1 The general rule

From time to time, a firm will realise that a client is not going to pay the amount owing to the firm. The firm will have to write off the amount owing for its professional charges and VAT and for any disbursements paid from the business bank account. The general rule for VAT used to be that there was no VAT relief, and VAT had to be accounted for to HMRC even if the debt was written off. Thus, the VAT was an additional element of the bad debt and increased the amount which had to be written off.

Entries:

CR Client's ledger account, business section
DR Bad debts account
} with the whole amount

14.5.2 VAT relief

However, VAT relief is now available once the debt has been outstanding for at least six months since the date payment was due. In this case, the solicitor will be entitled to a refund from HMRC.

Entries:

When debt is written off:
CR Client's ledger account, business section, with the full amount owing
DR Bad debts account with the full amount owing

When VAT relief becomes available:
CR Bad debts account with amount of VAT
DR HMRC with amount of VAT

Example

On 9 April, you send Green a bill for professional charges of £400 plus VAT. On 6 June, you write off Green's debt.

Six months after the due date of payment of Green's bill (31 October), you become entitled to VAT bad debt relief.

The accounts will look like this:

Client: Green
Matter: Miscellaneous

Date	Details	Business account			Client account		
		DR	CR	BAL	DR	CR	BAL
Apr 9	Profit costs	400		400DR			
	VAT	80		480DR			
June 6	**Bad debts**		**480**	–			

Profit costs account

Date	Details	Business account		
		DR	CR	BAL
Apr 9	Green		400	400CR

HMRC account				
Date	**Details**	**Business account**		
		DR	**CR**	**BAL**
Apr 9	Green		80	80CR
Oct 31	**Bad debts. VAT relief**	**80**		–

Bad debts account				
Date	**Details**	**Business account**		
		DR	**CR**	**BAL**
June 6	**Green**	**480**		480DR
Oct 31	**HMRC. VAT relief**		**80**	400DR

14.6 PETTY CASH

14.6.1 Need for petty cash account

Any firm will need some petty cash on the premises to meet small cash payments. When cash is withdrawn from the bank for petty cash, the entries will be:

CR Cash – business section
DR Petty cash account

When a payment is made, for example a roll of sticky tape is bought, the entries will be:

CR Petty cash account
DR appropriate ledger account, for example Sundries

14.6.2 Petty cash payments for clients

A firm will sometimes make a payment from petty cash on behalf of a client. The CR entry will be made on the petty cash account, not on the main cash account. The firm will want to DR the client ledger account to show that the client now owes the firm for the expense incurred. The DR entry must be made on the business section of the client ledger even if client money is held for the client. This is because petty cash is business money. Thus, by deciding to use petty cash, the firm has elected to use business money on behalf of the client.

Example

You hold £200 in the client bank account for Smith. You pay £20 expenses to an expert witness from petty cash.

Smith's client ledger account will look like this:

Client: Smith **Matter:**							
Date	**Details**	**Business account**			**Client account**		
		DR	**CR**	**BAL**	**DR**	**CR**	**BAL**
	Cash. Received on account					200	200CR
	Petty cash. Expert witness	20		20DR			

The corresponding credit entry will be on the petty cash account, not on the cash account. Notice that the 'Details' section of Smith's ledger account refers to 'petty cash', not to cash.

14.7 INSURANCE COMMISSION

Firms providing legal services may be offered commission from insurance companies or sellers of financial products. Where the firm is entitled to retain the commission, it represents an additional source of income; the firm will have a commission received account to which receipts are credited and a ledger account in the name of each company paying commission.

However, it will be relatively rare for the firm to be entitled to retain commission. Paragraph 5.1 of the SRA Code of Conduct for Firms requires those regulated by the SRA to 'properly account to clients for any financial benefit' received as a result of client instructions.

What does 'properly account' mean? Where a financial benefit has been received as a result of acting for a client, 'properly accounting' is likely to be:

- paying it to the client;
- offsetting it against fees; or
- keeping it only where you can justify keeping it, you have told the client the amount of the benefit (or an approximation if you do not know the exact amount) and the client has agreed that you can keep it.

There is a further reason for not retaining commission. Firms that wish to take advantage of the exemption allowing professional firms to avoid regulation by the Financial Reporting Council in relation to investment business must account for all commission to clients.

Exercise 14A

You act for Forsyth.

March

1	Forsyth sends £100 on account of costs.
2	You pay court fees of £40 from the client bank account.
3	The bank informs you that Forsyth's cheque has been dishonoured.
15	You re-present the cheque, instructing the bank that, assuming the cheque is honoured, you want £40 to be paid into the business bank account and £60 into the client bank account.
16	You pay an accountant's fee of £200 plus £40 VAT. The invoice is addressed to Forsyth. It is a disbursement.
18	You issue a bill for £400 plus £80 VAT.
19	Forsyth complains, and you reduce the bill by £40 plus £8 VAT.
31	You write off Forsyth's debt as bad, having transferred any balance in the client bank account to the business bank account.

Make the necessary entries in Forsyth's client ledger account and the cash account. Do not complete the balances on the cash account.

SUMMARY

(1) Cheques which are not made out to the firm cannot be paid into the firm's bank account. The cheque does not represent money in the firm's hands. The firm must forward the cheque to the payee, and does not need to record the receipt and payment in the accounts as there is no dealing with client money.

(2) A firm can draw against a client's cheque before it has cleared. However, this is not advisable. If the client's cheque is dishonoured, the firm will have breached the Rules and will have to remedy the breach by transferring sufficient cash from the business to the client bank account to cover the payment.

(3) If the firm reduces the amount charged for profit costs, the VAT is also reduced.

(4) If a client's debt is written off as bad, the firm will lose the amount charged for profit costs plus any disbursements paid from the business bank account. VAT bad debt relief can be obtained once the debt has been outstanding for six months.

(5) Petty cash is business money, so any payment made for a client using petty cash is a payment of business money.

(6) A firm will normally account to a client for commission received as a result of acting for a client.

SOLUTION

Exercise 14A

Notes:

March

1	This was received generally on account of costs and is client money.
2	You appear to have client money available and so can make the payment from the client bank account.
3	Drawing against an uncleared cheque is unwise. Here, as the cheque has been dishonoured, there has been a breach which must be remedied by transferring £40 from the business to the client bank account.
15	The re-presented cheque is split between the business and the client bank account. The portion representing reimbursement of the expense incurred for court fees is business money; the balance is client's money.
16	As the invoice is addressed to the client, the agency basis is used. Business money is used as you do not have sufficient client money.
19	This is an abatement. Simply make the opposite entries you would make if delivering a bill.
31	There is £60 in the client bank account which can be transferred to the business bank account. The rest of Forsyth's indebtedness, including VAT, must be written off as a bad debt.

No VAT relief is available at present. The debt has not been outstanding for six months since the due date for payment.

Client: Forsyth
Matter:

Date	Details	Business account			Client account		
		DR	CR	**BAL**	**DR**	**CR**	**BAL**
March							
1	Cash. On account					100	100CR
2	Cash. Court fees				40		60CR
3	Cash. Dishonoured cheque				100		40DR
3	Cash. To remedy breach	40		40DR		40	–
15	Cash. Re-presented cheque		40	–		60	60CR
16	Cash. Accountant	240		240DR			
18	Profit costs	400		640DR			
	VAT	80		720DR			
19	Profit costs – abatement		40	680DR			
	VAT – abatement		8	672DR			
31	Cash. Transfer		60	612DR	60		–
31	Bad debts		612	–			

Cash account

Date	Details	Business account			Client account		
		DR	**CR**	**BAL**	**DR**	**CR**	**BAL**
March							
1	Balances						
1	Forsyth. On account				100		
2	Forsyth. Court fees					40	
3	Forsyth. Dishonoured cheque					100	
3	Forsyth. To remedy breach		40		40		
15	Forsyth. Re-presented cheque	40			60		
16	Forsyth. Accountant		240				
31	Forsyth. Transfer	60				60	

CHAPTER 15

ACCOUNTING TO THE CLIENT FOR INTEREST

15.1	Introduction	171
15.2	The obligation to account	171
15.3	Use of separate designated deposit bank account	173
15.4	Use of general client bank account	176
15.5	SRA Consultation Paper	180

LEARNING OUTCOMES

After reading this chapter you will be able to:

- explain the circumstances in which a client is entitled to be paid interest on client money
- identify the two methods of accounting for interest
- explain the advantages and disadvantages of each method
- explain how interest is calculated.

15.1 INTRODUCTION

Solicitors may hold money belonging to other people for substantial periods of time. Inevitably some of those people will wonder whether they are entitled to be paid a sum in lieu of the interest they might otherwise be earning on that money. Principles 5 and 7 require those providing regulated services to act with integrity and in the best interests of the client, so it will frequently be appropriate for firms to account to clients for interest on client money held.

This chapter covers:

(a) the circumstances in which a client is entitled to be paid interest on client money;

(b) the use of separate designated client accounts; and

(c) the use of a general client bank account.

15.2 THE OBLIGATION TO ACCOUNT

15.2.1 When must a firm account for interest?

Paragraph 1.2 of the Code of Conduct for Firms requires: 'You do not abuse your position by taking unfair advantage of clients or others.' Paragraph 5.1 of the Code requires: 'You properly account to clients for any financial benefit you receive as a result of their instructions, except where they have agreed otherwise.' On general principles, it would clearly be wrong for firms to earn interest on money held in the client bank account without accounting for the benefit to clients.

In fact, Rule 7.1 of the Accounts Rules states specifically that firms must 'account to clients or third parties for a fair sum of interest on any client money held by you on their behalf, unless you have reached a separate agreement with your client'. Rule 7.2 states that firms 'may by a written agreement come to a different arrangement with the client or the third party for whom the money is held as to the payment of interest', but they must provide the client or third party with 'sufficient information to enable them to give informed consent'.

Whereas the old Rules imposed detailed rules on when interest was to be paid and how it was to be calculated, the new Rules require firms to set their own policy on the circumstances in which it is fair to account to clients for interest and how such interest is to be calculated.

The terms of the policy should be drawn to the client's attention at the start of the retainer unless it is inappropriate to do so, for example where the client has a continuing relationship with the firm.

Such a policy is likely to provide that interest will be accounted for unless it is less than a stated figure, say £20 or less. The figure will need to be set at a reasonable level and reviewed in the light of current interest rates.

15.2.2 How do firms deal with interest?

There are two possible ways of dealing with interest. Firms can choose to pay client money either (1) into a general client bank account or (2) into a separate deposit bank account designated for money of that particular client (a 'separate designated client account'). Whichever they choose to do, the requirement under the Rules is the same: the interest allowed must be a 'fair sum'.

Firms will usually open a separate designated bank account for a particular client's money when they recognise that they will be holding a substantial amount for a significant time and simply want to pass on to the client all the interest allowed by the bank. In the past, the income tax rules applying to bank interest made it impracticable for firms to retain any part of the interest earned. This was because, for tax years before 2016/17, banks deducted basic rate tax at source from interest earned on separate designated client accounts (subject to the tax status of the individual clients) and credited the net amount to the separate designated account. For tax years 2016/17 onwards, banks and building societies pay all interest gross. It is likely, however, that firms will continue to account to clients for all interest earned on money in specially designated accounts given the obligation to act in the client's best interests.

Where a client's money is left in the general client bank account, the firm has to decide by reference to its policy whether to allow interest and how to calculate it. The sum decided upon will be allowed from the business bank account and is, in effect, an expense of the business – a well-run firm will cover the expense by earning interest on client money and having that interest paid into its business bank account (see **15.2.3**).

15.2.3 Factors affecting choice of method

When the firm opens a separate designated client bank account, the bank calculates the amount and pays the amount of interest earned. If such an account is not opened, the firm has to pay an appropriate amount in lieu of interest from the business bank account. It might seem, therefore, that it is always preferable to open a separate designated client account. However, this is not so.

A firm which opened a separate designated client bank account for every client for whom money was held would end up with an enormous number of different client bank accounts, and this would be administratively inconvenient.

Moreover, solicitors are allowed under the Solicitors Act 1974 to put client money held in a general client bank account on deposit and keep any interest earned over and above what is required to be paid under the Rules. In general, the more money placed on deposit, the higher the rate of interest earned. The firm only has to pay the client the rate that is fair in relation to the amount held *for that client*. The result is that the firm may earn more interest on client money than is paid out to clients. This is likely to encourage the firm to use the second method.

15.3 USE OF SEPARATE DESIGNATED DEPOSIT BANK ACCOUNT

15.3.1 What is involved?

The firm simply opens a deposit account at the bank designated with the name of the client or third party and pays the client money into it. Unlike the general client bank account, this account will be reserved for money of the particular client or third party. The firm will account to the client for the interest allowed by the bank.

Where a firm opens separate designated deposit client accounts for clients, it will need to ensure that the recording requirements of Rule 8.1 are complied with:

(a) The client's ledger account must show receipts and payments of client money dealt with through the separate designated deposit account. This will require either a separate ledger account for designated deposit account transactions or separate columns on the ordinary client ledger account.

(b) The firm's cash book must include details of receipts and payments of client money dealt with through separate designated deposit accounts. This could be done by having a separate cash account for each designated deposit account or, more likely, a combined cash account showing transactions on all the designated deposit accounts.

The disadvantage of this method (as explained at **15.2.3** above) is that the firm loses the opportunity to benefit from interest earned by client money.

15.3.2 Accounting entries

The firm will instruct the bank to open a deposit bank account – the separate designated deposit account. The client money will either be paid directly into the separate designated deposit account, or, if it is currently held in the general client bank account, the firm will instruct the bank to transfer the appropriate amount from the current client bank account to the designated deposit bank account. The firm will record the receipt into the separate designated client bank account by making a DR entry on the deposit cash account.

Entries are also needed on the client ledger accounts to show what has happened to the money. You may prefer not to worry about the bookkeeping entries, in which case you can go straight to **15.4**.

The firm may choose to have additional columns on the client ledger to record receipts and payments through the separate designated deposit account. The client ledger would then look like this:

Client Matter:										
Date	**Details**	**Business**			**Client**			**Client-deposit**		
		DR	CR	BAL	DR	CR	BAL	DR	CR	BAL

When a separate ledger account is used, the business columns are normally redundant as you already have a client ledger account showing dealings with business money. We have, therefore, shaded the business columns on separate ledger accounts to indicate that they will not be used.

When transferring money from the general client bank account to a separate designated deposit account, there are two stages:

(1) To record a payment out of the general client bank account:

Entries:

CR Cash
DR Client ledger account (1) } Client section

(2) To record a receipt into the separate designated client bank account:

CR Client ledger account (2) (or additional deposit column on Client ledger account (1))
DR Deposit cash account

Note: If money is received and paid straight into a separate designated deposit account, Step (1) is not required.

The bank will pay interest earned into the separate designated deposit account. You will record the interest as a CR on the client's new ledger account and as a DR on the deposit cash account.

Banks do not normally allow payments directly from deposit accounts. Where money is on deposit and you wish to make a payment, you must transfer funds from the separate designated deposit bank account to the general client bank account. However, because you are holding client money, you can make the payment from the general client bank account provided you have initiated the transfer. You do not need to wait for the funds to be received into the general client bank account.

Example

You act for Dash Ltd, which is owed £2,200 by Bingley. You write to Bingley, and you receive a cheque from him for the money owed on 3 April. On 4 April, Dash Ltd tells you to hold the money for five weeks until 9 May. You instruct the bank to put the money on deposit in a separate designated client bank account. On 9 May, you tell the bank to close the account. They tell you that they have allowed £18 interest. The £2,218 is transferred to the general client bank account. You send Dash Ltd the £2,218.

Notes:

April

3 The money is received as client money and paid into the general client bank account.

Entries:

CR Dash Ltd (debt collection) ledger account }
DR Cash account } Client section

4 The bank will transfer the cash from your general client bank account to the separate designated client bank account. You will need an entry on your deposit cash account (DCA) to record the additional funds held in separate designated deposit accounts, and a new client ledger account (or additional deposit section on the old client ledger) to show that funds are held for Dash in a separate designated deposit account.

Entries:

CR Cash account }
DR Dash Ltd (debt collection) ledger account } Client section

DR Deposit cash account (DCA)
CR Dash Ltd (money held on deposit) ledger account

Note:

Had you known on 3 April that you would want to put the money on deposit, you could have paid the money straight into the separate designated deposit account without passing it through the general client bank account.

Entries:

DR DCA
CR Dash Ltd (money held on deposit) ledger account

May

9 Deal with the interest first. The interest has been earned on behalf of Dash Ltd and belongs to it. It is client money and the bank will pay it into the separate designated deposit account.

Entries:

DR DCA with interest
CR Dash Ltd (money held on deposit) ledger account with interest

Then pay out the total from the separate designated client bank account.

Entries:

CR DCA
DR Dash Ltd (money held on deposit) ledger account

Then receive the total into the general client bank account.

Entries:

DR Cash account
CR Dash Ltd (debt collection) ledger account } Client section

You can now pay Dash Ltd the total sum you are holding on its behalf.

Entries:

CR Cash account
DR Dash Ltd (debt collection) ledger account } Client section

The completed accounts look like this:

Client: Dash Ltd (1)
Matter: Debt collection

Date	Details	Business account			Client account		
		DR	CR	BAL	DR	CR	BAL
April							
3	Cash. Bingley					2,200	2,200CR
4	Cash. On deposit				2,200		–
May							
9	Cash. Off deposit					2,218	2,218CR
	Cash. Returned				2,218		–

Client: Dash Ltd (2)
Matter: Money held on deposit

Date	Details	Business account			Client account		
		DR	CR	BAL	DR	CR	BAL
April							
4	Deposit cash. A/C opened					2,200	2,200CR
May							
9	Deposit cash interest					18	2,218CR
9	Deposit cash. A/C closed				2,218		–

Cash account

Date	Details	Business account			Client account		
		DR	CR	BAL	DR	CR	BAL
April				XXX			XXX
3	Dash Ltd (1). Bingley				2,200		
4	Dash Ltd (1). On deposit					2,200	
May							
9	Dash Ltd (1). Off deposit				2,218		
9	Dash Ltd (1). Returned to client					2,218	

Deposit cash account (DCA)

Date	Details	Business account			Client account		
		DR	CR	BAL	DR	CR	BAL
April							
4	Dash Ltd (2). A/C opened				2,200		xxx
May							
9	Dash Ltd (2). Interest				18		xxx
9	Dash Ltd (2). A/C closed					2,218	–

You may choose to have a separate deposit section on the existing client ledger account instead of a separate client ledger account. In this case, the Dash Ltd example would appear as follows.

Client: Dash Ltd
Matter: Debt collection

Date	Details	Business	Client			Client – Deposit		
			DR	CR	BAL	DR	CR	BAL
April								
3	Cash. Bingley			2,200	2,200CR			
4	Cash. On deposit		2,200					
4	Deposit cash. A/C opened						2,200	2,200CR
May								
9	Deposit cash. Interest						18	2,218CR
9	Deposit cash. A/C closed					2,218		–
9	Cash. Off deposit			2,218	2,218CR			
9	Cash. Returned		2,218		–			

Cash account

Date	Details	Business account			Client		
		DR	CR	BAL	DR	CR	BAL
April	Balance						xxx
3	Dash Ltd (1). Bingley				2,200		
4	Dash Ltd (1). On deposit					2,200	
May							
9	Dash Ltd (1). Off deposit				2,218		
9	Dash Ltd (1). Returned					2,218	

Deposit cash account (DCA)

Date	Details	Business account			Client		
		DR	CR	BAL	DR	CR	BAL
April	Balance						xxx
4	Dash Ltd. A/C opened				2,200		xxx
May							
9	Dash Ltd. Interest				18		xxx
9	Dash Ltd. A/C closed					2,218	–

15.4 USE OF GENERAL CLIENT BANK ACCOUNT

15.4.1 What is involved?

The firm must bear in mind the requirement to allow a fair sum under Rule 7.1.

Assume that you hold £1,600 of client money for nine weeks on behalf of your client, Smith, in the general client bank account. Based on its policy, the firm must calculate a fair sum and allow it to the client.

The disadvantage of this method is that the firm has to calculate how much would have been earned in respect of each individual client to whom the rules apply. Also, at first sight, it appears that the firm will be out of pocket. However, as explained at **15.2.3**, this is not necessarily the case.

A well-organised firm will always put a proportion of its client money on deposit in a general deposit bank account. It will then be entitled to keep the interest earned on that general deposit bank account. Provided the firm organises its bank accounts sensibly, it should earn more interest on its general deposit bank account than it has to pay to individual clients. A firm can never put all of its client money on deposit since it must ensure that it has sufficient client money readily available to meet all day-to-day expenses for clients.

Often, the amount allowed in interest will simply reduce the amount that the client has to pay the firm for the services provided. However, if the client has already paid, the firm may actually send a cheque.

15.4.2 Accounting entries

You may prefer to skip the detail of the bookkeeping entries, in which case you may proceed straight to the Summary at the end of this chapter.

Using this method, the interest payment is an expense of the business and will be recorded on an interest payable account. It is equivalent to the firm paying any other business expense, such as electricity or wages.

The business money dealing will be recorded in a business cash account and on the business section of the client ledger account. If the money is transferred from the business bank account to the client bank account and held for the client, entries must be made on the client ledger and cash account to record the cash transfer from the business to client bank account.

Example

To enable you to make a direct comparison, we shall use the same basic facts as in the previous example, except that the money is not put into a separate designated deposit account.

Notes:

April

3 You receive the £2,200 on behalf of Dash Ltd and pay it into the general client bank account. Entries as before:

Entries:

CR Dash Ltd ledger account
DR Cash account
} Client section

May

9 You have to allow Dash Ltd £18 interest, and therefore have to account to Dash Ltd for £2,218. You can do this in one of two ways.

Method 1 Send two cheques: one drawn on the business bank account for the £18 interest, and the other drawn on the client bank account for the £2,200.

Entries must be made on the client ledger business section to record the dealing with business money.

Entries:

To record £18 owed to client in interest

DR Interest payable ledger account
CR Dash Ltd ledger account
} Business section

To record £18 business cash sent to client

DR Dash Ltd ledger account
CR Cash account } Business section

To record £2,200 client cash sent to client

DR Dash Ltd ledger account
CR Cash account } Client section

The accounts will look like this:

Client: Dash Ltd
Matter: Debt collection

Date	Details	Business account			Client account		
		DR	CR	BAL	DR	CR	BAL
April							
3	Cash. Bingley					2,200	2,200CR
May							
9	Interest payable		18	18CR			
9	Cash. Interest	18		–			
9	Cash. Returned				2,200		–

Cash account

Date	Details	Business account			Client account		
			CR	BAL	DR	CR	BAL
April							
3	Dash Ltd. Bingley				2,200		
May							
9	Dash Ltd. Interest		18				
9	Dash Ltd. Returned					2,200	

Interest payable account

Date	Details	Business account		
		DR	CR	BAL
May				
9	Dash Ltd.	18		18DR

Method 2 Transfer the £18 from the business bank account to the client bank account, and then send Dash Ltd one cheque drawn on the client bank account for £2,218. In this case, additional entries must be made on the client section of the client ledger and on the client section of the cash account to show that money has been held for the client in the client bank account.

Entries:

To record £18 owed to client in interest

DR Interest payable ledger account
CR Dash Ltd ledger account } Business section

To record £18 business cash paid out of business bank account

DR Dash Ltd
CR Cash } Business section

To record £18 received into client bank account

CR Dash Ltd ledger account
DR Cash account } Client section

Payment to Dash Ltd of £2,218 from client bank account

DR Dash Ltd ledger account
CR Cash account
} Client section

The accounts will look like this:

Client: Dash Ltd
Matter: Debt collection

Date	Details	Business account			Client account		
		DR	CR	BAL	DR	CR	BAL
April							
3	Cash					2,200	2,200CR
May							
9	Interest payable		18	18CR			
9	Cash. Interest	18		–		18	2,218CR
9	Cash. Returned				2,218		–

Cash account

Date	Details	Business account			Client account		
		DR	CR	BAL	DR	CR	BAL
April				xxx			xxx
3	Dash Ltd. Bingley				2,200		
May							
9	Dash Ltd. Interest		18	xxx			
	Dash Ltd. Interest				18		xxx
9	Dash Ltd. Returned					2,218	xxx

Interest payable account

Date	Details	Business account		
		DR	CR	BAL
May				
9	Dash Ltd.	18		18DR

Exercise 15A

You act for the executor of Swan, deceased, and for Cygnet, the residuary beneficiary of Swan's estate. You complete the administration and ask Cygnet for instructions on what to do with the money due to him (£200,000). Cygnet tells you to hold the money pending his instructions as he is hoping to buy a house in the near future.

March

20 You transfer Cygnet's residuary entitlement of £200,000 from the executor's ledger account to Cygnet's ledger account.

April

15 You realise that Cygnet will be entitled to interest on the money held for him. You calculate that he is entitled to £100 for the period from 20 March. You pay the sum from the business bank account into the client bank account.

16 You tell the bank to open a separate deposit bank account designated with Cygnet's name and to pay all the money held for Cygnet into that separate designated client account.

30 Cygnet tells you to send him the amount to which he is entitled. The bank credits £120 interest. You close the separate designated client account, transfer the money to the general client bank account and send Cygnet a cheque for the whole amount.

May	
6	Cygnet tells you he thinks he is entitled to more interest for the period 20 March–15 April. You agree and send him a business bank account cheque for £30. Show relevant cash accounts and client ledger entries for Cygnet.

15.5 SRA CONSULTATION PAPER

In the SRA Consultation Paper, 'Client money in legal services - safeguarding consumers and providing redress: The model of solicitors holding client money', issued on 14 November 2024, one of the issues addressed was the treatment of interest on client money. There are a range of views. The paper says:

> We have heard that some firms consider it to be fair if they pay their clients interest at the rate they would have received if their money had been held in a separate account and the firm then keeps any excess interest. Anecdotally, other firms have told us that they have an agreement with their bank not to receive interest on client accounts in return for free business banking. Members of the public taking part in deliberative research initially felt that a 'fair sum' meant receiving all of the interest that their money earned, but were happy to receive as much interest as they would have earned in their own account if the firm used the interest they retained to reduce fees in some way.

In a recent financial benchmarking survey, the Law Society estimated that firms could have made as much as £27 million (total net income) in interest on client money in 2022/2023. Increases to interest rates have made the issue more pressing.

One concern of the SRA is that retaining interest earned on client accounts may incentivise firms to hold more client money, or to hold it for longer, than necessary. The SRA has heard that some small firms rely on interest from client funds to remain viable or retain staff, especially in particularly price competitive areas such as conveyancing. On the other hand, firms have expressed the view that by retaining some of the interest earned on client money, they can keep costs down, improving affordability and therefore access to legal services.

The Paper says:

> We consider that it is likely to be in the client's best interest to receive all the interest from their money, and for firms to reflect their true operating costs through the fees that they charge. This is fairer to individual clients, more transparent and arguably would better promote effective competition.

The paper asks whether the SRA should amend the rules to prevent firms retaining any interest earned on money held on their behalf, subject to an appropriate de minimis to take account of the fact that sometimes the interest due to an individual client would be so small that it would be unreasonably burdensome to pay that interest to the client.

An article in the *Law Society Gazette* by Edouardo Reyes on 11 February 2025 included this view from Peter Steel, chair of the Law Society's regulatory processes committee:

> 'There appears to be no compelling case for change,' Steel argues. 'As long as firms have a clear interest policy, and there is full transparency at the outset of a retainer with the client as to what happens to the interest held on their money, it should remain the client's choice as to whether they instruct a firm that will pay interest over to them or another firm where interest may be used differently.'

In its response to the consultation, the Law Society said:

> Most firms comply with the SRA's rules and no persuasive evidence to the contrary has been presented for a rule change.
>
> Firms are not motivated to hold client money for longer than necessary, as this increases risk.
>
> Under the SRA Accounts Rules, firms must pay clients a 'fair' sum of interest unless an alternative agreement is reached with the client.

Where some firms can secure better interest rates by pooling client accounts, any retained interest can be taken into account to offset charges and reduce client costs.

Rules around transparency and safeguarding consumer interests already exist and, due to the likely temporary rise in interest rates, we see no reason for a change to the current rules.

SUMMARY

(1) Clients are normally entitled to interest on client money held by firms providing legal services.

(2) The firm can use one of two methods to meet the obligation to account for interest.

(3) The firm can open a separate deposit account designated with the name of the client and account to the client for all the interest earned on the account.

(4) Alternatively, the firm can pay the client interest from the business bank account. The amount due is calculated by reference to the firm's policy and must be a fair sum.

(5) A firm which pays interest from the business bank account will be out of pocket unless it puts a proportion of the money in the client bank account on deposit. The Solicitors Act 1974 allows solicitors to keep the interest earned on client money placed on general deposit.

SOLUTION

Exercise 15A

Notes:

March

20 This is an inter-client transfer from the ledger account of the executor to the ledger account of Cygnet. No entries will be made on the cash account as the money remains in the client bank account.

April

15 To record the payment of interest from the business bank account:

DR Interest payable
CR Cygnet (1) – Business section

CR Cash
DR Cygnet (1) } Business section

Since the interest is going to be held by the firm for Cygnet, it must be received into the client bank account:

DR Cash
CR Cygnet (1) } Client section

16 To record the transfer of the money into a separate designated deposit account:

CR Cash
DR Cygnet (1) } Client section

DR Deposit cash account (DCA)
CR Cygnet (2)

30 To record the bank's payment of £120 interest:

DR DCA
CR Cygnet (2)

To record the transfer of £200,220 back to the general client bank account:

CR DCA
DR Cygnet (2)

DR Cash
CR Cygnet (1) } Client section

To record the payment of £200,220 to Cygnet:

CR Cash
DR Cygnet (1) } Client section

May

6 To record the payment of £30 interest from business money:

DR Interest payable
CR Cygnet (1) – Business section

CR Cash
DR Cygnet (1) } Business section

As the £30 is paid out to Cygnet directly and is not held by the firm in the client bank account, no entries need be made on the client section of Cygnet's ledger account or on the client section of the cash account.

Client: Cygnet (1)
Matter: House purchase

Date	Details	Business account			Client account		
		DR	CR	BAL	DR	CR	BAL
March							
20	Executor of Swan Residuary entitlement (TJ)					200,000	200,000CR
April							
15	Interest payable		100	100CR			
15	Cash. Interest	100		–		100	200,100CR
16	Cash. On deposit				200,100		–
30	Cash. Off deposit					200,220	200,220CR
30	Cash. Returned				200,220		–
May							
6	Interest payable		30	30CR			
6	Cash. Interest	30		–			

Client: Cygnet (2)
Matter: Money held on deposit

Date	Details	Business account			Client account		
		DR	CR	BAL	DR	CR	BAL
April							
16	Deposit cash. A/C opened					200,100	200,100CR
30	Deposit cash. Interest					120	200,220CR
30	Deposit cash. A/C closed				200,220		–

Cash							
Date	**Details**	**Business account**			**Client account**		
		DR	**CR**	**BAL**	**DR**	**CR**	**BAL**
April	Balance			xxx			xxx
15	Cygnet (1). Interest		100		100		
16	Cygnet (1). On deposit					200,100	
30	Cygnet-deposit (1). Off deposit				200,220		
30	Cygnet (1). Returned to client					200,220	
May							
6	Cygnet (1). Interest		30				

Designated Deposit Cash							
Date	**Details**	**Business account**			**Client account**		
		DR	**CR**	**BAL**	**DR**	**CR**	**BAL**
April							
16	Cygnet (2). A/C opened				200,100		xxx
30	Cygnet (2). Interest				120		
30	Cygnet (2). A/C closed					200,220	

Interest payable				
Date	**Details**	**Business account**		
		DR	**CR**	**BAL**
Apr				
15	Cygnet (1).	100		100DR
May				
6	Cygnet (1).	30		130DR

CHAPTER 16

FINANCIAL STATEMENTS

16.1 Introduction 185
16.2 Layout 185

LEARNING OUTCOMES

After reading this chapter you will be able to:

- prepare a simple Financial Statement showing how much money is required from or due to a client.

16.1 INTRODUCTION

If you handle money for a client, you should always prepare a written statement explaining how the client's money held has been dealt with and how much, if anything, is due to or from the client.

The statement is particularly important in property transactions where it is likely to be sent to clients part-way through the transaction to inform them how much they will have to provide or how much will be available to them at the end of the transaction.

Errors made in such statements are a common cause of complaint from clients.

In this chapter you will learn how to prepare a simple Financial Statement.

16.2 LAYOUT

There is no set layout but the statement must be clear and easy for the client to follow.

A common layout is to show the statement in the form of a sum, starting with the purchase price, adding expenses and deducting receipts (or in the case of a sale, starting with the sale price, deducting expenses and adding receipts).

Note: Items to be deducted are frequently shown in brackets.

Example

FINANCIAL STATEMENT [date]
TO: MR AND MRS BOUNDS
PURCHASE OF 3 WICKET STREET

		£	£
Purchase price			300,000
less:	Prepaid deposit	(30,000)	
	Mortgage advance net of legal fees	(222,340)	
			(252,340)
			47,660
add:	Stamp duty land tax	5,000	
	Land Registry fees	100	
	Professional charges	400	
	Search fee	20	
	VAT on professional charges and searches	84	
			5,604
less:	Received on account of costs		(400)
DUE FROM YOU			52,864

Where a simultaneous sale and purchase are involved, it is good practice to show separate subtotals for the sale and for the purchase so that the client can see how much the purchase cost and how much is available from the sale. The statement may then show in a summary the total amount due to or from the client in respect of both transactions.

Exercise 16A

You act for Cara, who is selling 6 High Street for £165,000 to Pritti and buying 'The Cedars' for £180,000 from Vlad.

The Bayswater and District Building Society, for whom you act, is granting a mortgage on 'The Cedars' of £120,000, and there is a mortgage to redeem on 6 High Street of £140,000.

June

1 Cara gives you £200 on account of costs.

3 You pay search fees of £10 on 'The Cedars'. The fee is not a disbursement.

5 You receive a cheque from Cara for £18,000 (the deposit agreed on 'The Cedars') made out to Vlad's solicitors.

7 You send the cheque for £18,000 to Vlad's solicitors to hold as stakeholders. You receive a cheque for £6,000 from Pritti's solicitors which you are to hold as stakeholders.

16 You send a Financial Statement to Cara which shows the total required from her to complete both transactions. You also present your bill which includes £200 costs on sale and £300 costs on purchase plus VAT. Your charges to the building society, which Cara is to pay by way of indemnity, are £40 on the mortgage advance and £20 on the mortgage redemption, plus VAT in each case.

18 You receive from Cara the amount requested on 16 June and you receive the mortgage advance from the building society.

20 You complete the sale and purchase.

21 You pay Land Registry fees of £100 and stamp duty land tax of £1,100 on 'The Cedars' and transfer the amount due to you for costs, etc.

Prepare the financial statement sent to Cara on 16 June.

PRACTICAL POINT

You need to be clear which items relate to the sale and which to the purchase.

The following is a breakdown:

Sale	Purchase
Official Copies of title from Land Registry	Pre-contract searches and enquiries, eg local authority search, environmental search, mining search
Mortgage Redemption	Land Registry search
Estate Agent's Fees	Mortgage Advance
Bankruptcy Search if also acting for Mortgagee	Land Registration Fees
	Stamp Duty Land Tax
	Bankruptcy Search

SUMMARY

(1) If you handle client money, you must prepare a Financial Statement showing how the money has been dealt with.

(2) There is no required form for Financial Statements, but they must be clear, accurate and easy for clients to understand.

(3) Where a transaction involves the sale of one property and the purchase of another, it is good practice to show separate subtotals for the amount available from the sale and the amount required for the purchase.

SOLUTION

Exercise 16A

FINANCIAL STATEMENT 16 JUNE
TO: CARA
PURCHASE OF 'THE CEDARS'

		£	£
Purchase price			180,000.00
less	Prepaid deposit	(18,000.00)	
	Mortgage advance	(120,000.00)	
			(138,000.00)
			42,000.00
add	Our professional charges	300.00	
	Search fee	10.00	
	VAT on professional charges and search fee	62.00	
	Professional charges to building society and VAT payable by you	48.00	
	Land Registry fees	100.00[1]	
	Stamp duty land tax	1,100.00[1]	
			1,620.00
Required for purchase			**43,620.00**

SALE OF 6 HIGH STREET

Sale price			165,000.00
less	Mortgage redemption	(140,000.00)	
	Our professional charges	(200.00)	
	VAT	(40.00)	
	Professional charges to building society costs and VAT payable by you	(24.00)[2]	
			(140,264.00)
Available on sale			**24,736.00**
SUMMARY			
	Required for purchase		43,620.00
less	Available on sale		(24,736.00)
			18,884.00
less	Received on account		(200.00)
DUE FROM YOU			**18,684.00**

[1] Although you have not paid these on 16 June, you know that they will be required and will therefore include them on the Financial Statement.

[2] The VAT on the fees charged to the building society is not itemised separately as the invoice is addressed to the building society, not the client.

CHAPTER 17

ACCOUNTING PROBLEMS FOR SOLICITORS

17.1	Introduction	189
17.2	Number of ledger accounts required	189
17.3	Agency transactions	206

LEARNING OUTCOMES

After reading this chapter you will be able to:

- identify how many ledger accounts are required in particular transactions
- understand how to deal with instructing another firm to act as your agent in a client transaction.

17.1 INTRODUCTION

In this chapter you will look at some particular accounting complexities relating to the number of ledger accounts required, and to agency transactions.

17.2 NUMBER OF LEDGER ACCOUNTS REQUIRED

17.2.1 The problem

You must record receipts of client money for each client. This requires a separate ledger account for each client for whom money is held. You must consider carefully which client the firm is holding money for, and whether money ceases to be held for one client and becomes held for someone else as this will require an inter-client transfer.

17.2.2 Funds originally held for one client being held for another

This can happen in a number of different types of transaction.

Example

You act for the executors of a deceased person. You complete the administration of the estate and inform the residuary beneficiary of the amount of his entitlement. The residuary beneficiary asks you to hold the money for him pending completion of a transaction on his behalf.

The money will stay in your client bank account, so no entries are made on your cash account. However, you must mark the fact that the money is no longer held for the executors but is now held for the residuary beneficiary. You do this by an inter-client transfer.

Entries:

DR executors' ledger
CR residuary beneficiary's } Client section

Exercise 17A

You act for George and for George & Co Ltd. George is a director of George & Co. George is selling land to George & Co for £120,000. The sale is to be completed on 5 June.

On 1 June, George tells you that he will be investing in a venture capital trust and asks you to hold the proceeds of sale of the land until he gives you further instructions.

On 4 June, the company gives you the funds to complete the purchase. On 5 June, you complete the sale. On 7 June, George tells you to pay the sale proceeds to the Gallymead Venture Capital Trust.

How will you deal with the sale proceeds of the land?

17.2.3 Stakeholder money

You may receive a deposit to hold as stakeholder. This is clearly a receipt of client money and so must be held in the client bank account. Who is it held for?

You are holding it jointly for the buyer and the seller. It will not become the property of the seller unless and until completion takes place. Therefore, you cannot simply record the stakeholder money as held for the seller alone. Note, however, that it is normal for conditions of sale to provide that sellers who are buying a residence in England and Wales may use all or any part of a deposit to fund the deposit on the property being purchased. See Standard Conditions of Sale, 5th edn, SC 2.2.5.

The Guidance to Accountants issued by The Law Society on 16 December 2005 said that stakeholder money may be shown on the seller's ledger but must be clearly labelled as stakeholder money held for both buyer and seller. The new Rules do not say anything specific about stakeholder money. Rule 8.1 requires all receipts and payments of client money to be recorded in client ledgers identified by the client's name and an appropriate description of the matter to which they relate. This sounds as if separate ledger accounts are required. However, the SRA has confirmed in correspondence that the new rules allow firms to manage their client accounts in a way that suits them provided that client money remains protected and a clear audit trail shows the movement of money. It is, therefore, permissible to show stakeholder money on the seller's ledger account so long as it is labelled appropriately. For example:

Entries:

DR Cash
CR Seller's ledger, noting money held as stakeholder } Client section

This is convenient but there is a risk that the money held for the deposit might be used for other purposes if those responsible for making payments fail to notice that the money is stakeholder money. Clear labelling is very important.

Alternatively, you can have a separate stakeholder ledger in the joint names of the client and the buyer and credit the stakeholder money to that account.

Entries:

DR Cash
CR Joint stakeholder ledger } Client section

As soon as completion takes place, you start to hold the money for the seller alone. You must record this by making an inter-client transfer from the joint stakeholder ledger account to the seller's ledger account.

Entries:

On the day of completion:

DR Joint stakeholder ledger }
CR Seller's ledger } Client section

This is much more trouble than following the procedure suggested in the Guidance to Accountants. However, it has the advantage of keeping the entries relating to the stakeholder funds entirely separate from those relating to the money held for the seller alone. It therefore avoids the risk of making a payment from the client bank account for the seller using funds which are not yet available to the seller.

A deposit received as agent for the seller belongs to the seller alone and is credited directly to the seller's ledger account.

Entries:

DR Cash }
CR Seller's ledger } Client section

17.2.4 Bridging finance

A deposit received as stakeholder is not available to the seller until completion without agreement (see, for example, Standard Conditions of Sale (5th edn), SC 2.2.5). A seller who is purchasing a replacement property may have insufficient cash available to pay the deposit on the purchase. Where a deposit is not available or is insufficient, it is possible to take a bridging loan from a bank to cover the period from exchange of contracts on the purchase to completion of the sale, when cash will become available.

A bridging loan is a personal loan to the borrower and, once received, belongs to the borrower and not the lender. Hence, when a solicitor receives the cash (whether direct from the lender or via the borrower), it will be held to the order of the borrower and must be credited to the borrower's ledger account, not to a ledger account in the name of the lending bank.

On completion of the sale, the loan, together with interest, must be repaid to the lender.

17.2.5 Mortgages

17.2.5.1 Introduction

Many clients who buy property need to borrow money on mortgage. A client who sells property which is subject to a mortgage will have to redeem, ie repay, that mortgage after completion.

If you act for a client who is buying a property, you may also act for the lender, provided that there is no conflict of interest.

Where you are instructed to act for both the borrower and the lender, you must bear in mind that there are two separate clients. You must consider carefully for which client you are holding client money.

17.2.5.2 Mortgage advances – solicitor acting for buyer and lender

Money received from a lender as a mortgage advance is normally held for the lender until the day of completion.

Rule 8.1 requires receipts and payments of client money to be recorded on client ledgers identified by the client's name and an appropriate description of the matter. The previous Rules contained a specific exception for loans from institutional lenders that provide mortgages on standard terms as part of their normal activities. Firms were allowed to credit the mortgage funds to the borrower's ledger account provided it was clearly labelled. Rule 8.1 has no exceptions but, as explained at **17.2.3**, the SRA has confirmed in correspondence that the new rules allow firms to manage their client accounts in a way that suits them provided that client money remains protected and a clear audit trail shows the movement of money.

Firms that act for both lender and borrower on the same matter can therefore choose how to treat mortgage funds:

Method 1

The mortgage advance is credited to the borrower's ledger account, when received. The details column must include the name of the lender and the fact that it is a mortgage advance.

Method 2

The mortgage advance is credited to a separate ledger account in the name of the lender on receipt. On the day of completion, the funds become available to the borrower, so an inter-client transfer should be made to the borrower's ledger.

Method 1 is simpler but Method 2 gives a clearer audit trail.

Example

The Southern Cross Building Society advances £50,000 to Brown on 6 June for his house purchase. Completion takes place on 8 June.

Method 1

Client: Brown
Matter: House Purchase

Date	Details	Business account			Client account		
		DR	CR	BAL	DR	CR	BAL
June 6	Cash. Southern Cross Building Society. Mortgage advance.					50,000	50,000CR

Method 2

Client: Southern Cross
Matter: Mortgage Advance. Brown

Date	Details	Business account			Client account		
		DR	CR	BAL	DR	CR	BAL
June 6	Cash. Mortgage advance. Brown.					50,000	50,000CR
8	Brown. Transfer.				50,000		

Client: Brown
Matter: House Purchase

Date	Details	Business account			Client account		
		DR	CR	BAL	DR	CR	BAL
June 8	Southern Cross Building Society. Transfer. Mortgage advance.					50,000	50,000CR

Note: Frequently, the money advanced by way of mortgage will be paid direct to the seller's solicitor by the lender. In such a case, as the buyer's solicitor does not handle the mortgage advance, there will be no entries relating to the money in the accounts of the buyer's solicitor.

17.2.5.3 Professional charges on mortgage advance

You are entitled to charge the lender for work done in connection with the mortgage advance as well as to charge the buyer for the work done in connection with the purchase. The buyer will frequently have agreed with the lender to pay the costs charged to the lender. The normal rule is that costs and VAT *must* be debited to the ledger account of the person (Person A) to whom the legal services were supplied. If another person, B, is discharging the debt by way of indemnity, the debt can be transferred from A's ledger account to B's ledger account.

Entries:

DR Buyer's ledger account, business section with fees charged on the purchase and VAT
CR Profit costs account and HMRC account with the fees and VAT

DR Lender's ledger account, business section with fees charged on the mortgage and VAT
CR Profit costs account and HMRC account with the fees and VAT

Transfer debt from the lender's ledger account to the borrower's ledger account as follows:

Entries:

CR Lender's ledger account, business section with fees charged on the mortgage and VAT as one figure
DR Buyer's ledger account, business section with fees charged on the purchase and VAT as one figure

If the firm has chosen not to have a separate ledger account for the lender, the charges and VAT of the lender will have to be shown on the borrower's ledger account.

Example

On June 8 you charge Southern Cross £120 + £24 VAT for acting for it on the mortgage advance. Brown has agreed to pay the charges. You charge Brown £200 + £40 VAT for acting on the purchase.

Method 1

Client: Brown
Matter: House Purchase

Date	Details	Business account			Client account		
		DR	CR	BAL	DR	CR	BAL
June							
6	Cash. Southern Cross Building Society. Mortgage. advance.					50,000	50,000CR
8	Profit costs	200		200DR			–
	VAT	40		20DR			
8	Profit costs. Southern Cross.			360DR			
	Mortgage advance.	120					
	VAT	24		384DR			

Method 2

Client: Brown
Matter: House Purchase

Date	Details	Business account			Client account		
		DR	CR	BAL	DR	CR	BAL
June							
8	Southern Cross. Mortgage. Transfer.					50,000	50,000CR
8	Profit costs	200		200DR	50,000		–
	VAT	40		240DR			
	Southern Cross. Costs. Transfer	144		384DR			

Client: Sothern Cross
Matter: Mortgage Advance. Brown

Date	Details	Business account			Client account		
		DR	CR	BAL	DR	CR	BAL
June							
6	Cash. Mortgage advance: Brown					50,000	50,000CR
8	Brown. Transfer.				50,000		–
8	Profit costs	120		120DR			
	VAT	24		144DR			
8	Brown. Costs. Transfer		144	–			

17.2.5.4 Mortgage redemption – acting for both lender and seller

Many sellers have a balance left on their mortgage at the date of sale. The balance has to be paid off from the proceeds of sale.

It is uncommon to act for both lender and seller. However, it is possible. Where this is the case, some of the sale proceeds will be received for the seller and some for the lender. The whole of the receipt is client money and will be paid into the client bank account. You need to comply with the requirements of Rule 8.1 so you need to show who you are holding the client money for.

The clearest audit trail would be to credit the whole amount to the seller's ledger account initially, to give a full picture of the sums handled for the seller. You would then do an immediate inter-client transfer of the amount required to redeem the mortgage.

Entries:

CR Seller's ledger account } Client section
DR Cash account

Entries:

DR Seller's ledger account } Client section
CR Lender's ledger account

You will then pay the mortgage redemption money to the lender.

Entries:

DR Lender's ledger account } Client section
CR Cash account

Alternatively, you can take a more streamlined approach and split the credit entries at the time of receipt. If this is done, you will credit part of the proceeds to the seller's ledger account and part to the lender's ledger account. The whole amount is debited to the cash account client section.

Frequently, the money due for the mortgage redemption will be paid direct to the lender's solicitor by the purchaser. In such a case, as the seller's solicitor does not handle that money, there will be no entries relating to the money in the solicitor's accounts.

17.2.5.5 Legal fees on mortgage redemption

The seller may have agreed to pay the legal fees of the lender. The seller's solicitor will address a bill to the lender. The legal fees on the mortgage redemption must initially be debited to the lender's ledger account. The debt will then be transferred to the seller's ledger account to show that it is the seller who will discharge it, not the lender.

Entries:

DR Seller's ledger account, business section, with fees charged on the sale and VAT
CR Profit costs account and HMRC account with fees charged on the sale and VAT

DR Lender's ledger account, business section, with fees charged on the mortgage and VAT
CR Profit costs account and HMRC account with fees charged on the mortgage and VAT

Transfer debt from the lender's ledger account to the seller's ledger account as follows:

CR Lender's ledger account with fees charged on the mortgage and VAT as one amount
DR Seller's ledger account with fees charged on the mortgage and VAT as one amount

17.2.6 Examples

Below are examples of transactions involving two clients.

Example 1

Purchase – with mortgage advance

Your firm is instructed by Eliot, who is purchasing 'The Willows' for £157,000 with the aid of an £85,000 mortgage from Gravesend Building Society for whom you also act. The following events occur:

August

4 Eliot tells you that he has paid £500 preliminary deposit to the estate agents, Coombs.

5 You order online mining search (£5 plus VAT) from a commercial provider who takes payment by direct debit. You will use the search to provide advice to Eliot.

12 You receive £15,200 from Eliot being the balance of the 10% deposit required.

15 You receive and pay surveyor's invoice in Eliot's name of £164 including VAT. It is a disbursement.

20 You exchange contracts and pay the balance of the deposit.

29 You order bankruptcy search (£5 plus VAT) from a commercial provider who takes payment by direct debit. You will use the search as part of your service to Eliot.

30 You send financial statement and bill of costs to Eliot and bill to Gravesend Building Society. (Professional charges on purchase amount to £400 and on mortgage to £80 plus VAT.)

September

1 You receive mortgage advance of £85,000 from Gravesend Building Society.

1 You receive sum due for completion from Eliot.

2 You complete purchase of 'The Willows'.

3 You pay Land Registry fees of £200 and stamp duty land tax of £640 to close the account.

Show the entries necessary to record the above transaction in the client ledger and cash account, together with the financial statement sent on 27 August.

Notes:

August

4 You do not need to make any entries – but remember that, when contracts are exchanged and the 10% deposit is payable, £500 of the deposit has already been paid.

5 The money for the search is paid from the business bank account. The search is not regarded as a disbursement by HMRC (it is used to provide advice). The VAT exclusive amount is debited to Eliot's ledger account – Business section, with a note that it is part of your taxable supply. The VAT is debited to the HMRC account as input tax.

Entries:

CR VAT exclusive amount to cash account CR VAT to cash account DR VAT exclusive amount to Eliot ledger account	Business section
DR VAT to HMRC account	

12 The money is client money and is paid into the client bank account.

Entries:

CR Eliot ledger account DR Cash account	Client section

Remember that £500 has already been received by the estate agents. This money makes up the balance of the deposit.

15 The surveyor's invoice is addressed to Eliot, and so you must pay it using the agency method. The money in the client bank account is specifically for payment of the deposit. It cannot therefore be used for payment of this bill. The bill must be paid out of business money as you have no client money available.

Entries:

DR Eliot ledger account CR Cash account	Business section

20 The payment of the balance of the deposit can be made out of the client bank account as you have client money available.

Entries:

DR Eliot ledger account CR Cash account	Client section

29 As with the local search, this is part of your supply of legal services. It is paid from the business bank account so there will be CR entries on the cash account for the VAT exclusive amount and the VAT. The VAT exclusive amount is debited to Eliot's ledger account – Business section, with a note that it is part of your taxable supply. The VAT is debited to the HMRC account as input tax. The entries are identical to those made for the local search on 5 August.

30 Sending the Financial Statement does not require any entries in the accounts. The Statement simply shows the client how much is required. A suitable Financial Statement is shown at the end of this example. Note that it includes the future disbursements (Land Registry fees and stamp duty land tax).

Professional charges and VAT: A bill is sent so the usual entries are made for professional charges and VAT. Remember to charge the amount due on the mortgage advance as well as those on the purchase to Eliot. Remember to increase your VAT output tax to cover the VAT you must charge on the searches. We will use a separate ledger account for the Building Society although this is not essential. See **17.2.5.2** and **17.2.5.3** above. If not using a separate ledger account for the Building Society, you would debit the charges and VAT to Eliot's ledger account.

Entries:

Professional charges on purchase	DR Eliot ledger account CR Profit costs account	Business section
VAT	DR Eliot ledger account CR HMRC ledger account	Business section

Entries:

Professional charges on mortgage advance	DR Building Society ledger account CR Profit costs account	Business section
VAT	DR Building Society ledger account CR HMRC account	Business section

The costs and VAT of the Building Society will be paid by Eliot, so the whole amount should be transferred as one figure from the Building Society's ledger account to Eliot's.

Entries:

CR Building Society ledger account DR Elliot's ledger account	Business section

September

1 The £85,000 mortgage advance is client money. It is paid into client bank account. You are receiving the money on behalf of your client, Gravesend Building Society. You will credit the money to the Gravesend Building Society ledger account.

Entries:

CR Building Society ledger account DR Cash account	Client section

1 The £57,892 is the amount shown in the Financial Statement. The money is a mixture of business and client money. We have not split the cheque but have paid it all into the client bank account. The business element must be transferred promptly. The money for the professional charges (including the searches), the paid surveyor's fee and VAT is business money. The money for the future disbursements is also business money because the client has been billed. As we are paying the future disbursements so shortly after receipt, we have paid them directly from the client bank account rather than transferring the money to the business account and paying from there. The SRA has confirmed that this is acceptable (see 'Taking money for your firm's costs', published 20 September 2020, and **9.8.2** above) despite the obligation in Rule 4.2 to allocate funds to the correct account promptly. We transfer the rest of the billed amount immediately.

Entries:

Receipt into client account of mixed funds

CR Eliot's ledger account DR Cash account	Client section

The transfer from the client to business bank account for profit costs and disbursements is recorded in the usual way.

Entries:

Withdrawal from client bank account

DR Eliot ledger account
CR Cash account
} Client section

Receipt into business bank account

CR Eliot ledger account
DR Cash account
} Business section

2 The mortgage advance is now available to Eliot, so record this by using an inter-client transfer.

Entries:

CR Eliot ledger account
DR Building Society ledger account
} Client section

2 On completion, the balance of the purchase price owing is paid out of the client bank account.

Entries:

DR Eliot ledger account
CR Cash account
} Client section

3 The Financial Statement took into account the amount which would be payable for Land Registry fees and stamp duty land tax. There is therefore enough money in the client bank account to cover them, so the payment can be made from the client bank account.

Entries:

DR Eliot ledger account
CR Cash account
} Client section

The *completed* accounts look like this:

Client: Eliot
Matter: Purchase of 'The Willows'

Date	Details	Business account			Client account		
		DR	CR	BAL	DR	CR	BAL
Aug 5	Cash. Mining search (taxable supply £1)	5		5DR			
12	Cash. From Eliot. Balance of deposit					15,200	15,200CR
15	Cash. Surveyor's fee	164		169DR			
20	Cash. Seller's solicitor. Balance of deposit				15,200		–
29	Cash. Bankruptcy search (taxable supply £1)	5		174DR			
30	Profit costs	400		574DR			
	VAT	82		656DR			
	Gravesend Building Society. Costs. Transfer	96		752DR			
Sept 1	Cash. From Eliot For completion					57,892	57,892CR
1	Cash. Transfer profit costs and disbursements		752	–	752		57,140CR
2	Gravesend Building Society. Mortgage advance. Transfer					85,000	142,140CR
2	Cash. Seller's solicitor. Completion				141,300		840CR
3	Cash. Land Registry fee				200		640CR
	Cash. Stamp duty land tax				640		–

Client: Gravesend Building Society
Matter: Mortgage Advance. Eliot

Date	Details	Business account			Client account		
		DR	CR	BAL	DR	CR	BAL
Aug							
30	Profit costs	80		80DR			
	VAT	16		96			
	Eliot. Costs. Transfer		96	–			
Sep							
1	Cash. Mortgage advance. Eliot					85,000	85,000CR
2	Eliot. Transfer				85,000		

Cash account

Date	Details	Business account			Client account		
		DR	CR	BAL	DR	CR	BAL
	Balances			xxx			xxx
Aug							
5	Eliot. Mining search		5				
5	VAT		1				
12	Eliot. Balance of deposit				15,200		
15	Eliot. Surveyor		164				
20	Eliot. Payment of deposit					15,200	
29	Eliot. Bankruptcy search		5				
29	VAT		1				
Sep							
1	Gravesend Building Society. Mortgage advance				85,000		
1	Eliot. Balance for completion				57,892		
1	Eliot. Transfer profit costs and disbursements		752	–		752	
2	Eliot. Payment purchase price					141,300	
3	Eliot. Land Registry fee					200	
3	Eliot. Stamp duty land tax					640	

HMRC

Date	Details	Business		
		DR	CR	BAL
Aug				
5	Cash. Eliot. Local search	1		
29	Cash. Eliot. Bankruptcy search	1		
30	Eliot		82	
30	Gravesend Building Society		16	

Profit costs

Date	Details	Business		
		DR	CR	BAL
Aug				
30	Eliot		400	
30	Gravesend Building Society		80	

FINANCIAL STATEMENT 27 AUGUST

TO: ELIOT
PURCHASE OF 'THE WILLOWS'

		£	£
	Purchase price		157,000
less:	Prepaid deposit		(15,700)
			141,300
less:	Mortgage advance		(85,000)
			56,300
add:	Professional charges on purchase	400	
	Local land charges fee	5	
	Bankruptcy search fee	5	
	VAT on professional charges and searches	82	
	Professional charges on mortgage (inc VAT)	96	
	Non-taxable disbursements:		
	Surveyor's fee	164	
	Land Registry fee	200	
	Stamp duty land tax	640	
			1,592
	DUE FROM YOU		57,892

Example 2

Sale and purchase – mortgage redemption and advance

You are acting for Laura, who is selling 'Obrion' for £140,000 and buying 'The Towers' for £200,000. There is an existing mortgage of £20,000 on 'Obrion' in favour of Brighton Building Society. This is to be redeemed following completion of the sale. Brighton Building Society has also agreed to a new mortgage to Laura of £50,000 for the purchase of 'The Towers'. You have been instructed to act for Brighton Building Society in connection with the redemption and the new advance. Laura has agreed to pay the building society's legal fees in connection with the advance and redemption.

The following events occur:

May

17	You order from a third party provider official copy entries relating to 'Obrion' (£5 + VAT) and a local land charges search in respect of 'The Towers' (£5 + VAT). The agency takes payment by direct debit. You use these items to provide advice to Laura.
24	You receive £20,000 from Laura to use as the deposit on 'The Towers'.
28	You exchange contracts on sale and purchase and receive a £14,000 deposit on 'Obrion' as stakeholder. You pay deposit on 'The Towers'.
31	You send a completion statement in respect of 'Obrion' showing the balance due (£126,000).

June

1	You receive a completion statement in respect of 'The Towers' showing the balance due (£180,000).

2 You order a bankruptcy search from a third party provider. The agency takes payment (£5 + VAT) by direct debit. You use this item as part of your professional services.

3 You send a bill and a financial statement to Laura. Professional charges on sale are £400 plus VAT; on purchase £600 plus VAT. You send a bill to the building society. Professional charges on mortgage redemption are £40 plus VAT; and on the new mortgage advance £80 plus VAT.

8 You receive £13,692 from Laura, being the amount shown due in the financial statement.

9 You receive the mortgage advance of £50,000 from the building society.

10 You complete the sale and purchase.

11 You send the building society a cheque to redeem the mortgage. You pay stamp duty land tax (£1,100) and Land Registry fee (£250) in respect of 'The Towers'.

You pay the estate agent's commission of £980 including VAT. The invoice was addressed to Laura.

Show the entries necessary to record the above transaction in the client ledger and the cash account, together with the financial statement sent on 3 June.

Notes:

May

17 These payments for searches are made from the business bank account. You will CR Cash – Business and DR the VAT exclusive amount to Laura's ledger and the VAT to the HMRC ledger account.

Entries:

CR VAT exclusive amount to cash account
CR VAT to cash account
DR VAT exclusive amount to Laura ledger account
} Business section
DR VAT to HMRC account

24 Client money must be paid into client bank account.

Entries:

CR Laura ledger account
DR Cash account
} Client section

28 The £20,000 deposit received on the sale is client money so is paid into the client account. We have used a stakeholder ledger account in joint names of Laura and Buyer to record the receipt rather than crediting it directly to Laura's ledger account. However, the latter is acceptable so long as the entry in the details column makes it clear that the money is held for the buyer and Laura jointly.

Entries:

CR Joint stakeholder account
DR Cash account
} Client section

The £14,000 due for the deposit on the purchase will be paid out of client money.

Entries:

DR Laura ledger account
CR Cash account
} Client section

31 No entries are required. There are no additional items referred to, so at completion only the balance of the sale price (£126,000) will be received.

June

1 This confirms that only the balance of the purchase price (£180,000) will be payable at completion.

2 The search is dealt with in the same way as on 17 May.

3 The usual entries for professional charges and VAT are made. You will increase your VAT to cover the searches.

Remember that Laura is responsible for your charges to her and for your charges to the Brighton Building Society. If, as we are, you are using a separate ledger account for the Building Society, you must debit the legal fees on the mortgage advance and redemption plus VAT to the building society's ledger account and then transfer the debt to Laura's ledger account. If not using a separate ledger account for the Building Society, you would debit the charges and VAT to Laura's ledger account.

A financial statement is given at the end of this example.

8 The cheque is a combination of business and client money. We have not split it but have paid it into the client bank account. We must transfer the business element promptly. The money for the professional charges and VAT is business money. As in the Eliot example, the money received for the future disbursements is also business money. As we are going to pay the future disbursements quickly, we will leave the money in the client bank account and make the payment from the client bank account. The SRA has confirmed that this is acceptable (see 'Taking money for your firm's costs', published 20 September 2020, and **9.8.2** above) despite the obligation in Rule 4.2 to allocate funds to the correct account promptly. We transfer the rest of the billed amount immediately.

Entries:

Receipt from Laura

CR Laura ledger account } Client section
DR Cash account

Transfer money from the client to the business bank account in the usual way.

Entries:

Withdrawal from the client bank account

DR Laura ledger account } Client section
CR Cash account

Receipt into the business bank account

CR Laura ledger account } Business section
DR Cash account

9 The money is received on behalf of your client, Brighton Building Society, and if, as we are, you are using a separate ledger account for the Building Society, the money must be credited to its ledger account. If you dispensed with a separate ledger account, you would credit the advance to Laura's ledger account. You would have to label it with the name of the Building Society and describe it as a mortgage advance.

10 **Completion of sale:**

£126,000 is received from the purchaser's solicitor. It is client money and paid into the client bank account.

Entries:

CR Laura ledger account
DR Cash account
} Client section

Then transfer the deposit, which now belongs to Laura, from the joint stakeholder account.

Entries:

DR Joint stakeholder ledger account
CR Laura ledger account
} Client section

Redemption of mortgage:

Part of the sale proceeds (the £20,000 required to redeem the mortgage) is held for the building society. Transfer the redemption money from Laura to Brighton Building Society.

Entries:

DR Laura ledger account
CR Brighton Building Society ledger account
} Client section

Completion of purchase:

The mortgage advance is now available to Laura so record this by using an inter-client transfer.

Entries:

DR Building Society ledger account
CR Laura ledger account
} Client section

Send the seller's solicitor the balance required of £180,000 from the client bank account.

Entries:

DR Laura ledger account
CR Cash account
} Client section

11 Send Brighton Building Society £20,000 from the client bank account.

Entries:

DR Brighton Building Society ledger account
CR Cash account
} Client section

The Land Registry fees and stamp duty land tax can be paid from the client bank account.

DR Laura ledger account
CR Cash account
} Client section

11 The estate agent's bill is paid from the client bank account using the agency method.

Entries:

DR Laura ledger account
CR Cash account
} Client section

The *completed* accounts look like this:

Client: Laura
Matter: Sale of 'Obrion'; Purchase of 'The Towers'

Date	Details	Business account			Client account		
		DR	CR	BAL	DR	CR	BAL
May							
17	Cash. Official copies (taxable supply £1)	5		5DR			
17	Cash. Local land charges search (taxable supply £1)	5		10DR			
24	Cash. From Laura. For deposit on 'The Towers'					20,000	20,000CR
28	Cash. To Vendor's solicitor. Deposit on 'The Towers'				20,000		–
June							
2	Cash. Bankruptcy search (taxable supply £1)	5		15DR			
3	Profit costs. Sale	400		415DR			
	VAT	81		496DR			
	Profit costs. Purchase	600		1,096DR			
	VAT	122		1,218DR			
	Brighton BS. Transfer mortgage advance and redemption costs and VAT	144		1,362DR			
8	Cash. From Laura					13,692	13,692CR
8	Cash. Transfer profit and disbursements		1,362	–	1,362		12,330CR
10	Buyer's solicitor. Complete sale					126,000	138,330CR
10	Brighton Building Society					50,000	188,330CR
10	Laura and Buyer. Transfer deposit					14,000	202,330CR
10	Cash. Seller's solicitor. Complete purchase				180,000		22,330CR
10	Brighton Building Society. Transfer. Mortgage redemption				20,000		2,330CR
11	Cash. Stamp duty land tax. 'The Towers'				1,100		1,230CR
11	Cash. Land Registry fee. 'The Towers'				250		980CR
12	Cash, Estate agent. 'Obrion'				980		–

Client: Brighton Building Society
Matter: Mortgage advance and redemption. Laura

Date	Details	Business account			Client account		
		DR	CR	BAL	DR	CR	BAL
June							
3	Profit costs. Mortgage advance	80		80DR			
	VAT	16		96DR			
	Profit costs. Mortgage redemption	40		136DR			
	VAT	8		144DR			
	Laura. Costs. Transfer.		144	–			
9	Cash. Mortgage advance					50,000	50,000CR
10	Laura. Transfer Mortgage advance				50,000		–
	Laura. Transfer. Mortgage redemption					20,000	20,000CR
	Cash. To Brighton Building Society				20,000		–

Cash account

Date	Details	Business account			Client account		
		DR	CR	BAL	DR	CR	BAL
May				xxx			xxx
17	Laura. Official copies		5				
	VAT		1				
	Laura. Local land charges search		5				
	VAT		1				
24	Laura. For deposit				20,000		
28	Stakeholder				14,000		
	Laura. Deposit to vendors					20,000	
June							
2	Laura. Bankruptcy search		5				
	VAT		1				
8	Laura. Balance for completion				13,692		
8	Laura. Professional charges and disbursements	1,362				1,362	
9	Brighton Building Society. Mortgage advance.				50,000		
10	Laura. Purchaser's solicitors				126,000		
	Laura. Complete purchase					180,000	
11	Brighton Building Society. Mortgage redemption					20,000	
	Laura. Stamp duty land tax					1,100	
	Laura. Land Registry fee					250	
	Laura. Estate agent					980	

Client: Laura (and buyer)
Matter: Stakeholder

Date	Details	Business account			Client account		
		DR	**CR**	**BAL**	**DR**	**CR**	**BAL**
May							
28	Cash. Deposit on 'Obrion' re Laura					14,000	14,000CR
June							
10	Laura. Transfer deposit				14,000		–

HMRC

Date	Details	Business account		
		DR	**CR**	**BAL**
May				
17	Cash. Laura. Office copy entries	1		
17	Cash. Laura. Local search	1		
June				
2	Cash. Bankruptcy search	1		
3	Laura. Sale		81	
3	Laura. Purchase		122	
3	Brighton Building Society. Mortgage advance. Laura		16	
3	Brighton Building Society. Mortgage redemption. Laura		8	

Profit Costs

Date	Details	Business account		
		DR	**CR**	**BAL**
May				
3	Laura. Sale		400	
3	Laura. Purchase		600	
3	Brighton Building Society. Mortgage advance. Laura		80	
3	Brighton Building Society. Mortgage redemption. Laura		40	

FINANCIAL STATEMENT 3 JUNE

TO: LAURA

SALE OF 'OBRION'

		£	£
	Sale price		140,000
less:	Mortgage redemption		(20,000)
			120,000
	Professional charges on sale	400	
	Official copy entries	5	
	VAT on professional charges and searches	81	
	Professional charges on mortgage redemption (inc VAT)	48	
	Non-taxable disbursements:		
	Estate agent's commission (inc VAT)	980	(1,514)
	Available on sale		**118,486**
	PURCHASE OF 'THE TOWERS'		
	Purchase price		200,000
less:	Prepaid deposit		(20,000)
			180,000
	Mortgage advance		(50,000)
			130,000
add:	Professional charges on purchase	600	
	Local land charges search	5	
	Bankruptcy search fee	5	
	VAT on professional charges and searches	122	
	Professional charges on mortgage advance (inc VAT)	96	
	Non-taxable disbursements:		
	Stamp duty land tax	1,100	
	Land Registry fees	250	2,178
	Required for purchase		132,178
	SUMMARY		
	Required for purchase		132,178
less:	Available from sale		(118,486)
	DUE FROM YOU		13,692

17.3 AGENCY TRANSACTIONS

A firm providing legal services may decide to use another firm as its agent. This may happen in any type of transaction, but probably happens most often in the context of a litigation matter.

17.3.1 The agent firm

The agent firm treats the instructing firm like any other client. There will be a client ledger account in the name of the instructing firm, and the normal entries will be made to deal with any client money and the delivery of the bill.

17.3.2 The instructing firm

The professional fees charged by the agent are not a disbursement paid by the instructing firm on behalf of the client. The instructing firm is providing legal services to the client using an agent. The professional fees of the agent are, therefore, an expense of the instructing firm. The firm will charge more for its legal services in order to cover the expense of using an agent. Any true disbursements (eg court fees, counsel's fees) will be charged to the client as usual, and it is irrelevant whether the agent or the instructing firm pays them.

When the instructing firm pays the agent's bill, he sends one business bank account cheque for the total amount. There can be three different elements of that total: the agent's professional fees, VAT on those fees and any disbursements paid by the agent. The different elements will be recorded separately in the instructing firm's accounts.

Entries:

Agent's professional charges	CR Cash account DR Agency expenses account	Business section
Agent's VAT	CR Cash account DR HMRC account	Business section
Agent's disbursements	CR Cash account DR Client's ledger account	Business section

When the instructing firm sends its own client a bill, it adds the agent's professional charges to its own professional charges and passes on the agent's disbursements to the client.

Example

You act for Williams. You instruct Gibsons LLP, a firm of solicitors, as your agents. On 17 May, you receive their bill showing their professional charges of £200 plus VAT and a court fee of £70. You pay their bill on the same day. On 18 May, you send Williams a bill. Your own professional charges are £400 plus VAT.

Notes:

May

17 When you pay the agent's bill, you will pay a total of costs £200 plus £40 VAT and the court fee of £70, ie, a total of £310. However, you will make three separate pairs of DR and CR entries to record the three separate elements of the bill.

The accounts will look like this:

Cash account

Date	Details	Business account			Client account		
		DR	CR	BAL	DR	CR	BAL
May				xxx			xxx
17	Agency expenses		200				
	VAT		40				
	Williams		70				

Client: Williams
Matter: Miscellaneous

Date	Details	Business account			Client account		
		DR	CR	BAL	DR	CR	BAL
May							
17	Cash, Gibsons. Court fee	70		70DR			

Agency expenses account

Date	Details	Business account		
		DR	CR	BAL
May				
17	Cash. Williams	200		200DR

HMRC account

Date	Details	Business account		
		DR	CR	BAL
May				
17	Cash	40		40DR

18 When you issue your bill, you add the agent's professional charges to your own and make the usual entries for costs and VAT.

The accounts will look like this:

Cash account

Date	Details	Business account			Client account		
		DR	CR	BAL	DR	CR	BAL
May				xxx			xxx
17	Agency expenses		200				
	HMRC		40				
	Williams		70				

Client: Williams
Matter: Miscellaneous

Date	Details	Business account			Client account		
		DR	CR	BAL	DR	CR	BAL
May							
17	Cash, Gibsons. Court fee	70		70DR			
18	Profit costs (400 + 200)	600		670			
	VAT (80 + 40)	120		790			

Profit costs account

Date	Details	Business account		
		DR	CR	BAL
May				
18	Williams		600	600CR

Agency Expenses account

Date	Details	Business account		
		DR	CR	BAL
May				
17	Cash. Williams	200		200DR

HMRC account				
Date	Details	Business account		
		DR	CR	BAL
May				
17	Cash. Williams	40		40DR
18	Williams		120	80CR

SUMMARY

(1) If a firm has been holding client money for one client and then starts to hold some or all of it for another client, the firm must open a client ledger account for the transferee and record an inter-client transfer of the money.

(2) A deposit received as stakeholder is client money and must be paid into the client bank account. It is held for the buyer and seller jointly so it must be credited to a joint ledger account (usually called 'stakeholder'). It may still be possible to credit the deposit to the seller's ledger account with a note identifying it as stakeholder money held jointly for the seller and buyer. This was permitted under the old Rules but it is not clear whether this is still allowed.

On the day the sale is completed the cash becomes the seller's. The firm must make an inter-client transfer to show that the deposit is now held for the seller alone.

(3) Where a mortgage advance is received, the money is client money and must be paid into the client bank account. It should be credited to the ledger account of the lender.

(4) When one firm providing legal services instructs another to act as its agent, the professional charges of the agent firm are an office expense of the instructing firm, not a client disbursement. The instructing firm will increase its own professional charges to cover the costs of the agent.

SOLUTIONS

Exercise 17A

When the company gives you funds on 4 June, you must record a receipt of the company's money.

Entries:

DR Cash
CR George & Co Ltd } Client section

When the sale is completed on 5 June, you must show that the money is now held for George. You show this by doing an inter-client transfer.

Entries:

DR George & Co Ltd
CR George } Client section

When you complete the investment for George on 7 June, you must record a payment of George's money.

Entries:

DR George
CR Cash } Client section

CHAPTER 18

THIRD PARTY MANAGED ACCOUNTS

18.1	Introduction	211
18.2	Checks you should make before engaging a TPMA provider	212
18.3	Engaging with the client	212
18.4	What firms must tell clients	212
18.5	Systems and procedures	213
18.6	SRA Guidance	213
18.7	Proposals for change	213

LEARNING OUTCOMES

After reading this chapter you will be able to:

- explain the possible benefits of using third party managed accounts
- identify the checks that should be made before using such accounts
- identify the information that should be given about such accounts to the SRA and the client.

18.1 INTRODUCTION

Rule 11.1 allows firms to use a third party managed account (TPMA), rather than operating their own client account, to receive and make payments of client money.

Money held in a TPMA does not fall under the definition of client money in the SRA Accounts Rules as it is not held or received by the firm. As such, it does not have to be held in accordance with the SRA rules relating to the holding of client money.

However, Rule 11 does apply. Rule 11.1 provides that a TPMA can only be used if:

(a) use of the account does not result in you receiving or holding the client's money; and

(b) you take reasonable steps to ensure, before accepting instructions, that the client is informed of and understands:

  (i) the terms of the contractual arrangements relating to the use of the third party managed account, and in particular how any fees for use of the third party managed account will be paid and who will bear them; and

  (ii) the client's right to terminate the agreement and dispute payment requests made by you.

Rule 11.2 requires firms using TPMAs to obtain regular statements from the provider of the account and to ensure that these accurately reflect all transactions on the account.

Guidance issued by the SRA, 'Third party managed accounts' (updated 25 November 2019), reminds firms using TPMAs that they remain subject to other SRA regulatory requirements:

> Paragraph 4.2 of the SRA Code of Conduct for Solicitors, RELs and RFLs and Paragraph 5.2 of the SRA Code of Conduct for Firms set out your obligation to protect client money and assets. These remain relevant to funds held in a TPMA. In order to meet these obligations, and Principle 7 - the obligation to act in the best interests of each client, you will need to make sure that the decision to use a TPMA, and the TPMA used, is appropriate in each individual case.

Although using a TPMA comes with some costs, it can reduce overall firm overheads, especially if the firm only occasionally holds client money. For example, outsourcing the holding of client money can reduce professional indemnity insurance premiums and contributions to the Compensation Fund. Accountants' reports do not need to be prepared.

There are potential benefits beyond cost savings. Although it is impossible to eliminate all risk related to cyber crime, TPMAs could be a more secure way of handling client money. Using a TMPA may also help address a firm's money laundering risk.

18.2 CHECKS YOU SHOULD MAKE BEFORE ENGAGING A TPMA PROVIDER

In the Guidance referred to above, the SRA states that it expects firms to make sure that the TPMA provider is regulated by the Financial Conduct Authority (FCA). The TPMA provider must be either:

- an authorised payment institution; or
- a small payment institution which has adopted voluntary safeguarding arrangements to the same level as an authorised payment institution; or
- an EEA authorised payment institution.

These arrangements mean that the TPMA provider is authorised and regulated by the FCA. The TPMA must be an account held at a bank or building society operated as an escrow payment service (the third party receives and disburses money on your and your client's behalf).

18.3 ENGAGING WITH THE CLIENT

A firm entering into arrangements with a client to use a TPMA on behalf of the client must take appropriate steps to comply with Rule 11.1 and Rule 11.2 of the Accounts Rules and, according to the SRA guidance, must make sure that:

(a) it takes reasonable steps (see **18.4** below) to make sure that the client is informed of and understands their rights and obligations and what the use of the TPMA means in their case, including whether they are required to authorise payments, and any charges or fees they are liable to pay;

(b) it obtains regular statements and ensures that these reflect the transactions on the account correctly, and makes sure that the funds in the TPMA are only used for their designated purpose;

(c) it maintains an overview of the transactions on the account and keeps appropriate records to reflect this.

18.4 WHAT FIRMS MUST TELL CLIENTS

The SRA guidance referred to above provides that to comply with their obligations to clients, firms must take reasonable steps to ensure that the client understands the arrangement, before the agreement is entered into. Clients should understand in particular:

- how the money will be held and how the transaction will work (paragraph 8.6 of the SRA Code of Conduct for Solicitors, RELs and RFLs)
- their right to terminate the agreement (rule 11.1(b)(ii) of the accounts rules)
- their right to dispute payment requests made by you
- who will be responsible for costs associated with the agreement (rule 11.1(b)(i) of the Accounts Rules)
- that the TPMA is regulated by the FCA and that complaints about the TPMA provider should be made to that provider in accordance with their complaints procedure, and

- that the regulatory protections that apply to TPMAs are different to those that apply to client money held in a firm's client account (paragraph 8.11 of the SRA Code of Conduct for Solicitors, RELs and RFLs).

18.5 SYSTEMS AND PROCEDURES

Firms using TPMAs are, of course, still subject to the SRA Code of Conduct for Firms. Paragraph 2.1 of the Code requires them to have in place effective governance structures, arrangements, systems and controls to ensure that the business and employees comply with the SRA's regulatory arrangements.

This includes having appropriate internal systems for monitoring the transactions on the account and keeping appropriate records.

18.6 SRA GUIDANCE

In the Guidance referred to above, the SRA says that, while firms do not need permission to use a TPMA, it does expect firms to notify it, using its TPMA form. It will then update its records to show that firms are using a TPMA.

The form asks for the following information:

- the name and SRA number of your firm;
- the name of the TPMA provider;
- the TPMA provider's FCA authorisation number;
- the date on which you plan to start using a TPMA as part of your business.

If the same TPMA provider is used for several clients, it is only necessary to inform the SRA the first time that the TPMA provider is used. If more than one TPMA provider is used, the SRA expects to be notified of all providers.

If a firm switches between TPMA providers, or stops using the one currently engaged with, the SRA should be informed so it can update its records.

18.7 PROPOSALS FOR CHANGE

In the SRA consultation launched on 14 November 2024, 'Client money in legal services - safeguarding consumers and providing redress: The model of solicitors holding client money', the SRA questioned whether the current model of client bank accounts to hold client money continued to be appropriate.

Despite finding through online polls of over 2,000 consumers that 79% were comfortable or very comfortable with a regulated solicitor holding their money, the SRA considered that there are inherent risks in doing so, saying 'in recent years, we have seen those risks materialise in cases where large amounts of client money have been lost or misappropriated, causing detriment to consumers, as well as increased costs to the legal sector' (a reference to the collapse of the Axiom Ince Group).

Any change will not be swift. The consultation says:

> If we do decide that we will not allow firms to hold client money in the future, we recognise that this will take several years to achieve. Not least because we have heard that there are not yet sufficient alternatives available.

Most responses to the consultation were not in favour of this proposal. The Law Society said:

> Client accounts enable solicitors to address client needs promptly and efficiently.
>
> The proposed regulatory changes – such as restricting solicitors from holding client money or not holding it at all – are disproportionate and lack evidence of necessity.
>
> Our members overwhelming favour the retention of client accounts without restrictions, which are cheaper and more flexible than TPMAs.

In a collective response to the SRA's consultation on consumer protection, the law societies of Birmingham, Bristol, Leeds, Liverpool and Manchester said:

> The SRA has not adequately explained why it considers client money held to a solicitor's instruction in a TPMA would be safer than client money held in a separate client account .... Removal of client funds to TPMA merely pushes responsibility of failure of a TPMA to the FCA rather than the SRA. It gives no greater protection to consumers which is the SRA's entire purpose.

SUMMARY

(1) Firms can dispense with holding a client bank account by using a TPMA.

(2) Money held in such accounts is outside the definition of client money and so is not subject to the SRA Accounts Rules 2019.

(3) However, a firm which uses such accounts will be subject to the SRA Codes of Conduct.

(4) The client must be fully informed of the arrangement.

(5) The SRA expects to be informed when a firm decides to use or change a TPMA provider.

CHAPTER 19

COMPLIANCE

19.1	Introduction	215
19.2	Accountants' reports	215
19.3	Storage and retention of accounting records	217

LEARNING OUTCOMES

After reading this chapter you will be able to:

- explain the investigative powers of the SRA
- explain the need to deliver accountants' reports.

19.1 INTRODUCTION

There is no point in the SRA having rules governing how client money is treated if it is unaware of breaches. Some years ago therefore, the Rules were tightened to ensure that only accountants with auditor status inspected solicitors' accounts and that they were under an obligation to report breaches to the SRA. The rules on compliance were stringent.

In 2015 the SRA announced that it was making accountants' reports more targeted and relevant for firms and accountants alike. Solicitors' practices that present little or no risk – such as those firms that do not hold much client money – are now exempt from obtaining a report from their accountant.

The form that solicitors' accountants complete each year was also changed to give accountants more opportunity to exercise their professional judgement when preparing and finalising reports. Only qualified reports are now required to be submitted to the SRA, instead of all reports, as was previously the case.

As part of its response to the SRA consultation, the Law Society called on the SRA to reintroduce mandatory accountants' reports for all firms holding client money. In an article in *The Law Society Gazette* by Eduardo Reyes on 11 February 2025, Peter Steel, chair of the Law Society's regulatory processes committee, referred to the change in relation to the Axiom Ince collapse. He suggested that the previous rules requiring all firms to submit annual accountants' reports 'provided a degree of financial hygiene for practices, and often provided early warning of problem firms, for example, where no report was filed'. A second LSB report, on SSB Group, is awaited.

19.2 ACCOUNTANTS' REPORTS

Rule 12.1 provides that firms which have, at any time during an accounting period, held or received client money, or operated a joint account or a client's own account as signatory, must obtain an accountant's report for that accounting period within six months of the end of the period.

If the report is qualified to show a failure to comply with the rules, such that money belonging to clients or third parties is, or has been, or is likely to be placed, at risk, it must be delivered to the SRA within six months of the end of the accounting period. Only qualified reports need to be submitted to the SRA (Rule 12.1 (b)). The obligation to deliver qualified reports rests with the firm and its managers – and not the reporting accountants (although, in practice, accountants can and do send the reports to the SRA).

The SRA has issued guidance, 'Planning for and completing an accountant's report' (updated 14 September 2020). It says:

> We do not consider it appropriate to strictly define when a report must be qualified. We will rely on the accountant's professional judgement to assess the firm's compliance with the Accounts Rules and whether money belonging to clients or third parties, is, has been or may be placed at risk. We would expect an assessment to be based on an understanding of the seriousness of all the risks posed in the context of the firm's size and complexity, areas of work, systems and controls, compliance history and the likely impact on the firm and its clients if money were to be misused or not accounted for.

However, it does give some examples of 'Serious factors' – the presence of one or more of which is likely to lead to a qualification – and 'Moderate factors' – the presence of one or more of which may lead to a qualification depending on context (including factors such as the number of instances, whether the firm identified the breaches and what corrective action, if any, has been taken as a consequence):

> Serious factors include:
>
> - A significant and/or unreplaced shortfall (including client debit balances or business credit balances) on client account, including client money held elsewhere, for example a client's own account, unless caused by bank error and rectified promptly.
> - Systematic billing for fees and any disbursements that have not been incurred and payments in respect of that bill being made into the business account.
> - Evidence of any disregard for the safety of client money and assets.
> - Actual or suspected fraud or dishonesty by the managers or employees of the firm (that may impact upon the safety of money belonging to clients or third parties).
> - Accounting records not available or significantly deficient or bank accounts/ledgers failing to include reference to a client (rule 8.1, 8.2 and 8.3).
> - A failure to provide documentation requested by the reporting accountant (rule 12.8).
> - Client account bank reconciliations not carried out.
> - The client account is improperly used as a banking facility (rule 3.3). Please refer to our Warning Notice on this and associated case studies.

Rule 12.2 provides that firms are not required to obtain an accountant's report if:

(a) all of the client money held or received during an accounting period is money received from the Legal Aid Agency; or

(b) in the accounting period, the total balance of all client accounts plus any joint accounts and clients' own accounts operated by the firm does not exceed:

  (i) an average of £10,000; and

  (ii) a maximum of £250,000,

  or the equivalent in foreign currency.

SRA guidance, 'Accountant's report and the exemption to obtain one' (updated 25 November 2019), explains how to calculate whether or not the firm's balances fulfil the two exemption criteria.

Where a firm ceases to practise as an authorised body regulated by the SRA and to hold or operate a client account, or the SRA considers that it is otherwise in the public interest to do so, the SRA may require it to obtain or deliver an accountant's report to the SRA on reasonable notice (Rule 12.4). The effect of Rule 12.4 is that the SRA will only require firms to submit a report when a firm shuts down and closes its client account on a case-by-case basis, if it believes that it is necessary.

Any report obtained must be prepared and signed by an accountant who is a member of one of the chartered accountancy bodies and who is, or works for, a registered auditor.

Rule 12.6 provides that the SRA may disqualify an accountant from preparing a report for the purposes of this rule if:

(a) the accountant has been found guilty by their professional body of professional misconduct or equivalent; or

(b) the SRA is satisfied that the accountant has failed to exercise due care and skill in the preparation of a report under these Rules.

Rule 12.8 provides that firms must provide the accountant preparing a report with the following:

(a) details of all accounts held at any bank, building society or other financial institution at any time during the accounting period to which the report relates; and

(b) all other information and documentation that the accountant requires to enable completion of their report.

19.3 STORAGE AND RETENTION OF ACCOUNTING RECORDS

All accounting records should be securely stored and retained for at least six years (Rule 13.1).

SUMMARY

(1) The accounts of all firms regulated by the SRA have to be inspected by an accountant with auditor status once a year.

(2) Solicitors have to inform the SRA each time the reporting accountant is changed.

PART II SUMMARY

Solicitors' Accounts

Topic	Summary
Fundamentals	The SRA wishes to ensure that the highest possible standards are maintained by those providing legal services. Firms must keep other people's money separate from money of their own; they must keep other people's money safely in a bank or building society account and use each client's money only for that client's matters; they must keep proper accounting records to show receipts and payments made for each client.
The SRA Accounts Rules 2019	The Rules define client money and require firms regulated by the SRA to have a client bank account unless the firm comes within the exception in Rule 2.2. Client money must be kept separate from the firm's own money (Rule 4.1) and must be paid into the client bank account promptly (Rule 2.3). Mixed receipts must be allocated promptly to the correct account. Where money is held in the client bank account, funds can only be transferred to the firm's business account in payment of professional charges and disbursements after a bill or other written notification of costs has been issued. Rule 5 sets out the circumstances in which money may be withdrawn from the client bank account. The most important is Rule 5.3 which provides that money withdrawn for a particular client must not exceed the amount held for that client.
Need to record client transactions	Firms must have client ledger accounts for clients which record all receipts and payments of client money, together with professional charges made by the firm and payments made by the firm for the client from its own money (Rule 8).
Types of entry	There are really only four things that firms providing legal services ever record: the amount of professional charges and VAT owing when a bill is issued, a receipt of cash, a payment of cash and an inter-client transfer – this is where a firm which is holding client money for one client stops holding it for that client and starts holding it for another. The entries for the four events are set out in Chapter 11.

Topic	Summary
VAT and disbursements	When a firm makes a payment on behalf of a client which includes a VAT element, the treatment of the payment in the firm's records will depend on whether the invoice is addressed to the firm or the client. If it is addressed to the firm, the principal method must be used and the payment must be made from business money. If the invoice is addressed to the client, the agency method must be used and the payment can be made from office or from client money if any is available. See Chapter 12 for a full discussion of VAT. In order to be a disbursement, the goods or services must be provided to the client. If they are provided to the firm for use in the course of providing professional services to the client, they are not disbursements. In such cases, the firm recovers the cost of the goods or services by increasing its charges to the client.
Accounting to clients for interest	Rule 7 provides that firms must account to clients for a fair sum of interest earned on client money. If the money is left in the general client bank account, the firm must pay the client a sum from its business account representing a fair amount. Where a firm chooses to put money in a separate designated deposit account, it will normally account to the client for all interest allowed by the bank. Deposit interest is dealt with in Chapter 15.
Particular points in relation to property transactions	Money received as stakeholder is held for the buyer and seller jointly. It must either be recorded on a ledger account opened for the buyer and seller jointly, or, be shown on the seller's ledger but labelled as stakeholder money (if this treatment is still permitted under the 2019 Rules). Money received as a mortgage advance is held for the lender.
Particular points in relation to probate transactions	The client in a probate transaction is the personal representative. The administration of the estate is complete when the residuary beneficiary approves the estate accounts and is sent a cheque for the amount due. If the beneficiary asks the firm to continue holding the money, the firm must make an inter-client transfer to a new ledger account opened for the beneficiary.

APPENDIX 1 TO PART II

MULTIPLE CHOICE QUESTIONS

This Appendix contains multiple choice questions designed to test your knowledge of the material contained in Part II. Always read multiple choice questions carefully, and be particularly alert to words like 'always', 'must' and 'never'. Most (although not all) of the Rules contain exceptions, so any statement containing one of these words is likely to be wrong.

Questions

1. **Which ONE of the following is client money?**
   - A Money received in payment of a paid disbursement.
   - B Money received for professional charges following the issue of a bill.
   - C Money received for unpaid disbursements following the issue of a bill.
   - D Money received generally on account of costs.
2. **Which ONE of the following statements is WRONG?**
   - A A mixed receipt can be paid into the business account.
   - B Client money need not always be paid into the client bank account.
   - C Money received on account of costs and paid into the client bank account can never be transferred to the business account unless a bill has been issued.
   - D Any dealing with client money must be recorded under Rule 8.
3. **Which ONE of the following statements is CORRECT?**
   - A A mixed receipt of client and business money can be paid into the business bank account provided the client money element is transferred promptly to the client bank account.
   - B A mixed receipt of client and business money must be paid into the client bank account, and the business money element must be transferred promptly to the business bank account.
   - C A receipt of money to reimburse a firm for a paid disbursement is a receipt of client money if no bill has been issued.
   - D All firms regulated by the SRA must have a client bank account.
4. You pay a surveyor's fee of £300 + VAT on behalf of a client, registered for VAT, for whom you hold £500 on account of costs. The payment fulfils the criteria for a disbursement.

   Which ONE of the following statements is CORRECT?
   - A If the invoice is addressed to the client, the invoice must be paid from the client bank account.
   - B If the invoice is addressed to the firm, the invoice can be paid from the client bank account.
   - C If the invoice is addressed to the client, the invoice cannot be paid from the business bank account.
   - D If the invoice is addressed to the firm, the invoice must be paid from the business bank account.

5. **Which ONE of the following statements is CORRECT?**

   A Money received generally on account of costs cannot be transferred from the client to the business bank account in reimbursement of a disbursement paid from the business bank account unless a bill has been issued.

   B A client bank account must be held at a bank or building society in England and Wales and must include the name of the firm and the word 'client'.

   C There is no VAT relief on bad debts.

   D It is a breach of the SRA Accounts Rules 2019 to make a payment from the client bank account on behalf of a client before receiving confirmation that the client's cheque for money on account of costs has cleared.

6. **Which ONE of the following statements is CORRECT?**

   A A firm regulated by the SRA must account to a client for a fair sum of interest on any client money held.

   B It is a breach of the SRA Accounts Rules 2019 not to open a separate designated client account.

   C When paying interest, a firm must calculate the rate by reference to the best rate it is possible to get on the amount held.

   D Clients are always entitled to receive interest on client money.

7. You are holding £600 for a client on account of costs and have to pay a disbursement.

   Which ONE of the following statements is CORRECT?

   A You cannot pay the disbursement from the client bank account unless you issue a bill.

   B You cannot pay the disbursement from the client bank account if it exceeds £600.

   C You are permitted to withdraw more than £600 provided you ask the client to provide additional funds promptly.

   D You can never pay a disbursement from the client bank account.

8. You hold £500 on account of costs for the client. You pay a surveyor's fee of £200 + £40 VAT for the client. The invoice is made out to you. The payment fulfils the criteria for a disbursement.

   Subsequently you send the client a bill for £400 in professional charges. The client is registered for VAT.

   Which ONE of the following statements is CORRECT?

   A You can use client money to pay the disbursement.

   B You will send the client two VAT invoices: one for your own fees and one from the surveyor.

   C You will make no entries in the firm's VAT records in relation to the surveyor's fee.

   D You will send the client one VAT invoice covering the VAT on both the survey and the profit costs.

Answers

1. D
2. C
3. A
4. D
5. B
6. A
7. B
8. D

SRA ACCOUNTS RULES (EXTRACTS)

Introduction

These rules set out our requirements for when firms (including sole practices) authorised by us receive or deal with money belonging to clients, including trust money or money held on behalf of third parties. The rules apply to all firms we regulate, including all those who manage or work within such firms.

Firms will need to have systems and controls in place to ensure compliance with these rules and the nature of those systems must be appropriate to the nature and volumes of client transactions dealt with and the amount of client money held or received.

Part 2: Client money and client accounts

Client money

2.1 "***Client money***" is money held or received by you:

(a) relating to ***regulated services*** delivered by you to a ***client***;

(b) on behalf of a third party in relation to ***regulated services*** delivered by you (such as money held as agent, stakeholder or held to the sender's order);

(c) as a trustee or as the holder of a specified office or appointment, such as donee of a power of attorney, Court of Protection deputy or trustee of an occupational pension scheme;

(d) in respect of your ***fees*** and any unpaid ***disbursements*** if held or received prior to delivery of a bill for the same.

2.2 In circumstances where the only ***client money*** you hold or receive falls within rule 2.1(d) above, and:

(a) any money held for ***disbursements*** relates to costs or expenses incurred by you on behalf of your ***client*** and for which you are liable; and

(b) you do not for any other reason maintain a ***client account***;

you are not required to hold this money in a ***client account*** if you have informed your ***client*** in advance of where and how the money will be held. Rules 2.3, 2.4, 4.1, 7, 8.1(b) and (c) and 12 do not apply to ***client money*** held outside of a ***client account*** in accordance with this rule.

2.3 You ensure that ***client money*** is paid promptly into a ***client account*** unless:

(a) in relation to money falling within 2.1(c), to do so would conflict with your obligations under rules or regulations relating to your specified office or appointment;

(b) the ***client money*** represents payments received from the Legal Aid Agency for your ***costs***; or

(c) you agree in the individual circumstances an alternative arrangement in writing with the ***client***, or the third party, for whom the money is held.

2.4 You ensure that ***client money*** is available on demand unless you agree an alternative arrangement in writing with the ***client***, or the third party for whom the money is held.

2.5 You ensure that **client money** is returned promptly to the **client**, or the third party for whom the money is held, as soon as there is no longer any proper reason to hold those funds.

Client account

3.1 You only maintain a **client account** at a branch (or the head office) of a **bank** or a **building society** in England and Wales.

3.2 You ensure that the name of any **client account** includes:

(a) the name of the **authorised body**; and

(b) the word "client" to distinguish it from any other type of account held or operated by the **authorised body**.

3.3 You must not use a **client account** to provide banking facilities to **clients** or third parties. Payments into, and transfers or withdrawals from a **client account** must be in respect of the delivery by you of **regulated services**.

Client money must be kept separate

4.1 You keep **client money** separate from money belonging to the **authorised body**.

4.2 You ensure that you allocate promptly any funds from **mixed payments** you receive to the correct **client account** or business account.

4.3 Where you are holding **client money** and some or all of that money will be used to pay your **costs**:

(a) you must give a bill of **costs**, or other written notification of the **costs** incurred, to the **client** or the paying party;

(b) this must be done before you transfer any **client money** from a **client account** to make the payment; and

(c) any such payment must be for the specific sum identified in the bill of **costs**, or other written notification of the **costs** incurred, and covered by the amount held for the particular **client** or third party.

Withdrawals from client account

5.1 You only withdraw **client money** from a **client account**:

(a) for the purpose for which it is being held;

(b) following receipt of instructions from the **client**, or the third party for whom the money is held; or

(c) on the **SRA's** prior written authorisation or in **prescribed** circumstances.

5.2 You appropriately authorise and supervise all withdrawals made from a **client account**.

5.3 You only withdraw **client money** from a **client account** if sufficient funds are held on behalf of that specific **client** or third party to make the payment.

SRA Glossary (extracts)

authorised body	means: (a) a body that has been authorised by the SRA to practise as a licensed body or a recognised body; or (b) a sole practitioner's practice that has been authorised by the SRA as a recognised sole practice
client	means the person for whom you act and, where the context permits, includes prospective and former clients In the SRA Financial Services (Scope) Rules, in relation to any regulated financial services activities carried on by an authorised body for a trust or the estate of a deceased person (including a controlled trust), means the trustees or personal representatives in their capacity as such and not any person who is a beneficiary under the trust or interested in the estate
client account	has the meaning given to it in the SRA Accounts Rules
client money	has the meaning given in rule 2.1 of the SRA Accounts Rules
costs	means your fees and disbursements
interest	includes a sum in lieu of interest
mixed payments	means a payment that includes both client money and non-client money
regulated services	means the legal and other professional services that you provide that are regulated by the SRA and includes, where appropriate, acting as a trustee or as the holder of a specified office or appointment
third party managed account	means an account held at a bank or building society in the name of a third party which is an authorised payment institution or small payment institution that has chosen to implement safeguarding arrangement in accordance with the Payment Services Regulations (as each defined in the Payment Services Regulations 2017) regulated by the FCA, in which monies are owned beneficially by the third party, and which is operated upon terms agreed between the third party, you and your client as an escrow payment service

Note. Please check www.sra.org.uk for updates.

Index

abatements 164
accountants
functions 4–5
registered auditor status 216
reports 5, 111–12, 215–17
SRA compliance 215–17
accounts
see also **balance sheet; profit and loss account;** *and individual accounts eg* **cash account** *and individual accounts eg* **cash account**
classification of items 22
concepts, accruals 31–2
form 12–13
information provided 6–7
limitations 76
meaning 3
nature 4
reading *see* **reading accounts**
record keeping 3–4
taxation purposes 4, 5–6
users
external 4
government and regulatory 4
internal 4
VAT *see* **Value Added Tax**
accruals basis 31–2
acid test 83
adjustments
bad debts 36–7
closing stock 35–6
concept of accruals 31–2
depreciation 38–40
doubtful debts 37
outstanding expenses 32–3
prepayments 33–4
work in progress 34–5
agency transactions
agent firm 206
instructing firm 207–9
analysis of accounts ***see*** **reading accounts**
annual reports and accounts 73–4
auditors' report 74
chairman's report 74
directors' report 74
notes 74
statement of cash flow 73
statement of changes in equity 73–4
statement of comprehensive income 73
strategic report 74
appropriation account
companies 57–9
dividends 58–9
retained profits 59
taxation 57–8
partnerships 49
assets 7
balance sheet 26–8
assets – *continued*
depreciation *see* **depreciation**
auditors 5
report 74
audits
statutory requirement 5
'true and fair' view 5
average settlement period 84

bad debts
adjustments 36–7
general rule 165
VAT relief 165–6
balance sheet
assets 26–8
CA 2006 format 71
company accounts 59–63
date of preparation 26
depreciation 38–9
example 27
final accounts 25–8
liabilities 26–8
order of items 27
partnerships 50
preparation 25–8
purpose 22
UK Adopted IAS format 72–3
bank overdrafts 79
book value 39
disposal of fixed asset 41
bookkeeper
accuracy checks 18
day-to-day accounts 3
trial balance 17–18
bookkeeping, double entry ***see*** **double entry bookkeeping**
bridging finance 191
business bank account
client money into 101–2, 123–6
dealing with bills 155
Legal Aid Agency receipts 99
business money
see also **transfers of funds**
receipts of client money and 100–1
separate from client money 100–4
businesses
types 7

capital
double entry bookkeeping 11
maintenance of 56
capital accounts
partnerships 48
capital allowances
deferred taxation 63–4
capital redemption reserve 62
capital reserve 59, 61–2
capitalisation of reserves 62

cash account 16–17
chairman's report 74
cheques
see also **receipts in payment of bill**
dishonoured 162–4
made out to client or third party 161
splitting 153–4
unsplit cheque 154–5
classification of items
profit and loss account 22
client bank account 28, 93
accounting systems 108–9
client money into 99–100
controls 108–9
dealing with bills 155
deputies 98–9
general account 176–9
improper use 97–8
interest 110
accounting entries 177–9
requirements 176–7
when accounted for 171–2
joint accounts 110–11
lack of capacity 98–9
Legal Aid Agency receipts 99
money laundering 94–5, 97
not used for banking facilities 93–9
proposed abolition 90, 213–14
record keeping 108–9
residual balance 105–7
separate designated deposit account 173–6
SRA warning notice 95–7
use of 93–9
withdrawals, purpose 105
client money 92–3
accountant's report requirement 111–12, 215–17
into business bank account 123–6
into client bank account 99–100
joint accounts 110–11
separate from business money 100–4
SRA consultation paper 90, 180–1, 213–14
third party managed accounts 110, 211–12
transfers *see* **transfers of funds**
withdrawal from client bank account 105–7
closing stock
adjustments 35–6
trading account 35–6
commission 167
companies
directors 53
dividends 54
investment in shares 54
nature 53–4
separate legal entity 53
shareholders 53, 54
company accounts
annual reports and accounts 73–4
appropriation accounts 57–9
dividends 58–9
retained profits 59
taxation 57–8
balance sheet 59–63
capital redemption reserve 62
company accounts – *continued*
capital reserve 59, 61–2
consolidated *see* **consolidated accounts**
debentures 56
deferred taxation
capital allowance 63–4
concept 63–4
depreciation 63
example 64–5
object of 64
dividends 58–9
earnings per share 85
formats 69–73
issue of shares 54–6
at par 55
at premium 55
maintenance of capital 56
profit and loss account 57–9
appropriation section 57–9
purchase of own shares 56
raising capital, share issue 54–6
reading 76–7
see also **reading accounts**
reserves
capital 59, 61–2
capital redemption 62
capitalisation of 62
debenture redemption 60
general 59
reserve funds 61
revaluation 61–2
revenue 59–61
share premium account 61
sinking fund 61
retained profits 59, 60, 61, 62
revaluation reserve 61–2
revenue reserve 59–61
share capital 54–6
share premium account 61
sinking fund 61
statutory regulation 67–8
see also **regulation of accounts**
taxation 57–8
deferred 63–5
compliance (Solicitors Regulation Authority)
accountant's reports 215–17
consolidated accounts 63
parents 63
subsidiaries 63
costs
definition 92, 103
counsel's fees
VAT 144
'credits' 12
current account
movements on 50–1
partnerships 49
current ratio 82–3

debenture redemption reserve 60
debentures 56
'debits' 12

debts
bad *see* **bad debts**
doubtful 37
deferred taxation
capital allowances 63–4
concept 63–4
depreciation 63
example 64–5
object 64
deposit bank account
accounting entries 173–6
interest 173
requirements 173
depreciation
adjustments 38–40
balance sheet 38–9
calculation 39
date of purchase and sale 40
deferred taxation 63
disposal of fixed asset 41
profit and loss account 38–9
reducing balance method 39
revaluation 40–1
straight line method 39
designated deposit client account 173–6
directors 53
report 74
disbursements
anticipated 93, 102–3
definition 92
items not qualifying as 137–9
payment 102–4, 123
Practice Note 137
receipts for unpaid 99–100
dishonoured cheques 162–4
disposal of fixed assets
at book value 41
not at book value 41
distribution *see* dividends
dividends 54
company accounts 58–9
double entry bookkeeping
assets 26–8
capital 11
credits 12
day-to-day accounts 9
debits 12
errors 18
example 13–15
form of accounts 12–13
ledger accounts 16–17
liabilities 26–8
principles 10–12
proprietor separate from business 11
purpose 9–10
reasons for use 9
recording transactions 13–15
rules for recording transactions 10–11
trading stock 25
trial balance 17–18, 21–2
doubtful debts
adjustments 37
drawings accounts 17

earnings per share 85
efficiency ratios 83–4
average settlement period 84
stock turnover 84
errors
double entry bookkeeping 18
expenses 7
adjustments 32–3

fees
definition 92, 103
final accounts
accruals basis 31–2
adjustments *see* **adjustments**
balance sheet 25–8
importance 29
profit and loss account 22–5
purpose 21–2
trading account 25
Financial Reporting Standards 6
financial statements
layout 185–6
purpose 185
fixed asset disposal
at book value 41
not at book value 41

gearing 84–5
gross profit margin ratio 82
group accounts *see* consolidated accounts

HM Revenue and Customs 4, 5
see also **taxation**

income 6–7
income statement 71–2
inflation 80
insurance commission
solicitors' accounts 167
inter-client transfers 123, 126–7
recording transfer 126–7
requirements 126
interest
accounting entries 173–6, 177–9
choice of method 172
client bank account
accounting entries 177–9
requirements 176–7
client money 110
deposit bank account
accounting entries 173–6
requirements 173
obligation to account 171–2
separate designated deposit bank accounts 173–6
solicitors' accounts 171–81
SRA consultation paper 180–1
International Accounting Standards Board 6, 69
International Financial Reporting Standards 69
investment ratios 85

ledger accounts 16–17
numbers of 189–206
Legal Aid Agency receipts 99

liabilities 7
balance sheet 26–8
liquidity 79, 82
acid test 83
current ratio 82–3

matching 32
medical records
VAT 138
money laundering 94–5, 97
money *see different kinds eg* client money; business money
mortgages 191–206
acting for buyer and lender 191–2
acting for lender and seller 194
advances 191–2
costs on redemption 194–5
examples 195–206
professional charges on advances 192–4
redemption 194–5

net profit margin ratio 82

Office of Public Guardian 98–9
overdrafts 79

partnerships
appropriation account 49
balance sheet 50
capital accounts 48
changes in partners 51
current account 49
movements on 50–1
nature 47–8
profit and loss account 49
profit sharing 48–9
reading accounts 77
taxation 51
payments in advance 33–4
petty cash
need for account 16, 166
payments for clients 166
solicitors' accounts 166
prepayments
adjustments 33–4
professional charges 15
solicitors' accounts 118–19, 123
VAT 135–6
profit costs 15
solicitors' accounts 118–19, 123
VAT 135–6
profit and loss account
appropriation account
companies 57–9
partnerships 49
CA 2006 format 70–1
classification of items 22
company accounts 57–9
depreciation 38–9
final accounts 22–5
income and expenses 22–3
period covered 22
preparation 23–5
purpose 22
profit and loss account – *continued*
trading business 25
UK Adopted IAS format 71–2
profit and loss reserve 60
profit sharing
partnerships 48–9
profitability 79, 80–2
earnings per share 85
gross profit margin ratio 82
investment ratios 85
net profit margin ratio 82
ratios 80–2
return on capital employed ratio 81
sales to capital employed ratio 81–2
trend analysis 80
profits, retained/reserved 59, 60, 61, 62
proprietor
need for financial reports 4

ratio analysis
acid test 83
average settlement period 84
current ratio 82–3
efficiency 83–4
gearing 84–5
gross profit margin ratio 82
liquidity 82–3
net profit margin ratio 82
profitability 80–2
purpose 80
return on capital employed ratio 81
sales to capital employed ratio 81–2
stock turnover 84
reading accounts
ability to pay debts 79
bank overdrafts 79
company accounts 76–7
efficiency 83–4
gearing 84–5
inflation 80
information required from 76–7
liquidity 79, 82–3
partnerships 77
persons reading 75–6
preliminary steps 77–8
profitability 79, 80–2
gross profit margin ratio 82
net profit margin ratio 82
ratios 80–2
return on capital employed ratio 81
sales to capital employed ratio 81–2
trend analysis 80
purpose 75
ratio analysis
efficiency 83–4
liquidity 82–3
profitability 80–2
purpose 80
sole traders 77
statement of cash flow 73
receipts in payment of bill
see also **cheques**
anticipated fees 102–3

receipts in payment of a bill – *continued*
client bank account 101–2
client money 101–2
dealing with 155
direct transfers 154–5
from Legal Aid Agency 99
mixed business and client money 100–1
splitting cheque 153–4
unsplit cheque 154–5
solicitors' accounts 153–5
splitting cheque 153–4
unpaid professional disbursements 99–100
unsplit cheque 154–5
records
accountant's role 5
cash transfers 124–6
client bank account 108–9
importance 3–4
inter-client transfers 126–7
transfers 124–7
two sets 113
VAT 6
redemption of mortgage 194–5
redemption reserve 60
reducing balance method
depreciation calculation 39
regulation of accounts 6
accounting principles 68–9
FRS 102 69
IFRS 69
international regulation 69
role 67
SRA compliance 215–17
standards 6
UK Adopted IAS 69
UK GAAP 69
reserve funds 61
reserves
capital 59, 61–2
capital redemption 62
capitalisation of 62
debenture redemption 60
general 59
reserve funds 61
revaluation 61–2
revenue 59–61
share premium account 61
sinking fund 61
retained profit 59, 60, 61, 62
return on capital employed ratio 81
revaluation
depreciation and 40–1
revaluation reserve 61–2
revenue reserve 59–61

sales to capital employed ratio 81–2
search fees
solicitors' accounts 137–8
VAT 137–8
separate designated deposit client account
interest 173–6
share capital 54–6
share premium account 55, 61
shareholders 53, 54
shares
companies buying own 56
investments in 54
issue 54–6
at par 55
at premium 55
types 55–6
sinking fund 61
sole traders
reading accounts 77
solicitors
SRA compliance 215–17
VAT and 135–44
see also **Value Added Tax**
solicitors' accounts
abatements 164
agency transactions
agent firm 206
instructing firm 207–9
bad debts 165–6
bridging finance 191
business bank account *see* **business bank account**
business money *see* **business money**
cash account 16–17
cheques *see* **cheques**
client bank account *see* **client bank account**
client money *see* **client money**
dealing with bills 155
dual cash account 114
dual ledger for each client 115
financial statements 185–7
format of accounts
dual cash account 114
dual ledger for each client 115
requirements 114
funds originally held for one client held for another 189–90
insurance commission 167
interest *see* **interest**
ledger accounts 189–206
Legal Aid Agency receipts 99
mortgages *see* **mortgages**
number of ledger accounts 189–206
payments 116–17
persons bound by rules 91
petty cash 166
principles 90–1
professional charges 118–19, 123
profit costs 118–19, 123
receipts 115–16
cheques to client or third party 161
in payment of bill *see* **receipts in payment of bill**
records
transfers 124–7
two sets 113
retention 217
SRA Accounts Rules 89–112
stakeholder money 190–1
storage 217
transfers *see* **transfers of funds**
two sets of records 113

Solicitors Regulation Authority
accountants' reports 215–17
consultation paper on client money 90, 180–1, 213–14
third party managed accounts 211, 212, 213
solvency *see* liquidity
SRA Accounts Rules 2019 89–112
future 91
persons bound by 91
principles 90–1
text 223–5
third party managed accounts 211–12
stakeholder money 190–1
statement of cash flow 73
statement of changes in equity 73–4
statement of comprehensive income 73
statement of financial position 72–3
stock turnover 84
straight line method
depreciation calculation 39
strategic report 74

taxation
accounting requirements 4, 5–6, 63–5
company accounts 57–8
deferred *see* **deferred taxation**
partnerships 51
VAT *see* **Value Added Tax**
third party cheques 161
third party managed accounts (TPMAs)
benefits 212
change proposals 90, 213–14
client money 110, 211–12
engaging with client 212
information to client 212–13
provider checks 212
Solicitors Regulation Authority 211, 212, 213
systems and procedures 213
trading account
closing stock 35–6
need for 25
preparation 25
trading business 7
double entry bookkeeping 13–15
profit and loss account 25
trading stock
closing stock 35–6
double entry bookkeeping 25
transfers of funds
business bank account, client money into 101–2, 123–6
cash transfers 123–6
client bank account, withdrawals from 105–7
client money
into business bank account 101–2, 123–6
payment of disbursements 102–4, 123
transfers of funds – *continued*
withdrawal from client bank account 105–7
inter-client 123, 126–7
payment of disbursements 102–4, 123
anticipated 93, 102–3
paid disbursements 103–4
payment of profit costs 123
reasons for 123
recording 124–7
types 123
trial balance 21–2
double entry bookkeeping 17–18
preparation of profit and loss account 23–5

UK Adopted International Accounting Standards 69
accounts formats 71–3
UK Financial Reporting Council 6
UK GAAP 69

Value Added Tax
accounts 134–5
bad debt relief 165–6
collection 134–5
counsel's fees 144
disbursements
agency method 141–2
conditions 136
counsel's fees 144
meaning 136–9
non-taxable 141
principal method 142–4
search fees 137–8
taxable 141–4
treatment of 140–4
general principle 131–5
input tax 133
medical records 138
'non-disbursements' 139–40
output tax
business 132
supply of goods 131
supply of services 132
taxable person 132
taxable supply 132
professional charges 135–6
records 6
search fees 137–8
solicitors and 135–44
tax invoices 134
time of supply 133–4
value of supply 133

work in progress
adjustments 34–5